BISMARCK AND THE
HOHENZOLLERN CANDIDATURE
FOR THE SPANISH THRONE

ACKNOWLEDGMENTS

I WISH to express my most sincere gratitude to M. Renouvin, Membre de l'Institut, Doyen de la Faculté des Lettres de Paris, who has helped me most generously with his advice in the different stages of the preparation of this book. I have received from M. Baumont, Membre de l'Institut, Professor at the Sorbonne, and French Chief Editor of the German diplomatic documents, valuable support and encouragement. I am very greatly indebted to the Hon. Margaret Lambert, British Chief Editor of the German diplomatic documents, for her stimulating criticism and counsel.

I wish to thank too Professor J. Boyd, Taylor Professor of the German Language and Literature in the University of Oxford, and Mr C. R. Bingham, of Queen's College, Oxford, who has helped me in the final redaction of the Introduction.

Dr Xavier de Salas, Director of the Spanish Institute in London, has kindly helped me in gaining access to the Spanish diplomatic archives in Madrid, of which those for 1870 are not yet normally open to historians.

Finally, I have much pleasure in thanking Mr Peter Calvocoressi for the enlightened interest he has taken in this volume.

CONTENTS

FOREWORD

By Dr G. P. GOOCH

━━━━━━━━━━━━━━━━━━━━━━━━

LARGE-SCALE movements and events result from a combination of remote and proximate circumstances. The fundamental cause of the Franco-German war of 1870 which changed the face of Europe was French fear of the increase of Prussian power since the Austrian war of 1866 and the determination to prevent its further growth. The immediate cause was the Hohenzollern candidature for the Spanish throne, left vacant by the expulsion of Queen Isabella in 1868. Her son Alfonso was too young to rule, and General Prim, the most powerful figure on the Spanish stage, felt that the Bourbons who had reigned since 1700 had been a failure. Why should not a monarch be sought beyond the frontier? His choice fell on Leopold, son of Prince Anton, of the Catholic branch of the Hohenzollern family which had remained in south Germany when Frederick, Burgrave of Nuremberg, went north to become the first Elector of Brandenburg. Since Prince Anton had recently permitted his son Carol to ascend the throne of Rumania, another son seemed likely to accept a far more glittering prize.

The first reaction of Prince Leopold was negative. He had no desire to leave his Fatherland, and the chequered record of the Spanish Bourbons since the time of Napoleon rendered the outlook uninviting. Though Prince Anton shared his son's apprehensions, both were prepared to sacrifice their feelings if King William, as the head of the House of Hohenzollern, believed acceptance to be in the interests of Prussia. When the old monarch expressed his dislike of the project but declined to intervene on the ground that it was not his business, it seemed as if Spain would have to look elsewhere.

It was at this moment, in March 1870, that Bismarck advances to the centre of the stage. A Hohenzollern on the Spanish throne, he explained to his master in a lengthy Memorandum, would be a distinct advantage to Prussia and Germany. It would inspire gratitude in the Spanish people for delivering them from an anarchical situation. The acceptance of the Rumanian crown by a German prince had led to a marked increase in trade, and with another German prince in Madrid even greater commercial benefits might be reaped. Still more important would be the enhanced renown of the German name throughout the world, and the prestige of the Hohenzollerns would at last equal that of the Hapsburgs. To reject the offer would deeply wound the pride of Spain, who would

9

probably turn to Bavaria, the friend of Paris, Vienna and the Vatican rather than of Berlin. Failure to secure a foreign prince might lead to the establishment of a republic, which would in turn strengthen the republican party in France. Prince Leopold could count on an almost unanimous vote in the Cortes, for monarchical sentiment was strong. Physical danger to the prince need not be anticipated. If the Spanish offer were rejected, he, Bismarck, would disclaim all responsibility for the consequences. That is hardly the letter of a man "tolerably indifferent to the entire question", as he describes himself in his apologia.

King William's marginal comments show that he was completely un-convinced, and throughout the prolonged discussions he never concealed his anxieties; but so great was the Chancellor's authority that finally Prince Leopold, with his father's consent, accepted the invitation. When the offer had been made the King of Prussia had declined to say Yes, and now that it was accepted by his kinsman he declined to say No, though he consented "with a very heavy heart". The news created intense indignation in France. The Government threatened war, and the acceptance was withdrawn by Prince Leopold and his father, who had no desire to set the world aflame. When, however, the French Emperor, hoping for an even more spectacular diplomatic victory, demanded a promise that the offer, if repeated at some future time, would never be accepted, King William, who was taking the waters at Ems, declined further discussion of the subject with the French Ambassador. Bismarck promptly reported the snub inflicted on France to the European capitals in a shortened version of his master's telegram from Ems; the Emperor declared war, was defeated and dethroned. Meanwhile an offer of the Spanish throne had been accepted by the Duke of Aosta, a member of the House of Savoy. The French Government had lost its head in the crisis, and France paid the penalty in the loss of Alsace and part of Lorraine.

Such is the familiar story, known in outline to every student of modern history. In the following seventy years many dispatches and diaries have thrown light on the Hohenzollern candidature, but now for the first time we can reconstruct the whole story from the German archives captured and brought to England at the close of the Second World War. In this volume, in which the editor provides every possible assistance to the reader in the Introduction, notes and appendices, we can follow almost from day to day the exchanges between Madrid, Sigmaringen on the Danube, and Berlin, not only of the principal actors in the drama but of Bismarck's agents in Spain. The general impression derived from the new material remains unchanged, namely that the initiative came from Madrid, that the offer met with an extremely cool reception by both branches of the Hohenzollern family, and that final acceptance was due to the steady pressure of the Iron Chancellor. While the family shrank from a gamble for the highest stakes, Bismarck welcomed the prospect of a conflict with

France in which military victory seemed reasonably certain and which he believed would remove the last obstacles to the voluntary incorporation of the south German states in a federal empire with the King of Prussia at its head. Of his desire for war there is of course not a trace in his letters and dispatches, but his disclaimer of responsibility for Prince Leopold's decision is unconvincing.

While Leopold, his father and King William come very well out of the searching test of the opening of the archives, Bismarck emerges as the *Realpolitiker* who was ready to lie and to unleash a major war in furtherance of his policy. "If we did for ourselves what we do for our country," exclaimed Cavour, "what rascals we should be." The Iron Chancellor agreed with the Piedmontese Premier in regard to the difference between public and private morality, for *raison d'état* has always been a religion of the majority of statesmen. It is curious that he should have taken so much pains to conceal his share in engineering the struggle which earned him the gratitude of his countrymen and left the Prussianized Reich the strongest military power in the world. Luckily for historians, attempts to mislead posterity rarely succeed, however long we have to wait for the truth.

The significance of these captured documents—some already known, many others printed for the first time—is twofold. In the first place they complete our knowledge of some of the most critical months in recent history. Secondly, they reveal the most gifted—if not the wisest—of nineteenth-century statesmen at work behind the scenes, a Vulcan forging his thunderbolts. History on a grand scale is usually made by men who stick at nothing in pursuit of their own glory, such as the two Napoleons, Hitler and Mussolini, or in the supposed interests of their country, such as Richelieu and Frederick the Great, Bismarck and Cavour. At the close of his eventful life the Iron Chancellor confessed that he had made three wars, adding that he had settled all that with his Maker. Fortunately for his peace of mind he passed away before the impermanence of the Hohenzollern Empire and the insecurity of the frontiers of the Reich were revealed in the testing fires of war.

G. P. GOOCH

INTRODUCTION

THE documents from the German Foreign Ministry Archives reproduced here have been kept secret since 1870, and this Introduction is an attempt to discover why they were so closely guarded and how historians were prevented from examining them.

On 16 July 1870, in the *Bundesrat*, Bismarck denied emphatically any participation by the Prussian Government in the negotiations which led to the offer of the Spanish Crown to Prince Leopold of Hohenzollern; the Prussian Government, he stated, had heard about it only through a Havas telegram of 3 July 1870.[1]

Bismarck's declaration was then dictated by obvious reasons of political expediency, but in 1881 Bismarck gave Sybel unrestricted access to the files of the Foreign Ministry for "the publication of a historical work on Prussian History in the years 1850-1870".[2]

A few days after Bismarck's dismissal, however, on 5 April 1890, a meeting of the Cabinet decided that henceforth Sybel's volumes on *The Founding of the German Empire* should be submitted before publication to a commission composed of Marschall, the State Secretary and head of the Foreign Ministry, and of two civil servants, Rottenburg and Raschdau.[3] The commission was to examine whether Sybel's publication could be permitted as harmless from a political point of view.[4]

On 29 July 1890 Caprivi reported to the Emperor on Sybel's account of the Hohenzollern candidature and proposed that the publication of Sybel's *Founding of the German Empire* should be discontinued, at least temporarily, and more particularly that the publication of Volume VI should not be permitted. The arguments advanced by Caprivi are to be found in the note he wrote about his interview with William II:[5]

BERLIN, 31 July, 1890

In the report to the Kaiser at Wilhelmshaven on 29th inst., I reported to His Majesty with regard to the discussion of the candidature to the throne of Spain in Sybel's work "The Founding of the German

[1] "Dem Auswärtigen Amte des Norddeutschen Bundes, wie der Regierung Seiner Majestät des Königs von Preussen waren diese Vorgänge vollständig fremd geblieben. Sie erfuhren erst durch das am 3. d.Mts. abends aus Paris abgegangene Havas'sche Telegramm, dass das Spanische Ministerium beschlossen habe, dem Prinzen die Krone anzubieten." (From the protocol kept in the file: *IA Frankreich No. 70. Band 5.*)

[2] Anlage I zum Gutachten Frantzius v. 7.8.1890, AS 1509: 19 March 1881, letter Bismarck to Sybel, AS 361, in *IA Bo 32 g. Bd. 5.*

[3] A 4904, pr. 13 April 1890, in *IA Deutschland 158 g. Bd. 1.*

[4] Letter of Caprivi to Sybel, 8 April 1890, in *IA Deutschland 158 g. Bd. 1.*

[5] 31 July 1890, AS 1463, in *IA Bo 32 g. Bd. 5.*

Empire", that I must pronounce myself against the publication of both drafts[1] submitted by Privy Councillor von Sybel, and this must further lead us to doubt whether Volume VI should appear at all for the time being.

Sybel's second draft, too, questions the ideas hitherto publicized and officially confirmed about the causes of the 1870-71 war and might be expected to cast doubts at home and abroad upon the trustworthiness of our political attitude at that time. This would be just as unlikely to remain without repercussions on the position of the present government, as were the articles recently published in the *Hamburger Nachrichten* about our relations with Austria and Russia,[2] which have raised the question in the press whether our attitude deserves to be trusted. Thus any account in Sybel's book deviating from the accredited legend would be harmful, not least in Germany itself, if the collaboration of the *Bundesrat* were sought for a future war and if it were then held against us that our declarations might have the same value as those made to the *Bundesrat* in 1870. In France, moreover, in order to make our present policy more difficult, every word which might serve to stir up the mistrust already existing about the causes of the 1870 war would be exploited against us.

[1] Sybel had submitted a first draft on 11 June 1890 to Caprivi, who had had it examined by Raschdau, a *Vortragender Rat* in the Political Section of the German Foreign Ministry and a member of the *ad hoc* commission created by the council of the Cabinet on 5 April 1890 (see above). Raschdau thought the publication of Sybel's manuscript would be harmful (see AS 1137 and AS 1151 in *IA Bo 32 g. Bd. 5*). After a conversation with Raschdau, Sybel submitted on 17 June 1890, as a second draft, an abridged version of the Hohenzollern candidature (Annex to AS 1151, in *IA Bo 32 g. Bd. 5*).

Even in his first draft Sybel had been careful not to disclose the whole truth about the Hohenzollern candidature, for he commented upon his first version:

> In der dort gegebenen Darstellung habe ich zwei Thatsachen nicht erwähnt, welche zwar dem Inhalt derselben nicht den geringsten Eintrag thun, deren Veröffentlichung aber [Marginal note of Caprivi: "auch ohne das!"] trotzdem feindseligen Beurtheilern Anlass zu missbräuchlichen und gehässigen Folgerungen geben könnte.
>
> 1. Der Kronprinz hat fortdauernd [Marginal note of Caprivi: "zuerst wohl nicht"] auf den Erbprinzen für Annahme der Candidatur eingewirkt. Offenbar widerlegt dies nicht den Satz, dass damals [Marginal note of Caprivi: "dieses 'damals' ist ein sehr kurzer Zeitraum, der die Beurtheilung nicht verändern wird"] die preussische Regierung mit der Sache nicht befasst war.
> 2. Salazar erklärte Anfangs dem Fürsten von Hohenzollern, er könne nicht nach Deutschland kommen: statt dessen möge Bucher, der damals in Düsseldorf war, [Marginal note of Caprivi: "u[nd] poussirte"] nochmals nach Madrid reisen. Bismarck sah die Nothwendigkeit nicht ein, genehmigte aber den Urlaub unter der Weisung, Bucher reise als Vertrauensmann des Fürsten, und habe vor allen Dingen jede Hereinziehung der preussischen Regierung in der Unterhandlung zu verhüten. (Annex to AS 1117, in *IA Bo 32 g. Bd. 5*.)

[2] This is an allusion to articles, inspired by Bismarck, on the Russo-German Reinsurance Treaty.

On the other hand it is not possible to palm off on to Sybel's book the version of events given hitherto. It would be unworthy of its author and of the work as a whole, and dangerous in so far as people might still be alive in Spain who know the real facts and might feel constrained to enter into a public discussion of the question.

Such a version would moreover hardly be in the interest of Prince Bismarck, either, and with a person of his communicative mood one would have to expect that he would protest; he would be inclined not to let one of his most prominent diplomatic achievements be hushed up in a book composed in his honour with official support.

So it seems to me conclusive, that the writing of history, when contemporaries are still living, raises such problems here that no way out is to be found and it only remains to discontinue altogether the publication of the work, even at the risk of causing unpleasantness for the deserving author, and perhaps creating pecuniary problems and exciting the wrath of Prince Bismarck.

Moreover I remarked to His Majesty that, besides, the attitude of the late Emperor William I to the Spanish candidature and to the 1870 war might appear in a wrong light, as it was impossible to tell the whole truth, and that the Princely House of Hohenzollern would appear in a definitely unfavourable light.

His Majesty approved of my view and added that He Himself would have been disposed anyhow to prevent the further appearance of the book. Already the first volume had unpleasantly affected the German Princes. Above all Her Majesty the Empress was indignant about the part which the book ascribed to Her father, and all the more so as the family had in its hands papers which might make it possible to contradict Sybel's interpretation. The brother of Her Majesty had already taken steps in that direction.

Therefore the continuation of the publication of the work was to be prevented as far as possible.

CAPRIVI. 31.7.90

Caprivi informed Sybel of the Kaiser's decision[1] and at the same time asked advice from the Foreign Ministry legal adviser, Frantzius, as to the rights which Sybel might be able to assert against the suppression of his work. In his answer[2] Frantzius distinguished between forbidding Sybel the use of official sources and the *opinion* of the Chancellor (shared by the Emperor) that Sybel's work should be discontinued. Evidently Sybel could do nothing against the veto on the use of official sources. But Frantzius recommended that, should Sybel persist in his intention of continuing *The Founding of the German Empire*, the Foreign Ministry could

[1] 31 July 1890, letter of Caprivi to Sybel, zu AS 1463, in *IA Bo 32 g. Bd. 5.*
[2] Dated 7 August 1890, AS 1509, in *IA Bo 32 g. Bd. 5.*

censor his manuscripts with the greatest severity from the standpoint of his use of official material. Sybel would then, in spite of the loss of his book, have no ground for complaint.

In his letter to Sybel[1] Caprivi had merely expressed the *opinion* of the Kaiser that the time had not yet come for using documentary evidence on the circumstances which preceded the war of 1870. When Caprivi met Sybel on 7 August 1890, the latter declared the *opinion* of the Kaiser was equivalent to a veto, and Sybel doubted whether he would be able to finish his work without using official sources.[2]

In fact, as we know, Sybel completed his work, omitting all references to the secret files of the diplomatic archives. He found himself, however, in an awkward position in 1895 when some intimate papers were published concerning the King of Rumania, brother of Leopold of Hohenzollern, the candidate for the Crown of Spain.[3] Sybel then tried, but without result, to impress on Hohenlohe, who had succeeded Caprivi as Chancellor, that he did not any longer feel bound by the obligation which Caprivi had imposed upon him of ignoring the secret documents of the Foreign Ministry on the Hohenzollern candidature.[4]

About the same time Hohenlohe had to deal with an attempt, coming from a different quarter, to lift the veil of secrecy from the Hohenzollern candidature. The Prussian envoy in Baden, Eisendecher, reported that a professor of history named Oncken had received from Prince Leopold of Hohenzollern-Sigmaringen an authorization to use some important but hitherto unrevealed documents on the candidature.[5] In a conversation with Eisendecher the Prince had declared that this would help to dispel some lasting errors and clarify some points which remained obscure.

Hohenlohe explained to the Emperor that Oncken's revelations might well include precisely what was omitted from Sybel's publication, and in so doing possibly endanger the memory of William II's grandfather.[6] At Hohenlohe's suggestion William II wrote to Leopold of Hohenzollern asking him either to withdraw the permission given to Oncken or to arrange for Oncken's manuscript to be censored by the Foreign Ministry.[7] The Prince of Hohenzollern answered that, though pressed for several years from different sides to release the documents kept in the Sigmaringen archives, he had always refused, feeling that a disclosure of all the events

[1] 31 July 1890; cf. above.
[2] Caprivi's marginal note on Frantzius' report.
[3] *Aufzeichnungen aus dem Leben des Königs Karl von Rumänien*, Vol. II.
[4] 13 February 1895, Sybel to Hohenlohe, AS 163, in *IA Deutschland 158 g. Bd. 1.*
[5] 4 October 1895, Ber. 462, A 10787, in *IA Deutschland 158 g. Bd. 1.*
[6] 11 October 1895, Immediabericht, AS 961, in *IA Deutschland 158 g. Bd. 1.*
[7] 20 October 1895, letter of William II to the Prince of Hohenzollern, AS 961 I, in *IA Deutschland 158 g. Bd. 1.*

connected with the candidature was still premature.[1] Oncken, continued Leopold, had not obtained full access to the Sigmaringen archives; he had merely been invited for a few days to the Weinburg near the Bodensee, where, whilst he was allowed to take some notes, certain documents were read aloud to him. These documents contained nothing which could be detrimental to the memory of William II's grandfather; nevertheless Leopold had enjoined on Oncken the duty of not publishing for the moment the revelations made to him, and proposed he should use them in a few years as material for a new edition of his book *Das Zeitalter des Kaiser Wilhelm*. In his own justification Leopold added that in his opinion his father's part had not received very favourable treatment from Sybel, the suggestion being made that his father had acted through motives of personal ambition. Nevertheless Leopold gave the assurance that Oncken would be requested to publish nothing without the consent of the Foreign Ministry.

The Foreign Ministry was then approached in January 1897 about the proposed inclusion in Oncken's book *Unser Heldenkaiser* of three letters addressed by King William in 1870 to Prince Karl Anton of Hohenzollern. The Foreign Ministry objected to the publication of the letter dated 21 June 1870, which contained an allusion to the early history of the candidature.[2] Hohenlohe this time explained to the Kaiser that the contents of the letter would indicate a difference of opinion between King William and Bismarck and, still worse, would reveal that Bismarck's point of view concerning the Spanish candidature had prevailed.[3] The letter also disclosed that Bismarck had concerned himself with the candidature during the winter of 1869-70, which was in contradiction with his declaration to the *Bundesrat* on 16 July 1870. William II commented there in the margin: *"Das wäre nicht das erste Mal, dass Bismarck gelogen hat."* However, the Kaiser agreed to Hohenlohe's proposal to have the document omitted from Oncken's book.

It is remarkable that the Foreign Ministry was perfectly aware by that time of the fact that historians had ceased to believe the official version, especially since the publication in 1894 of the biography of King Charles of Rumania.[4] This publication had, in the view of the German Foreign Ministry, indirectly merely reinforced the French conviction, that Bismarck had brought about the Hohenzollern candidature with the intention of provoking a war; but this French theory would, they considered,

[1] 25 October 1895, letter of Prince of Hohenzollern to William II, AS 1016, in *IA Deutschland 158 g. Bd. 1*.

[2] Aufzeichnung Klehmet, 2.1.1897, AS 4, in *IA Deutschland 158 g. Bd. 2*. For the text of King William's letter of 21 June 1870 see Documents below.

[3] Immediatbericht Hohenlohe, 8 January 1897, AS 40, in *IA Deutschland 158 g. Bd. 2*.

[4] Aufzeichnung Klehmet, 6 January 1897, AS 23, in *IA Deutschland 158 g. Bd. 2*.

receive much stronger support if the very words of the King of Prussia were to be divulged.

In the same year, 1897, a Colonel von Werthern informed Hohenlohe[1] of his intention to publish a biography of Versen, the Prussian emissary sent to Spain in April 1870 at the request of King William to enquire into the strength and reliability of the Spanish army, whilst Bucher was negotiating the Hohenzollern candidature with the Spanish Government. Versen had also been negotiating on behalf of Bismarck with Leopold of Hohenzollern and had contributed to the latter's acceptance of the Spanish Crown on 19 June 1870. Colonel von Werthern had obtained access not only to Versen's correspondence but, more important still, to his diary for the period 18 May-22 July 1870, and was forwarding to Hohenlohe a transcription of Versen's diary, the text of which is given in an Appendix to the present volume. Of course the Foreign Ministry objected to the publication by Colonel von Werthern of a chapter dealing with Versen's mission to Spain, especially as Werthern's editorial venture led him to revelations surpassing those of the King of Rumania and showing that Bismarck, as the motive power behind the secret negotiations, was well aware that an outbreak of French national hatred against the Hohenzollerns might ensue. As von Werthern was a colonel on the active list, the Foreign Ministry suggested that the Kaiser's military cabinet should indicate to Werthern that he was disclosing State secrets, which it was in the interest of Germany and Prussia not to reveal. The Foreign Ministry also suggested in this connexion that at least a hint should be dropped to Werthern that a publication of his chapter might be considered as "treason".[2]

In 1890 William II had approved his Chancellor's view that Sybel should be prevented from publishing his version of the Hohenzollern candidature. The Kaiser had also indicated that he would be in favour of a policy of altogether prohibiting the publication of *The Founding of the German Empire*. The fundamental views of William II on the writing of German history for the second half of the nineteenth century are stated in the following memorandum by Bülow in 1902:

> His Majesty has already told me previously on the occasion of a biography planned by Duke Ernst Günther,[3] of his grandfather, and of his *father*, that it should if possible not be published yet, and on no account be published without handing in the manuscript here for perusal beforehand. His Majesty declared on this occasion that things should not be published which might offend King Christian of Denmark, whom he respected very much, or offend his daughters in St

---

[1] 12 April 1897, Freiherr von Werthern to Hohenlohe, AS 338, in *IA Deutschland 158 g. Bd. 3*.

[2] Aufzeichnung Klehmet, 1 May 1897, AS 353, in *IA Deutschland 158 g. Bd. 3*.

[3] Of Schleswig-Holstein.

Petersburg and London, nor even should those things be published which might be used to discredit the late Emperor William I and the policy of Prince Bismarck towards Schleswig-Holstein.

I think it is imperative that *Wirklicher Legationsrat* Rücker-Jenisch[1] should (in a friendly manner) leave no doubt in Duke Ernst Günther's mind that His Majesty the Kaiser definitely expects that the manuscript will be submitted before any publication dealing with any phase of German history during the second half of the last century. Hereby Herr Jenisch might casually remark, that His Majesty considers publications about the said political era as in principle still premature.

BÜLOW, 19.3.[1902][2]

In 1903 Theodor von Bernhardi's son submitted to the Foreign Ministry the latter part of his father's memoirs. The manuscript contained some indications on the character of Bernhardi's visit to Spain during 1869–70 when he busied himself not only with art and literature but also with Spain's political situation and the question of the succession to the throne. It appeared that Bernhardi had been constantly in touch with the Prussian Legation in Madrid and had entered into contact with a number of Spanish personalities: Prim, Serrano, Countess Montijo and others. Though nowhere clearly expressed in the diaries submitted to the Foreign Ministry, the assumption was that Bernhardi had been sent to Spain on a semi-official mission. The Foreign Ministry objected to those passages which suggested that Bernhardi had been receiving instructions from the General Staff through Moltke and "reporting" regularly to Keudell and the Foreign Ministry, and that his reports had excited great interest in Berlin, an interest which was shared even by the King.[3] The reader of Bernhardi's memoirs, it was feared by the Foreign Ministry, would only too easily draw the conclusion that Bernhardi's trip to Spain was connected with the question of the succession to the throne, indeed, a sort of forerunner of Bucher's and Versen's trips during the spring of 1870. This would throw a completely new light on the Hohenzollern candidature, which Bismarck and the Prussian Government would seem to have planned since the beginning of 1869. Furthermore, Prussian history, and in particular Sybel's official version, already endangered by the memoirs of the King of Rumania, would suffer yet another blow. The Foreign Ministry recommended that, should the official version of the Hohenzollern candidature be maintained, the passage referring to instructions from Berlin to Bernhardi should be suppressed, a recommendation which was

---

[1] *Wirklicher Legationsrat* Rücker-Jenisch was in this case playing the part of an intermediary between the Duke of Schleswig-Holstein and the German Foreign Ministry (see March 1902, Aufz. Richthofen, A 3423, in *IA Ae 61 Schleswig. Bd. 28*).

[2] In *IA Ae 61 Schleswig. Bd. 28*.

[3] Aufzeichnung Klehmet, 3 October 1903, AS 1228, in *IA Deutschland 158 g. Bd. 3*.

accepted by Bernhardi's son, who incidentally may well have censored parts of the manuscript himself, even before submitting it to the German Foreign Ministry.

In 1910-11 the Foreign Ministry had again to fight a threat of indiscretion from Sigmaringen. Zingeler, the archivist of the Hohenzollern-Sigmaringen family, had been planning a publication on 8 September 1911 to celebrate the hundredth anniversary of Prince Karl Anton's birth. The Hohenzollern candidature was to occupy a prominent place in the publication of papers relating to Karl Anton. The Foreign Ministry found this project the most dangerous it had so far to counter.[1] The indiscretions committed by the King of Rumania were of import, but they did not bear the mark of authenticity as they were supposed to derive merely from an indirect source. Zingeler, with his access to the archives of Sigmaringen, was actually planning to contradict the official version of the candidature, which Bismarck had maintained in his memoirs in 1898.[2]

In the eyes of the Foreign Ministry, Zingeler's publication would be an irreverence towards Bismarck and at the same time throw such light on the real course of events that the official "fiction" would be completely demolished; this was the more likely as Zingeler intended to reproduce decisive documents on the famous Council of Ministers, of which some details had already been given by Keudell in 1901,[3] but whose existence Bismarck had denied in his memoirs. The Foreign Ministry vetoed the Zingeler publication as it stood, considering its own position all the stronger as the Kaiser had some time earlier expressed the definite view that no publication concerning any aspect of German history during the second half of the nineteenth century should take place without the Foreign Ministry's having scrutinized the manuscript beforehand.[4] Bethmann-Hollweg's comment was: "*Die Aktenstücke dürfen unter keinen Umständen veröffentlicht werden.*"[5] With the assent of Prince William of Hohenzollern-Sigmaringen,[6] Zingeler undertook a complete reconstruction of his

[1] Aufzeichnung Griesinger, 6 February 1911, AS 217, in *Asservat 36*.

[2] The Foreign Ministry pointed particularly to the following passages from *Gedanken und Erinnerungen*:

Page 80: "Politisch stand ich der ganzen Frage ziemlich gleichgültig gegenüber."

Page 81: "Die Memoiren Sr. Majestät des Königs von Rumänien sind über Einzelheiten der ministeriellen Mitwirkung in der Frage nicht genau unterrichtet. Das dort erwähnte Minister-Conseil im Schlosse hat nicht stattgefunden."

Page 82: "Von Seiten unseres Auswärtigen Amtes waren die ersten schon unberechtigten Anfragen Frankreichs über die spanische Thronkandidatur am 4. Juli der Wahrheit entsprechend in der ausweichenden Art beantwortet worden, dass das Ministerium nichts von der Sache wisse."

[3] Keudell, *Fürst und Fürstin Bismarck*. 1901.

[4] See Bülow memorandum of 19 March 1902.

[5] 24 March 1911, marginal comment to AS 498, pr. 21 März 1911, in *Asservat 36*.

[6] 5 April 1911, letter of Prince William of Hohenzollern-Sigmaringen to Bethmann-Hollweg, AS 580, in *IA Deutschland 158 g. Bd. 4*.

chapter on the candidature, which actually met with the approval of the Foreign Ministry,[1] Bethmann-Hollweg,[2] and the Kaiser.[3]

In 1911 Hans Delbrück, the Prussian historian, became involved in a controversy with Emile Ollivier when, to prove Bismarck's peace-loving intentions, he made reference[4] to some instructions which Bismarck was supposed to have sent to Bucher during the negotiation of the Hohenzollern candidature.[5] Emile Ollivier denied the authenticity of Delbrück's document.[6]

Delbrück asked for Foreign Ministry permission to consult the correspondence between Bismarck and Bucher at the time of the latter's journey to Spain in 1870,[7] so that he could prove the authenticity of the letter disputed by Emile Ollivier. Delbrück was not permitted to read the secret documents on the candidature, and was told by the Foreign Ministry that the letter he had been referring to as allegedly sent by Bismarck to Bucher did not exist.[8]

[1] 1 May 1911, Aufzeichnung Wedel, zu AS 700, in *IA Deutschland 158 g. Bd. 4.*

[2] 3 May 1911, Erlass Bethmann-Hollweg, AS 700, in *IA Deutschland 158 g. Bd. 4.*

[3] 5 May 1911, Bericht Jenisch, AS 737, in *IA Deutschland 158 g. Bd. 4.*

[4] Delbrück had published an article entitled "Ollivier über den Krieg 1870", in *Die Preussischen Jahrbücher*, Bd. 137, 2. Heft. Berlin, 1909.

[5] Delbrück had quoted Bismarck's alleged instructions to Bucher from Fester's article in the *Deutsche Rundschau*, of July 1909. Later Hesselbarth reproduced (both in Spanish and in German translation) this "Instruktionsbrief" originally published by Pirala, *Historia Contemporánea*, Vol. 3, p. 392. Madrid, 1874. (Hermann Hesselbarth, *Drei psychologische Fragen zur spanischen Thronkandidatur Leopolds von Hohenzollern*, pp. 34-5. Leipzig, 1913.)

[6] "Vous invoquez ensuite la lettre espagnole dont j'ai publié le texte. Cette lettre n'a certainement pas été une instruction adressée à Lothar Bucher. Cet envoyé extraordinaire du chancelier n'avait pas été expédié à Madrid sans être muni d'instructions complètes qui n'avaient pas à lui être renouvelées à quelques jours de là sous une forme embrouillée. Bismarck savait qu'en certaines négociations, véritables complots, on n'écrit pas ce qu'on peut dire. Le destinataire est Bernhardi ou quelque autre personnage de l'entourage de Prim. Cette lettre exprime, en effet, la prévision que l'excitation française n'aboutira pas à un fait de guerre. En prescrivant à son complice une démarche qui amènera la guerre, Bismarck lui fait entendre qu'il ne la prévoit pas. Un tel langage peut-il être pris au sérieux? L'artifice banal de ceux qui préparent une guerre n'est-il pas de se répandre en protestations pacifiques? Leur dessein est de ceux que l'on n'avoue pas même à son ombre et à plus forte raison à ses agents: on les maintient dans l'illusion afin qu'ils puissent, avec plus d'assurance, endormir les soupçons de celui sur lequel on se dispose à fondre. 'Si tu veux tromper un prince, dit Guicciardini, trompe ton ambassadeur auprès de lui.' Les hypocrisies de la lettre espagnole ne sont qu'une ruse préparée d'avance pour le jour où l'on se défendra d'avoir été le provocateur." (Annex to AS 827, pr. 24 Mai 1911, in *IA Deutschland 158 g. Bd. 4.*)

[7] 19 May 1911, letter from Delbrück to Bethmann-Hollweg, AS 827, in *IA Deutschland 158 g. Bd. 4.*

[8] 30 June 1911, letter from Langwerth to Delbrück, zu AS 906, in *IA Deutschland 158 g. Bd. 4.* Actually the result of the research undertaken by the Foreign Ministry in connexion with Delbrück's enquiry was the following statement:
"Ein an Bucher oder eine dritte Person gerichteter Brief Bismarcks mit dem von

Another historian, Ernst Marx, who in 1911 published in Stuttgart a short study entitled *Bismarck und die Hohenzollernkandidatur in Spanien*, was equally unsuccessful in his efforts to gain access to the secret files on the candidature. Marx was told that for "political reasons" he could not have access to documents of the Foreign Ministry other than those which Sybel had been allowed to use.[1]

For the same "political reasons" Brandenburg was also refused permission to read a series of documents of 1870 connected with the Hohenzollern candidature and the origins of the war,[2] and was allowed to look only at those files and documents which Sybel had been able to use for his *Founding of the German Empire*.

At that same time when historians like Delbrück and Brandenburg had to rest content with negative answers from the Foreign Ministry, another *Bismarckforscher*, Hermann Hesselbarth, met with a rather extraordinary piece of luck. Hesselbarth received a letter dated 12/25 September 1911 from St Petersburg, signed by a certain Bohnen, who described himself as a "Reichsdeutscher" and a businessman, and who was director of a German industrial enterprise in St Petersburg.[3] Bohnen began his letter by stating that he had been much interested by Hesselbarth's work *Die Entstehung des deutsch-französischen Krieges* and that Hesselbarth in turn would be much interested by the communication he was about to make. The following was Bohnen's story: fourteen years earlier in Spain a friend had shown him some notes concerning the Hohenzollern candidature, a copy of which was appended to the letter. The notes, which reproduced a series of telegrams exchanged between Bismarck and Salazar in 1870, had been taken by *Hofrat* Kleefeld, who in the sixties and seventies of the last century was in charge of the chancery of the Prussian Legation in Madrid. Kleefeld had married a Spanish lady and at his death in Valladolid towards 1886 had left his private papers to a Spaniard named Barrasa—the friend of Bohnen, as appeared from a subsequent letter.[4] In Kleefeld's papers was to be found the "Discreta y simpática Relación en que se refieren los pasos que se han dado por el caballero Ole Ole sin narices para obtener un lucrativo empleo en España en el año de 1870", which came to constitute the hard core of Hesselbarth's

Professor D.[elbrück] in den P[reussischen] Jahrb[üchern] (S. 312) wiedergegebenen Inhalte hat sich in den Akten nicht ermitteln lassen. Auch enthalten die Akten keinen Bericht von Bucher, der auf einen solchen Brief Bezug nimmt oder schliessen lässt. Die Gedankengänge des Briefes entsprechen der Bismarck'schen Auffassung, die Form ist offenbar apokryph."

[1] 23 January 1912, zu AS 296, in *IA Spanien 32. Bd. 6*.

[2] 1 January 1912, letter Bethmann-Hollweg to Brandenburg, zu A 17137, in *IA Deutschland 158 g. Bd. 4*.

[3] *Asservat 36*, Ser. 8559, Fr. Nr. E599.210-29.

[4] 15/28 November 1911, letter from Bohnen to Hesselbarth, in *Asservat 36*, Ser. 8559, Fr. Nr. E599.230-2.

publication *Drei psychologische Fragen zur spanischen Thronkandidatur Leopolds von Hohenzollern.*[1]

"Ole Ole sin narices" was a phonetic transcription—invented by Spanish humorous periodicals—of the name Hohenzollern-Sigmaringen, a word almost impossible to pronounce in Spanish. Kleefeld had introduced in his notes a further and somewhat childish touch of mystery by writing all names in the reverse order of their letters: Bismarck was written as "Kramsib", Thile as "Eliht", Bucher as "Rehcub", Versen as "Nesrev", Salazar as "Razalas", Prim as "Mirp", Sagasta as "Atsagas", Zorrilla as "Alliroz", Berlin as "Nilreb", and Varzin as "Nizrav". In addition to this a sort of code had been agreed between Salazar and Berlin, so that many points appeared obscure to Hesselbarth, who had only the text of the exchanged telegrams; he tried to obtain more information through the German Ambassador to Madrid, Prince Ratibor. Hesselbarth, however, did not reveal the existence of the documents which had come into his possession and referred only to the pseudo-letter of instructions to Bucher published by Pirala.[2]

Hesselbarth wanted Prince Ratibor to ask the Spanish Foreign Ministry three questions concerning "M. de Gama", who he thought had belonged to the diplomatic service:

"(1) *Quel rang obtenait-il?*
(2) *Est-il mort au service?*
(3) *Descendait-il du célèbre Vasco?*"

The Foreign Ministry, informed by Prince Ratibor of Hesselbarth's enquiry, decided that Hesselbarth's questions should not be forwarded to the Spanish Foreign Ministry, because they might well disclose the identity of Gama as Salazar y Mazarredo, a secret which the historians had not yet succeeded in piercing.[3] Concerning the Pirala publication of Bismarck's alleged instructions to Bucher, the Foreign Ministry remarked that it was probably better not to cast too much doubt on the existence of the document since German historians—Delbrück the year before and now Hesselbarth—were using it to prove that Bismarck did not want war with France.[4]

[1] Leipzig, 1913, pp. 28-34.

[2] 28 February 1912, letter of Hesselbarth to Prince Ratibor, zu AS 491, in *IA Deutschland 158 g. Bd. 4.*

[3] 22 March 1912, Aufzeichnung Rosenberg, zu AS 491, in *IA Deutschland 158 g. Bd. 4.*

[4] Strictly speaking, the German Foreign Ministry did not oppose Hesselbarth's publication but it was not told either that new documents had come into Hesselbarth's possession. The German Foreign Ministry knew about Hesselbarth only through Prince Ratibor's report of 14 March 1912 (AS 491, in *IA Deutschland 158 g. Bd. 4*) forwarding Hesselbarth's query concerning the identity of "Gama" and the authenticity of Bucher's "Instruktionsbrief" in which "Gama" was mentioned; this did not necessarily indicate that Hesselbarth had discovered new material as he was quoting Bucher's

In fact, Hesselbarth in his book reproduced the "Instruktionsbrief"[1] together with the Bismarck-Salazar telegrams, combining both sources to elucidate some of the mysteries associated with the Hohenzollern candidature. These mysteries dissolve in the light of the fuller documentation contained in the secret files here published.

One dark corner remained, however, on which Hesselbarth could have thrown some light: it is the fatal incident described as "Intermezzo" concerning a telegram of 20 June 1870 from Salazar to Madrid.[2] An error of transmission had caused the Cortes to be dispersed without electing a King, although Leopold had agreed to stand as candidate. Hesselbarth wrote: *"Der Depeschenirrtum und die Vertagung der Cortes. Keiner Erläuterung bedarf das Intermezzo."*[3] Hesselbarth knew that Kleefeld thought there had been no error of transmission but a deliberate falsification committed by Canitz, the Prussian Minister to Madrid, who had been from the beginning an opponent of the Hohenzollern candidature and who would thereby have found his opportunity to bring about its failure.[4] Hesselbarth's silence on this point can only be attributed to his desire not to reveal that his source of information was ultimately Kleefeld. The reader will be in a position to compare Kleefeld's explanation with the documents published below concerning the careful enquiry ordered by Bismarck, who was anxious to discover where the error of transmission had taken place.[5]

"Instruktionsbrief" from Pirala, *Historia Contemporánea*, Volume III, p. 392. The German Foreign Ministry, however, on the basis of Hesselbarth's letter to Prince Ratibor, wrote to Hesselbarth saying that he should call at the Foreign Ministry in Berlin to discuss orally his research on the question of the Hohenzollern candidature (23 March 1912, letter of Zimmermann to Hesselbarth, zu AS 491, in *IA Bo 32 g. Bd. 6*). Hesselbarth, who was a teacher at the *Realgymnasium* of Lippstadt in Westphalia, did not call personally at the Foreign Ministry, but delegated *Geheimer Archivrat* Dr Bailleu, whose title was *Zweiter Direktor des Preussischen Staatsarchivs*. The communication made by Rosenberg to Bailleu (17.2.1913, Notiz Rosenberg, AS 204, in *IA Deutschland 158 g. Bd. 4*) was on the lines of the Rosenberg memorandum which we have summarized (see 22 March 1912, Aufzeichnung Rosenberg, zu AS 491, in *IA Deutschland 158 g. Bd. 4*). Hence the German Foreign Ministry was faced with a *fait accompli* when Hesselbarth's book *Drei psychologische Fragen* appeared in 1913.

[1] Hesselbarth, *Drei psychologische Fragen*, pp. 34-5.

[2] Hesselbarth, op. cit., p. 33. Hesselbarth—or rather Kleefeld—gave wrongly the date of 20 June 1870, for, though Salazar had written the telegram on 19 June, it was brought by Versen to Berlin on 21 June and sent from there the same day, arriving in Madrid at 5 p.m. (see Doc. No. 199 and Appendix A, Versen's diary, pp. 279-281).

[3] Hesselbarth, op. cit., p. 57.

[4] 12/25 September 1911, letter of Bohnen to Hesselbarth, in *Asservat 36*, Ser. 8559, Fr. Nr. E599.210-29.

[5] In 1924, contrary to his earlier intention, Hesselbarth decided to reveal what had been his source and first asked the Foreign Ministry to confirm the authenticity of the documents he had published (9 April 1924, *P.A.* 501, in *Asservat 36*, Ser. 8559, Fr. Nr. E599.195-6). In fact, the Foreign Ministry had not yet discovered who had originally been guilty of the indiscretion; after a close examination of Hesselbarth's material it

On the eve of the First World War the German Foreign Ministry did not show any sign of wavering in its policy of keeping secret the early history of the Hohenzollern candidature, although the secrets it wanted to preserve had partly become public knowledge through Hesselbarth's publication of 1913. A two-volume work published by Richard Fester, also in 1913, *Briefe, Aktenstücke und Regesten zur Geschichte der Hohenzollernschen Thronkandidatur in Spanien*[1] gathered together all previous revelations, including those of Hesselbarth, on the secret negotiation of the candidature. This book of reference, still used today, shows how far German Foreign Ministry practice was lagging behind the progress of historical research.

In February 1920, after the long silence of the First World War, the Foreign Ministry received from Dr Willy Cohn, a *Studienassessor* in Breslau, a request to be allowed to consult the documents concerning the Hohenzollern candidature and the origins of the war, and more particularly the reports of Werthern, the Prussian Minister to Munich.[2] The Foreign Ministry answered that similar requests had been previously refused, as it was impossible to depart from the principle that political files could not be made available to historians before their transfer to the State Archives.[3]

This principle, however, was not invoked against Professor Platzhoff and Dr Rheindorf, who asked jointly in August 1921 to be allowed to study the files concerning the political history of the war of 1870. In a marginal note to the draft reply to Platzhoff and Rheindorf, the Foreign Ministry stated its intention of excluding from the files to be communicated those concerning the Hohenzollern candidature: it did not wish to give historians the proof that Bismarck's declaration of July 1870 in

had come to the conclusion that the leak had occurred in Madrid, not in Berlin, and had adopted the view advanced by two expert historians, Platzhoff and Rheindorf, that Salazar was the guilty party (18 August 1924, zu *P.A.* 501/24, in *Asservat 36*, Ser. 8559, Fr. Nr. E599.203-5). Following Hesselbarth's communication, data were extracted from the personal files showing that Alexander Kleefeld, who was born in Danzig on 2 June 1814 and died in Valladolid on 18/19 November 1886, had been employed at the Prussian Legation from 1849 until his retirement in 1875; Kleefeld had married not a Spanish lady, as Hesselbarth had been told, but the daughter of a businessman from Dresden, Bertha Jahn, who died in Valladolid in 1889. The heir was Friedrich Barraza Díaz, a Spanish cavalry officer, who obviously was the one who had given to Hesselbarth, through Bohnen, the Kleefeld documents (zu *P.A.* 501, in *Asservat 36*, Ser. 8559, Fr. Nr. E599.197). The Foreign Ministry did all in its power to prevent Hesselbarth from publishing any details about his source of information, and showed some concern on learning that Kleefeld not only had copied the few documents published by Hesselbarth, but also had collected during his long career six or seven volumes of notes with the ultimate purpose of serving history (*Asservat 36*, Ser. 8559, Fr. Nr. E599.199-209 and E599.175-7).

[1] Leipzig und Berlin, 1913.

[2] 21 February 1920, letter of Willy Cohn to the Foreign Ministry, A 2995, in *IA Deutschland 158 g. Bd. 5.*

[3] Zu A 2995, 12 March 1920, in *IA Deutschland 158 g. Bd. 5.*

the *Bundesrat* did not correspond to reality; that would only unnecessarily create new difficulties for German policy.[1] Besides, in an interview at the Foreign Ministry, Platzhoff declared that he was merely interested in the political history of the war itself and that he renounced in advance any idea of studying the documents on the Spanish affair. The Platzhoff-Rheindorf incident shows that the Foreign Ministry, with regard to the Hohenzollern candidature, was following the practice of secrecy established before the First World War.

In 1923, an American professor from Harvard, Robert Howard Lord, displayed a direct interest in the Hohenzollern candidature and wrote to the Foreign Ministry:

> The documents in the Berlin archives which I should most like to see are—especially—the reports of the Prussian envoys in Madrid and Paris, 1869-July 1870; and correspondence available on the subject emanating from Bismarck, King William, the Hohenzollern Princes, Prim, Salazar, Bucher, Versen, Bernhardi.[2]

Lord's wish was not granted, and he was allowed to consult merely the "open" files on the last days before the 1870 war.[3]

The Foreign Ministry asked Platzhoff and Rheindorf soon afterwards for their expert advice on the advisability of publishing the secret files. Their report, dated 14 March 1924, evaluated the contents of the secret files, pointing to the several instances on which they throw a new light from the viewpoint of historical research. Besides they assumed, though incorrectly, that the source of Hesselbarth's publication was Salazar, or rather documents which he left behind. As a conclusion to their study, Platzhoff and Rheindorf advised the Foreign Ministry against publication of the secret files.

Here is the full text of the Rheindorf-Platzhoff report; the first part,

---

[1] Zu H.A. 186, 8 September 1921, in *H.A. 24. Bd. 2.*

[2] Letter of 3 August 1923 from Lord to the Director of the Archiv des Auswärtigen Amtes, H.A. 521/23, in *H.A. 24. Bd. 5.*

[3] In fact his request received the marginal comment:

Professor Lord hat die folgenden Akten eingesehen:

Spanien 32 (offene Akten) Bd. 1-7.
Frankreich 70 Bd. 1, 2, 2a, 3, 4, 4a.
Türkei 24 Bd. 30-33.

Dagegen sind die *geh*[eimen] Akten betr. die Hohenzoll. Thronkandidatur in Spanien Prof. Lord nicht vorgelegt worden. Ich habe vielmehr, nach Rücksprache mit H. Min. Dir. v. Schubert, Prof. Lord mitgeteilt, dass diese Akten einer eventuellen amtlichen Publikation (die natürlich auch im Auftrage oder mit Genehmigung des AA. von einem freien, privaten Forscher gemacht werden könne), vorbehalten seien. Über den Zeitpunkt einer solchen Publikation liessen sich z. Zt. Angaben noch nicht machen. Prof. Lord zeigte volles Verständnis für diese Darlegungen. Z. d. A. M[eyer] 25.8.

entitled "The secret documents and the present state of historical investigation,"[1] may help the reader to find his way through documents published in the following pages:

RHEINDORF-PLATZHOFF REPORT ON THE SECRET DOCUMENTS ON THE CANDIDATURE FOR THE SPANISH THRONE

I. *The Secret Documents and the Present State of Historical Investigation*

Up to the beginning of the 20th century the antecedents of the war of 1870–71 and therewith of the Hohenzollern candidature for the Spanish throne were portrayed by historians exactly as Bismarck had represented them in his speeches and public proclamations at the outbreak of war and later in his *Reflections and Reminiscences*, i.e. it was taken for granted that the candidature of the Hereditary Prince, Leopold, was a question concerning only Madrid and Sigmaringen, in which the Prussian Government and Bismarck played no part. In the last decade before the World War, this view was invalidated by the publications of Keudell, Zingeler, Hesselbarth, Fester and others. It became known that the Spanish Government in February 1870 addressed itself not only to the Hohenzollern Princes but also to the King of Prussia and to Bismarck, that Bismarck had made strong representations to the King and the Hohenzollern Princes in favour of acceptance of the offered crown, that he entered into direct negotiations with the Spanish Government through the Spanish negotiator, Salazar, and by sending Bucher and Versen to Madrid, and that the final acceptance by the Hereditary Prince was to be ascribed to his efforts. Not all enigmas had been solved. New queries cropped up, but since with the material available no further progress could be made, historians after 1914 gave up the attempt to throw light on all the obscure aspects of the problem.

The secret files of the German Foreign Office present an uninterrupted narrative of the negotiations from February 1870 to the "bursting of the Spanish bomb" on 3 July 1870. They confirm the results of more recent investigations and certain of the shrewd conjectures put

---

[1] In fact, all documents contained in the secret files have remained so far unpublished, with the exception of five documents reproduced by Thimme in *Bismarck. Die gesammelten Werke*, Bd. VIb, doc. nos. 1521, 1548, 1557, 1562, 1564. As already stated, Lord could publish in his work, *The Origins of the War of 1870*, only documents from the open files. As this series of open files consulted by Lord had been formed from innocuous documents only, starting with 4 July 1870, the secret files we publish here could contain nothing but new material.

When in Varzin at Bismarck's side, Bucher had kept a file of all documents concerning the Hohenzollern candidature for the period of 2 to 19 July 1870. This file was later added intact to the series of secret files of the German Foreign Ministry in Berlin. From this file, the *Varzin Akten* (*IA Bo 32 Adhibenda*), which had remained uncensored, we have chosen to retain only those documents which were not to be found in the open files consulted by Lord.

forward in connexion with them by Hesselbarth and Fester. They contain in addition a series of new disclosures, hitherto entirely or largely unknown, connected with the question of the Spanish throne, especially with Bismarck's attitude to it and his line of conduct in general and in particular. The new information they furnish may be summarized as follows:

1. It was not until February 1870 that the Spanish Government approached King William and his Government, consequently it was only from that time onwards that Bismarck took up and pursued the idea of placing a Hohenzoller on the Spanish throne. No support is forthcoming for the theory, put forward by the French and also found in certain German works, that Bismarck seriously contemplated such a contingency earlier. However, the secret material still leaves the question open whether the first Spanish offer to the Hohenzollern in September 1869 came to Bismarck's knowledge and, if so, what attitude he took towards it.

2. Bismarck's memorandum of 9 March 1870 to the King—the most important source for his attitude—was made known in substance as early as 1901 by Keudell (*Fürst und Fürstin Bismarck*) but was wrongly dated, was not in the original wording and suffered from considerable omissions made by Keudell certainly on political grounds. It is especially noteworthy that he did not disclose Bismarck's argument that rejection by the Hohenzollern would have a Bavarian candidature as its consequence, thereby putting a dynasty on the Spanish throne "which looked for support to France and Rome, maintaining contact with anti-national elements in Germany and affording them a secure, if remote, rallying point". Further hitherto unknown features of the memorandum are Bismarck's proposal in the interests of absolute secrecy to discuss the question not at a Cabinet meeting but in a more limited circle; further, his brusque refusal to be responsible for a rejection of the proposal; and finally, the marginalia on the document in King William's own hand pointing out its disputable passages and the great risk involved in acceptance of the candidature.

3. Both the Prussian Crown Prince and Prince Karl Anton of Hohenzollern, who at first were against the candidature, were by March won over to the plan by Bismarck himself. The enquiry, made known by Zingeler, which the Crown Prince addressed to the Queen of England as to the British Government's attitude to the whole question was sent with the knowledge of the King and Bismarck, since the Crown Prince informed them both of London's reply.

4. The mysterious Mr Gama, one of the intermediaries between Berlin and Madrid, whose identity all the efforts of scholars had hitherto failed to establish, is a cover name for Salazar.

5. The much debated question whether Bucher carried written

28

instructions with him on his two journeys to Madrid is to be answered in the negative. It is confidently to be assumed that on both occasions his instructions were purely verbal. The tenor of his instructions for his first journey in April 1870 can be deduced from his reports from Spain on his conversations with Marshal Prim.

6. From these hitherto unknown reports of Bucher's it becomes clear that he took a very favourable view of Prince Leopold's prospects in Spain. In the questions over which the Hohenzollern felt the deepest concern, namely relations with the Holy See, the Civil List, the attitude of the army and the outcome of the election of the King, he believed all obstacles to have been removed.

7. With the rejection on the part of the two Hohenzollern Princes, the Hereditary Prince, Leopold, and his brother Frederick, at the beginning of May their candidature came for the time being to an end. That Bismarck played a pre-eminent part in its renewal at the end of May is made clear by the documents published by Zingeler and Hesselbarth. The diplomatic files furnish proof that Leopold's conversion was entirely Bismarck's work, and that it was also Bismarck who, by his letter to Prim of 1 June 1870, resumed negotiations with the Spanish Government.

8. The role played by Hereditary Prince Leopold in the whole affair appeared in an unflattering light in the material already published. The diplomatic files reveal that in the whole question he had virtually no will of his own, allowing himself to be led by his father whatever his own personal scruples. Just as in July 1870, when confronted with the French pressure for war, Prince Karl Anton withdrew the candidature without consulting his son, in the same way at the end of May he had announced acceptance in principle without Leopold's knowledge although reserving the final decision for him.

9. Of the Hereditary Prince's final negotiations with Versen, Bucher and Salazar at Reichenhall in June 1870, only the bare fact was previously known. The files give the exact details about which Bismarck was all the time kept informed by cipher reports from Versen.

10. After the Hereditary Prince had given his definite acceptance to the Spaniards in the middle of June, thereby ending the negotiations, Bismarck, returning to Varzin, entirely withdrew from the matter, leaving all further moves to the Spaniards. Thenceforward the tone of his communications conveyed that the question of the Spanish Throne was one concerning only Spain and the Hohenzollern, that neither the King of Prussia nor his responsible Minister had any voice in it. This is the same version as he was to put forward at the sitting of the Bundesrat of 16 July 1870 and have immediately published. Accordingly, he strongly disapproved of Bucher's going to report to the King at Ems after the Hereditary Prince's acceptance of the crown.

In his marginal comment written on Bucher's report of 22 June 1870 he expresses this later attitude of his very clearly. No note exists of the reasons determining this change of attitude.

11. It is no longer a secret that King William was from the outset opposed to the candidature and only gave consent to its acceptance under pressure from Bismarck and on the appeals of the Crown Prince and Karl Anton. What was not hitherto known is that he was not let fully into the secret and was intentionally kept in the dark by Bismarck on many points.

12. One of the greatest enigmas till now has been the question why, after Leopold's acceptance, Prim did not immediately proceed to the election of the King and on 23 July prorogued the assembled Cortes until 1 November, thereby postponing the election until after that date. In his *Neue Beiträge zur Geschichte der Hohenzollern'schen Thronkandidatur in Spanien*, pp. 170 ff., Fester already put forward the conjecture that this step was due to an error in the decoding of Salazar's telegram to the President of the Cortes of 20 June[1], the date for his arrival in Madrid having been deciphered not, as given in the telegram, 26 June but as 9 July. Fester leaves the question open whether the slip was due to "deliberate falsification" or to an oversight. The diplomatic files show that the telegram arrived correct in Madrid but at one single point was wrongly decoded by the cipher clerk at the Prussian Legation. This slip was fateful in that it frustrated Bismarck's purpose of making the election of the Spanish King a *fait accompli* and that the premature publication of the candidature opened up the possibility of French interference.

II. *Hesselbarth's Spanish Material and the Secret Files*[2]

A great part of the secret correspondence by telegram between Bismarck, the Secretary of State, Thile, Bucher, Canitz, the Minister at Madrid, and Salazar was published in 1918 by Hesselbarth in his book *Drei psychologische Fragen zur spanischen Thronkandidatur Leopolds von Hohenzollern*, pp. 28 ff., and was critically investigated by him, Fester and Marx, and in the main correctly interpreted. A collation of this material with the secret files reveals that in Hesselbarth's book a few documents of the collected correspondence are missing and that in what has been reproduced there occur certain errors which often spoil the sense. This raises the question, whence did Hesselbarth

---

[1] Salazar's telegram to the President of the Cortes is wrongly described by Hesselbarth as of 20 June. It was written by Salazar on 19 June and sent from Berlin on 21 June. (See Doc. No. 199 and Appendix A, Versen's diary, pp. 279-281).

[2] At the time when Platzhoff and Rheindorf wrote their report Hesselbarth had not yet told the German Foreign Ministry that his information originated not from the papers of Salazar but from those of Kleefeld.

obtain his material? He himself says (p. 36) that he had a transcription from Spain in which, however, the collector of the documents was not named.

The most likely assumption is that the material comes from Salazar, or, since he died on 19 February 1871, from the private papers left by him. The following reasons speak in favour of this:

1. Salazar was in possession of the Berlin telegrams addressed to him under his cover name and probably also kept copies of the telegrams he sent to Berlin via the Prussian Legation.

2. Among the documents there occurs as the "Intermezzo" a note written in Spanish relating to the above-mentioned error in the deciphering of Salazar's telegram of 20 June[1]. That the note was written by Salazar can hardly be doubted. For it was he who had the greatest interest in getting the error cleared up, and Bismarck had sent him through Canitz a communication about the error. The final sentence of the "Intermezzo" shows that it was not written until after the outbreak of war.

Against the assumption that Hesselbarth's material goes back to Salazar it might be objected that it contains four documents from the correspondence between Bismarck and Canitz. But they do not appear textually in Hesselbarth's collection. Of Canitz's telegram of 17 March 1870 (Hesselbarth, No. 3) the middle portion is lacking. From the telegram of 18 March (Hesselbarth, No. 4), in which Canitz expresses his objections to the Hohenzollern candidature, only one argument is cited, the danger of civil war. Bismarck's reply of 20 March (Hesselbarth, No. 6) is not quite textual though it renders the sense correctly and completely except for the final passage about secrecy. The content of Canitz's long letter to Bismarck of 26 March (Hesselbarth, No. 10) in which the Minister motivates in detail objections to the candidature is reduced to a single rather colourless sentence and erroneously described as a telegram.

This leads to the assumption that the collector of the Hesselbarth documents did not copy from the original dispatches. The greater probability is that they were read out to him or that he received a brief communication of their content. That could hold good only of Salazar. The possibility suggests itself in view of the close contact existing at that time between him and Canitz in connexion with the candidature question. Salazar no doubt took short notes of the communications made to him by Canitz and laid them with his own papers.

Against the assumption, supported by outside and inside evidence, that Salazar was the collector and owner of the Hesselbarth documents, another supposition, namely that the documents were unlawfully

[1] See p. 30, n.1.

copied from the archives of the German Legation at Madrid, scarcely deserves consideration. For in spite of the doubts expressed by the Minister, von Hatzfeldt, in his report of 4 May 1877, it is hardly probable that an unauthorized person can have gained access to the secret correspondence and copied it. Even if this had actually been so, there is nothing to explain why this person copied precisely those documents and not the whole lot and why he merely summarized the contents of certain of them.

The document in the Spanish collection about which discussion and controversy have been most intense is the so-called "Letter of Instructions" first published by Pirala in *Historia Contemporánea* (Volume III, Madrid 1876, pp. 392 ff.) without any indication of source and from there reproduced by Hesselbarth. Hesselbarth regards it as instructions for Bucher. As stated above, the diplomatic files do not contain written instructions to Bucher either for his first or for his second journey to Spain. It may confidently be assumed, moreover, that none were issued to him since they would have been on the one hand superfluous with a negotiator so fully initiated into Bismarck's policy and on the other highly dangerous on security grounds. Furthermore, Marx in his *Bismarck und die Hohenzollern-Kandidatur* (pp. 46 ff.) rightly points out that the so-called "letter of instructions", or at any rate part of it, cannot have been written earlier than the end of June, i.e. after Bucher's return, since it postulates the existence of Leopold's requests for the consent of his father and the King of 14 and 16 June respectively and his letter of acceptance to Prim of 23 June. Hence it cannot be doubted that the document in question is not instructions for Bucher. Then what is it?

Certainly Bismarckian ideas occur in it (e.g. "the Prince is of age and master of his decisions") and also certain Bismarckian turns of phrase, above all in the concluding sentence. But anyone who has made a study of Bismarck's diction would on formal and stylistic grounds rule out all possibility of this document's having originated either with Bismarck or with the German Foreign Ministry. Fester (p. 167 AS) justly draws attention to the fact that Pirala's original source was in French. The rhetorical questions contained in it point to Romance authorship. A similar rhetorical question occurs in the "Intermezzo" written by Salazar. This suggests that the so-called "letter of instructions" may also have emanated from Salazar's pen. If Romance, i.e. Spanish, authorship is assumed, there can be a question of nobody other than Salazar. Not only was he familiar with all the details of the long-drawn-out negotiations but his repeated conversations with Bismarck, Bucher, Canitz and Versen had given him full insight into Bismarck's views, thought processes, arguments and turns of phrase, and may explain their occurrence in the document. Thus what we have to deal with is not a "letter of instructions" to Bucher but notes made by Salazar for his own use on the basis of his conversations with the German diplomat and in which he committed sayings of Bismarck's to paper. This is corroborated by the fact that the "letter" manifestly consists of several parts, of which at least the passage relating to Leopold's letter of acceptance was not written until after the finish of negotiations with the Hohenzollern, a circumstance which in itself is a further indication that the origin of the "letter" is to be sought in notes jotted down by Salazar. This interpretation of the "letter of instructions" fits in flawlessly with the above outlined theory that Hesselbarth's whole material is based on notes of Salazar's while at the same time furnishing further support for the theory. How Pirala or Hesselbarth came into possession of Salazar's papers does not concern us here.

III. *Opinion on the Advisability of an Eventual Publication of the Secret Files*

From the standpoint of historical studies the publication of the secret files would without doubt be in the highest degree desirable. For thereby all guessing about the course taken by the Hohenzollern candidature would be brought to an end once and for all—and investigation at last established on a firm basis of fact. In spite of this the undersigned feel it their duty—however much as historians they deplore the renunciation—strongly to deprecate any such publication on weighty political grounds.

True, since the appearance of the books by Zingeler, Hesselbarth and others, the disclosure of the entire truth would now no longer create the same sensation in learned circles as it would have done 20 or 30 years ago. But now that since 1914 silence has again descended on the question even in historical writings, it would on grounds both of domestic and of foreign policy seem most inopportune to call it to life again. The objections expressed in the reports of 1890 and 1911, with which we fully associate ourselves, in the completely changed circumstances of Germany today carry still more weight than they did at the time they were formulated.

In the field of domestic policy publication would revive the old controversy over the origins of the 1870 war which in the nineties was carried on between the parties around the Ems telegram. The very fact that the secret files throw no light on Bismarck's reasons for taking up the candidature and that, rather, his motives must indirectly be gathered from his policy taken as a whole and from the general political situation, this very fact would open the door wide to a coloured or tendencious interpretation of Bismarck's action and thus drag the great struggle for German unity into the arena of party strife. In particular the discrepancy between what Bismarck did and his subsequent official explanations would not be understood aright in circles unversed in historical and political matters and would be regarded as a reproach if not even as a crime. They might well lose their faith in his whole policy and his achievement in regard to the rise of Germany. Moreover, in the present tense state of feeling within the Reich one must reckon with the fact that Bismarck's memorandum of 9 March 1870 with its references to the House of Wittelsbach and to Catholicism would, in Bavaria and in Catholic circles, be a cause of offence and annoyance which in certain circumstances might have disastrous consequences.

Still more so would this be the case abroad. The inner connexion between the Franco-German War of 1870 and the World War has become today a commonplace of public opinion to no small extent through the Treaty of Versailles, which in Part III, Section V, speaks expressly of the "wrong" done by us in 1871. The publication of the secret files would provide fresh material, highly damaging to Germany, in favour of this point of view. Although, or rather by the very fact that, in the documents Bismarck says not a word as to his ultimate object in the candidature question, particularly as to the reaction it would produce in France, it is possible to draw the conclusion that he wanted to create a *casus belli* and provoke the conflict. To be sure, judicious historians in England, America, and Italy concur with German historians in seeing the real cause of the war of 1870 in the openly expressed determination of the French nation and Government not to tolerate German unification and to despoil us of the fruits of the victories of 1866, and they regard the candidature for the Spanish throne as merely the external occasion of the conflict. But even here the publication of the secret files, especially under the impression of the prevailing anti-German feeling and propaganda, might enable the view to gain the upper hand that Bismarck at least created the occasion for the war and thereby brought about the armed conflict between the two peoples which might perhaps otherwise have been avoided. We Germans carry so heavy a burden of "guilt for the war of 1914" which has been laid upon our shoulders that we must not ourselves provide evidence enabling the responsibility for the war of 1870 to be laid also to our door.

The French especially, in view of their policy as a whole, would certainly never let this weapon against us escape them. Even today, nay more than ever today, they see Bismarck as the "falsifier of the Ems telegram", the man who bears the war guilt of 1870. Poincaré has developed this theme again and again not only in his speeches but in various writings on the origins of the war of 1870. His work *Les Origines de la Guerre*—which on publication was presented by the Rhineland Commission to the historians at Bonn University—opens with the Spanish throne candidature and represents Bismarck as its instigator. He and the circles backing him would without doubt make capital in their own favour and our disfavour out of any publication of the secret files, reading their own estimate of Bismarck's policy into the documents and using the documents as confirmation of it. They would welcome with joy the opportunity to arouse afresh and prejudice against us public opinion in France itself as well as among its allies and the neutrals.

From whatever political standpoint one regards the question of publication one always arrives at the same result, namely that politically it would have the most disastrous consequences for ourselves. For the same reason it is also not advisable to allow individual historians access to the secret files. Apart from the fact that a selection is very difficult to make and would create a precedent, the documents are of no value to research until they are thrown completely open. Moreover, the European political scene as a whole from 1866 to 1871 would barely be modified by an exact knowledge of the question of the Spanish throne. At that time European politics stood under the sign of Napoleon's policy of the encirclement of Prussia, against which Bismarck sought to lay his countermines in Spain. If the bomb had not burst there it would certainly have burst somewhere else and on another occasion. For the clash between Prussia-Germany and France, between French claims to the "prépondérance légitime de la France" in Europe and Germany and the will of the German people to restore its national unity and be master in its own house was inevitable from 1866 onwards. On it the candidature for the Spanish throne had no influence.

It need hardly be said that the undersigned will not make use of the secret documents that have come to their knowledge either in speech or in writing. They request that the present memorandum may be dealt with not as a routine communication but be treated as a confidential document.

BERLIN, 14 *March* 1924
[Signed] Rheindorf. Platzhoff[1]

Friedrich Thimme, the editor of the *Grosse Politik*, had in 1922 asked the Foreign Ministry to be allowed to consult in his spare time the files of the period 1862 to 1890 in preparation for the publication of Bismarck's *Gesammelte Werke* with which he was associated.[2] Thimme added the assurance that he would as a matter of course retain for publication only those documents which politically would not be open to objection.[3]

---

[1] *Asservat 36*, Ser. 8559, Fr. Nr. E599.089-101.

[2] 9 September 1922, letter of Thimme to the Foreign Ministry, zu H.A. 447, in *H.A. 24. Bd. 4.*

[3] "Es ist selbstverständlich, dass für den Abdruck, bei dem es sich überhaupt nur um Schriftstücke von programmatischer Bedeutung, also um eine Auslese der wichtigsten

On the eve of the publication in 1931 of the volume dealing with the Hohenzollern candidature, Thimme went to the Foreign Ministry asking whether Canitz's official correspondence of 1870 was in the German Embassy in Madrid; Thimme wanted to compare with their originals the documents published by Hesselbarth in 1913.[1] In fact, Canitz's correspondence concerning the Hohenzollern candidature had been transferred to Berlin as early as 1877, but Kaempfe, a Secretary of Legation who was in charge of the Political Archives and who received Thimme, answered without hesitation that he would of course gladly ask Madrid about it and let Thimme know. Thimme expressed his thanks. Kaempfe then glanced at the Hesselbarth documents, and said "as a private opinion" that they seemed to him quite unreliable as a historical source.

Reporting on his conversation with Thimme, Kaempfe recommended not to tell him the honest truth ("ihm nicht reinen Wein einzuschenken") but to wait four or five weeks, and, after the appearance of Thimme's volume, due in two or three weeks, to tell him that nothing was known in the Madrid Embassy about the documents in question.

As far as we can ascertain, the administration of the Political Archives in the German Foreign Ministry during the Nazi era did not have to deal with the problem of the secret files on the Hohenzollern candidature.

Schriftstücke Bismarckscher Provenienz handelt, nur solche Schriftstücke heranzuziehen sein werden, bei denen ein politisches Bedenken nicht vorliegen kann, wofür ich nach den bei der grossen Aktenpublikation gesammelten Erfahrungen einen leidlich sicheren Blick zu haben glaube."

[1] 31 March 1931, note by Kaempfe, I.S. 184, *Asservat 36*, Ser. 8559, Fr. Nr. E559.104-6.

BIBLIOGRAPHICAL NOTE AND COMPARISON WITH THE SPANISH DIPLOMATIC ARCHIVES

I. DOCUMENTARY SOURCES

1. The documents here printed come from the German Foreign Ministry files *IA Bo 32 secreta*.[1] *Die Berufung eines Prinzen von Hohenzollern auf den Spanischen Thron.*

Under this heading there are six files, starting at 17 February 1870. Originally these six files were entirely secret; later the documents from 4 July 1870 in file No. 2 onwards (and having no connexion with the secret negotiations for the candidature) were reclassified as "open" files and these were the source of Lord's book *The Origins of the War of 1870*.

There are two further files under the heading *IA Bo 32 secreta*:

Vol. 1a was made up at a late date and consists of the papers from the Prussian Legation in Madrid relating to the Hohenzollern candidature; these were transferred to Berlin in 1877 for security reasons.

Vol. Adhibenda. As already explained in the Introduction, the documents in file *IA Bo 32 Adhibenda* were collected by Bucher during the period 2-19 July 1870, when he was with Bismarck at Varzin. The Varzin documents were kept as a single file in the secret series, not divided into "secret" and "open" documents. For the present publication we decided to use from the file *Adhibenda* only those documents which are not also to be found in the open files consulted by Lord.

Except for such documents in the file *Adhibenda* as should have been classified "open", and except for press cuttings and printed pamphlets, we have made a point of reproducing in full all documents from the "secret" files belonging to the period *preceding* the Franco-Prussian war.

2. In the Introduction, we have made use of the later documents from *IA Bo 32* dealing with the prolonged secrecy of the Hohenzollern candidature documents. The following files have also been used:

IA Bc 70.[2] *Krieg mit Frankreich 1870*

    Bd. 5   : 20. Juli.
    Bd. 8, 8a : 23. Juli.
    Bd. 10   : 25. Juli.

IA Deutschland No. 158 geheim. Benutzung der politischen Akten des Auswärtigen Amts zu publicistischen Zwecken. Bd. 1-5 : 1890-1920.

IA Ae 61.[3] *Schleswig—Die Verhandlungen über die Abstimmung in den nördlichen Distrikten Schleswigs in Folge des Artikels V des Prager Friedens. Bd. 28 : vom 1 Januar 1901.*

---

[1] According to the filing system then in operation, *IA Bo* stood for: *I (Politischer Schriftwechsel) A (Europa) B (Die ausserdeutschen Staaten) o (Spanien).*
[2] In *IA Bc 70*, *c* means *Frankreich.*
[3] In *IA Ae 61*, *Ae* means *Deutschland, Dänemark (Wegen Holstein und Lauenburg).*

P.A. 24.[1] *Die private (wissenschaftliche) Benutzung des Politischen Archives. Bd. 1-29 : 1. März 1920-31. Dez. 1944.*

Asservat 36. Vorgänge betr. die Hohenzollernsche Thronkandidatur in Spanien 1869-70, und die Veröffentlichung daraus bezüglicher Geheim-dokumente durch Prof. Hesselbarth in Stift Rappel, 1911-25. Dabei Gutachten Platzhoff-Rheindorf, Berlin 14. III. 1924.

3. A transcript of Versen's diary, reproduced here as an Appendix, is to be found in the file *IA Deutschland No. 158 g. Bd. 3* already mentioned.

4. One would have expected to find some interesting material in the Bucher papers, but in 1893 the German Foreign Ministry was only able to buy from Bucher's brother papers of "literary" value, consisting for the most part of press cuttings from the time when Bucher was a journalist in London. Bucher's political papers had, according to a declaration made by Bruno Bucher to the German Ambassador in Vienna, either been destroyed by Bucher himself or forwarded after his death to Bismarck:

> Herr Bucher once more repeated what he had stated to me already on an earlier occasion, namely that at the time of his brother's death in October last year there had been, besides these folders,[2] a sealed packet of documents labelled "Property of Prince Bismarck" which had been at once forwarded by him from Berlin to the Prince's address.

> This documentary material, as being long since out of his hands, could not come in question in my negotiations with Herr Bucher, and there remain only a few private letters on non-political matters addressed to the late Lothar Bucher of which his brother wishes to retain possession. At my request he has today permitted me to look these through and I have found his statements confirmed. All other letters which are said to have contained political allusions have, as Herr Bucher declared to me, been burned by him.[3]

II. PRINTED LITERATURE

A complete bibliography of the Hohenzollern candidature would be out of proportion with the aim of this volume, as it would have to include practically the whole literature on the origins of the 1870 war. We mention here only works which are cited in the Introduction and which are connected in some way with the German diplomatic documents.

The first author concerned with the German diplomatic papers on the Hohenzollern Candidature was Heinrich von Sybel in his seven volumes *Die Begründung des deutschen Reiches durch Wilhelm I* (Munich, 1889-94). He himself indicated that after the fall of Bismarck permission to use the secret papers was withdrawn; hence the shortcomings of Volumes VI and VII dealing with the period 1866-70, which includes the negotiations for the Hohenzollern candidature.

The publication of papers relating to the King of Rumania was, it seems, prepared in Sigmaringen: *Aus dem Leben König Karls von Rumänien* (Stuttgart,

---

[1] *P.A.* means *Politisches Archiv.*

[2] That is, the papers acquired by the German Foreign Ministry.

[3] 1 March 1893, dispatch No. 66 of Reuss to the Foreign Ministry, AS 215, in *IA Deutschland No. 122 nr 2e. Bd. 1.* vom Januar 1893.

1894-1900, 4 vols.). Volume II, published in 1894, contained letters from his father, Prince Karl Anton von Hohenzollern-Sigmaringen, revealing that the Prussian Government had been involved in the negotiations for Leopold's candidature for the throne of Spain. These revelations moved Sybel to publish some explanations concerning his own work on the Hohenzollern candidature: *Neue Mittheilungen und Erläuterungen zu Band 6 und 7 der Geschichte der Begründung des deutschen Reiches durch Wilhelm I* (Historische Zeitschrift, LXXV, 1895, pp. 38-92).

In 1897 Wilhelm Oncken, who had gained access to some Sigmaringen papers, published *Unser Heldenkaiser* (Berlin, 1897).

The Versen papers were consulted by Werthern for a biography, but at the request of the German Foreign Office he refrained from publishing Versen's diary: Freiherr von Werthern, *General von Versen. Ein militärisches Zeit- und Lebensbild. Aus hinterlassenen Briefen und Aufzeichnungen* (Berlin, 1898).

In *Gedanken und Erinnerungen*, published in 1898, Bismarck maintained the version he had given to the *Bundesrat* in July 1870 and, in spite of the clear statements in the memoirs of the King of Rumania, denied that a Crown Council on the Spanish question had been held in March 1870. Keudell's book *Fürst und Fürstin Bismarck* (Berlin und Stuttgart, 1901) gave evidence about this Crown Council.

In 1906 appeared the ninth and last volume of the Bernhardi papers: *Aus dem Leben Theodor von Bernhardis* (Leipzig, 1896-1906, 9 vols.), Vol. 9: *In Spanien und Portugal. Tagebuchblätter aus den Jahren 1869-1871.* It deals with the Hohenzollern candidature. Bernhardi has been something of a mystery man. We publish here among the German diplomatic papers his reports to the *Auswärtiges Amt.* What did he report to Moltke? Unpublished material from Bernhardi may yet some day come to light.

Then in 1911 there began a series of publications by Karl Theodor Zingeler, the keeper of the Sigmaringen papers:

> *Karl Anton, Fürst von Hohenzollern, ein Lebensbild nach seinen hinterlassenen Papieren* (Stuttgart und Leipzig, 1911).
> *Das fürstliche Haus Hohenzollern und die spanische Thronkandidatur* (Deutsche Revue, XXXVII, 1, 1912, pp. 59-68).
> *Briefe des Fürsten Karl Anton von Hohenzollern an den Grossherzog Friedrich I von Baden* (Deutsche Revue, XXXVII, 2, 1912, pp. 148-62 and 294-309).
> *Briefe des Fürsten Karl Anton von Hohenzollern an seine Gemahlin Josephine, geborene Prinzessin von Baden* (Deutsche Revue, XXXIX, 2, 1914, pp. 338-346; XXXIX, 4, 1914, pp. 112-20).

The controversy between Delbrück and Ollivier concerning the alleged instructions of Bismarck to Bucher took place in 1911. As we know, Delbrück did not have access to the German diplomatic archives. His views on the Hohenzollern candidature are to be found in the following publications:

> *Der Ursprung des Krieges von 1870* (Preuss. Jahrb., Bd. 70,1892, pp. 729-46).
> *Zum Ursprung des Krieges von 1870* (Preuss. Jahrb., Bd. 79, 1895, pp. 341-8).
> *Das Geheimnis der napoleonischen Politik im Jahre 1870* (Preuss, Jahrb., Bd. 82, 1895, pp. 1-55).

Erinnerungen, Aufsätze und Reden (Berlin, 1905).
Ollivier über den Krieg 1870 (Preuss. Jahrb., Bd. 137, 1909, pp. 305-34).

Ollivier's point of view is reproduced in *L'Empire Libéral*, Vols. XI-XIV, (Paris, 1895-1912).

Erich Brandenburg used German diplomatic archives, but was refused access to the secret files on the candidature:

> *Briefe und Aktenstücke zur Geschichte der Gründung des deutschen Reiches 1870-71* (Leipzig-Berlin, 1911, 2 vols.).
> *Die Reichsgründung* (Leipzig, 1916, 2 vols.).
> *Untersuchungen und Aktenstücke zur Geschichte der Reichsgründung* (Leipzig 1916).

Ernst Marx published without the help of original sources *Bismarck und die Hohenzollern Kandidatur in Spanien* (Stuttgart, 1911).

Hermann Hesselbarth's book *Drei psychologische Fragen zur spanischen Thronkandidatur Leopolds von Hohenzollern* (Leipzig, 1913) included telegrams exchanged between Bismarck and Salazar, which went through the Prussian Legation in Madrid.

Richard Fester collected previous revelations, including those of Hesselbarth, on the Hohenzollern candidature in *Briefe, Aktenstücke und Regesten zur Geschichte der Hohenzollernschen Thronkandidatur in Spanien* (Leipzig, 1913, 2 vols.). Fester is also the author of several studies:

> *Bismarck und die Hohenzollernsche Thronkandidatur* (Deutsche Rundschau, Bd. 140, 1909, pp. 24-59).
> *Neue Beiträge zur Geschichte der Hohenzollern'schen Thronkandidatur in Spanien* (Leipzig, 1913).
> *Die Genesis der Emser Depesche* (Berlin, 1915).

After the First World War the American historian, Robert Howard Lord, published a wide selection of the documents contained in the "open" files of the German Foreign Ministry on the candidature in *The Origins of the War of 1870* (Cambridge, Mass., 1924).

An important documentary source on the origins of the 1870 war is Hermann Oncken: *Die Rheinpolitik Kaiser Napoleons III von 1863 bis 1870* (Berlin und Leipzig, 1926, 3 vols.). Oncken was not allowed access to the secret files on the candidature; he used mainly the Austrian archives, and used the Prussian archives very little. Concerning the latter, Oncken gives, in one instance at least, the impression of being biased. In a footnote to document 823 (vol. 3, pp. 372-3) he mentions Bismarck's dispatch to Bernstorff of 7 June 1870, which was later published in full by Thimme: *Bismarck. Die Gesammelten Werke* (Vol. VIb, doc. No. 1560). Although this dispatch runs directly against Oncken's main thesis one would have expected Oncken to reproduce it alongside the Austrian documents. Only a few lines of Bismarck's dispatch, however, are reproduced in the footnote, and they are accompanied by a commentary tending to refute Bismarck's affirmations.

Thimme published a few important documents on the early history of the candidature in Volume VIb of Bismarck's *Gesammelte Werke, Friedrichsruher*

Ausgabe (Berlin, 1924-33). Volume VIb was published in 1931. The existence of secret files on the Candidature was not revealed to Thimme.

Jochen Dittrich used the Sigmaringen archives for his article: *Bismarck, Frankreich und die Hohenzollernkandidatur* (Die Welt als Geschichte, 1953, 1, pp. 42-57).

The official publication of the Prussian diplomatic archives (*Die auswärtige Politik Preussens 1858-81. Diplomatische Aktenstücke, hg. von der Historischen Reichskommission*) undertaken under the Weimar regime did not reach the period of the candidature, as Volumes IV and V of the 3rd series, planned to cover 1869-71, were never published.

III. Comparison with the Spanish Diplomatic Archives

A comparison of the German documents published in this volume with their counterparts in the Spanish archives would permit a critical study and might reveal lacunae in the German documentation.

The possibility of such lacunae is strongly suggested by a careful reading of a Spanish author, Antonio Pirala, who, as early as 1876, in the third volume of his *Historia Contemporánea*,[1] mentioned documents not to be found in the German archives, notably a letter of 14 July 1869[2] sent by a Berlin banker to the Regent of Spain, General Serrano, recommending the Prince of Hohenzollern as the most suitable candidate. Pirala claims also to have seen an important document expressing some of Bismarck's views and running as follows:

> It is possible that we are seeing a transitory ferment in France and without doubt it behoves us to avoid all that might serve to contribute to or increase it. If this be so, would it be opportune to bring in my name in connexion with these negotiations? I think not; on the contrary my person should be left entirely out of the whole affair. In actual fact I am not officially involved, *engagé*. It is a question of a voluntary move on the part of the Spanish nation on the one hand and on the other of the Prince who is of age, master of his own actions and a private individual. Whether or not there have been reasons for obtaining the consent of the father and of the head of the family is a matter of a private nature, not an affair of State. To apprise the King of such a project is the duty of the Minister of the Royal Household. But I have helped with advice not in my quality as Prime Minister but rather as being in charge of Foreign Affairs, as confidential counsellor, like the other servants of the State who are in the secret. I believe that the Spanish Government will do better not to publish anything more than General Prim's letter of 17 February and the reply to it. In this way we shall be in an impregnable position with regard to the European public. If there is an uproar in France we shall simply ask, what do they want? Do they want to dictate the decisions of the Spanish nation and of a German private individual? Then will be the occasion to make use of what you, Doctor, suggest to me. Nevertheless there will be an outcry about intrigues, they will be furious with me without specifying the grounds for their attack.

[1] Pirala (Antonio), *Historia Contemporánea. Anales desde 1843 hasta la conclusión de la actual guerra civil.* Madrid, 1875-80. 6 vols.

[2] Pirala, *Historia Contemporánea*, Vol. 3, p. 392.

As to my reply, all that now remains at issue is the question of a policy towards the General. I have answered his letter. I hope that he will be in no doubt as to my most respectful sentiments towards his person and as to my support for the project, the realization of which now depends solely on him and the Cortes. I have not carried the affair to the stage it has now reached without considerable inconvenience, which M. Gama, with his knowledge of the whole situation, will be able to appreciate and explain to the General.[1]

We have indicated in the Introduction that in 1911 this document became the centre of a controversy between Ollivier and Delbrück. Hesselbarth, who reproduced the above quotation in full, considered it to be part of Bismarck's instructions to Bucher. The German Foreign Ministry, however, when questioned by Delbrück concerning the authenticity of the document, judged it apocryphal. Ollivier made a good point when he said that Bucher, who knew Bismarck's thoughts so intimately, had no need of written instructions. On the other hand the chances are that the document did exist, for it remains to be proved that Pirala produced a fake.

How can we explain the absence of a copy in the German secret files? It is not impossible that the document was eliminated by Bismarck himself from the series on the Hohenzollern candidature.

Dr G. P. Gooch remarks in the Foreword to this volume that none of the documents referred to the possibility of a war with France as a result of a Hohenzollern candidature. The document quoted by Pirala does precisely deal with the possible reactions of France, and in order to form a final opinion on it, it would be necessary to trace Pirala's original source.[2]

Pirala says also that Versen came to Madrid to propose a military alliance.[3] The German documents do not mention this, and it would certainly be worth consulting the documents seen by Pirala on this point.[4]

Finally Pirala gives an interesting detail concerning Bismarck's interview on 22 March 1869 with Rancés, the Spanish representative in Vienna, formerly in

[1] Pirala, *Historia Contemporánea*, Vol. 3, p. 392.

[2] Apart from the lacuna suggested by the Pirala document, there is a missing reference in the German archives—Bismarck's letter to Abeken of 20 June 1870, from which we would have learned a great deal about Bismarck's intentions. (See reference to this document in Abeken's letter to Bismarck of 22 June 1870.)

[3] Pirala, *Historia Contemporánea*, Vol. 3, p. 394.

[4] Pirala's affirmation concerning a proposed military alliance is confirmed by a biography of Sagasta, the Spanish Foreign Minister, for which the author used some of Sagasta's papers (Alvaro de Figueroa y Torres, Conde de Romanones, *Sagasta o el político*. Madrid, 1930). Rascón, the Spanish Minister in Berlin, reported an interview with Bismarck in the following terms:

I answered that I had no instructions and he replied that I should give my personal opinion, whereat I said that, considering the character of the men who form the present Government, I thought that in spite of not possessing a numerous army Spain would make war on France although the latter displayed no hostility towards her; and he answered that the important thing was not numbers but to split up the French forces. He ended by saying that he would send to Madrid a diplomatist with a knowledge of Spanish to settle the terms of the aid which Spain would give to Germany in the coming war (p. 110).

Berlin. Pirala says that Bismarck then put forward Leopold von Hohenzollern as a candidate for the throne of Spain.[1] This fact, if proved, would be of particular interest in view of the later claim made by Benedetti, the French Ambassador in Berlin, that he himself had made a report to Paris at that time about the possibility of a Hohenzollern candidature.[2] There is little doubt that Benedetti did so, but Benedetti's assumption that Rancés came to Berlin to foster a Hohenzollern candidature seems entirely unwarranted. On the one hand, Thile, the German Secretary of State, denied to Benedetti the existence of a Hohenzollern project.[3] Admittedly Thile's word should not be taken as

---

[1] *Historia Contemporánea*, Vol. 3, p. 391. This is Pirala's text: "The partisans of Montpensier, of Don Fernando and of Espartero were still agitating when for the first time Count von Bismarck put forward the name of Hohenzollern to occupy the Spanish throne." In a footnote Pirala adds: "Sr. Rancés, our Spanish Minister at Vienna, was present in 1869 to offer his congratulations to the King of Prussia on the occasion of the festivities on 22 March for that Sovereign's birthday; and it seems that in conversation with Bismarck he expressed some certainty that Montpensier would be chosen. This alarmed the Count and he found means through the press of putting forward the name of Prince Leopold of Hohenzollern."

[2] Benedetti, *Ma Mission en Prusse*, p. 302. Paris, 1871.

[3] The report of Benedetti on his interview with Thile of 31 March 1869 was incorporated by Gramont in his circular of 24 July 1870 on the origins of the war of 1870, which was communicated to the Spanish Government:

Berlin, 31 *March*, 1869.

MONSIEUR LE MARQUIS. [Marquis de la Valette, the French Foreign Minister at the time.]

Your Excellency yesterday asked me by telegraph to ascertain whether the Prince of Hohenzollern's candidature for the throne of Spain was put forward seriously. I had occasion this morning to see Herr von Thile and thought I might ask him if I must attach any importance to the rumours which had been circulating on this subject. I did not conceal from him that I was anxious to have exact information, pointing out that such an eventuality interested the Emperor's Government too directly for it not to be my duty to call attention to its dangers in the event of there being grounds for believing that it might come to something. I told my interlocutor that my intention was to inform you of our conversation.

Herr von Thile gave me the most formal assurance that he had at no time had knowledge of any indication of a nature to authorize such a conjecture and that the Spanish Minister at Vienna had not made any allusion to it during his visit to Berlin. The Under Secretary of State, in thus expressing himself and without anything said by me calling for such a manifestation, judged it his duty to pledge his word of honour.

According to him, M. Rancés confined himself to having a talk with Count von Bismarck, who perhaps desired to take advantage of that diplomatist's visit to gather information on the state of things in Spain and or the way they were shaping in the question of the choice of the future sovereign.

This in substance is what Herr von Thile told me, reverting several times to his initial statement that there had not been and never would be a question of the Prince of Hohenzollern for the Crown of Spain.

Pray accept the assurance of my high esteem.

(In bundle 2287: *IIA Política. Alemania 1866–1873*.) Benedetti published in his memoirs a more complete version of this report (*Ma Mission en Prusse*, pp. 305–6). So did the editor of the *Origines diplomatiques de la guerre de 1870–1871* (vol. 24, doc. 7363).

proof, but a more disturbing piece of evidence is the fact that Rancés was personally a warm supporter of the Montpensier Candidature.[1] If Pirala was accurately informed, Benedetti would have been guessing right although starting from false premises, for, according to Pirala, Bismarck would seem to have replied to Rancés mentioning the name of Leopold von Hohenzollern after Rancés had expressed to Bismarck his confident expectation that the Montpensier candidature would triumph.[2]

Unfortunately it has not been possible to check any of these points in the Spanish archives as the documents on the secret negotiations could not be found

---

[1] This appears clearly in a report written several weeks later by the Prussian representative in Vienna:

No. 170   Vienna, 9 June, 1869
                                             A 2192. Submitted 11 June, 1869

The Spanish Minister, Señor Rancés, called on me a few days ago prior to his departure for the Carlsbad cure, it seemed especially on purpose to tell me that his colleague in Berlin, Sr. Rascón, had reported having met with the most friendly reception there. Sr. Rancés on this occasion once again developed the theme of his view of the state of things in Spain, emphasizing that his opinion remained unchanged that the Duc de Montpensier was still to be regarded as the only possible candidate for the Spanish throne. Marshal Serrano and Admiral Topete, who represented army and navy opinion, were—he said—strongly in favour of this settlement and even Prim was not against it although for reasons of prudence he did not say so. The suitable moment would have to be awaited in order that the Constituent Cortes might proceed to this election, and this might take time because the Cortes were in no haste to disperse and, moreover, many organic laws were before them for debate and decision. That Queen Isabella should return to Spain or her son, the Prince of Asturias, come to the throne, a settlement favoured by the Emperor Napoleon, was beyond the realm of possibility. Many attempts were being made to influence the present Regent in this sense, but entirely without success.

Señor Rancés assumes that his Berlin colleague, Rascón, shares his views on the future occupancy of the throne of Spain, while perhaps not expressing them without a certain reserve. But Rancés regards this circumstance as important from his own point of view, since apart from Paris he regards Berlin as a centre of active policy in regard to Spain. From the Vienna Cabinet he expects no initiative in the matter but on the contrary unqualified adherence to French views and wishes. For that reason he has never discussed Spanish affairs with Count Beust and regards his post here as one of inactivity.

Señor Rancés agrees that for the Imperial French Court the Montpensier settlement is the most distasteful because of the Orléans connexion but he does not think that in the event the Emperor Napoleon would actively oppose it although, according to his information, Spanish conditions are a subject of constant concern to the Emperor of the French and would doubtless be more so if there was to be war.

Signed WERTHER (in file of the German Foreign Ministry archives: IA Bo 28. Vol. 4)

[2] But Benedetti, as he himself admitted in his memoirs, was completely ignorant of the secret negotiations started in February 1870 by Prim's letters to Bismarck, the Prussian King and Leopold von Hohenzollern (Ma Mission en Prusse, p. 314).

in Madrid.[1] Prim was War Minister and worked at the War Ministry. A search for the documents undertaken in Madrid in the Ministry of the Army, which replaced the War Ministry, has been fruitless.[2]

The archives of the Spanish Ministry for External Affairs,[3] however, help to answer some questions connected with the Hohenzollern candidature.[4]

The candidature of the Duke of Genoa is as fully documented as can be expected from the files of a Foreign Ministry. They show chronologically how the Hohenzollern candidature was taken into consideration in February 1870. A circular of 17 December 1869 instructed the Spanish representatives in the main capitals abroad to prepare public opinion for the candidature of the Duke of Genoa. Hence the Spanish Government was seriously contemplating this Italian prince, and when the Spanish Chargé d'Affaires in Florence wired on 21 December that the rumour of a Hohenzollern candidature had made a bad impression there, he received this answer on the same day:

> The Government has no other candidate than the Duke of Genoa. It is untrue that Prince Leopold has been considered, and still less true that negotiations

---

[1] Pirala described his sources as "documentos officiales y cartas reservadas" (*Historia Contemporánea*, Vol. 3, p. 394).

[2] Are these documents in the archives of the *Presidencia del Gobierno*?

[3] Here is the list of the files—or rather bundles—which were actually consulted:

2878. *IIC. Sección histórica. Candidaturas para el Trono. Don Fernando. Duque de Génova. Hohenzollern. 1870.*

This bundle consists of five files: two dealing with the candidature of the Duke of Genoa, which we have used for this note; two files deal with the Hohenzollern candidature, which Lord examined in the 1920's for his book *The Origins of the War of 1870*; the last file deals with the candidature of Don Fernando of Portugal.

2287. *IIA. Politica. Alemania. 1866–1873.*
2319. *IIA. Politica. Austria. 1851–1875.*
2457. *IIA. Politica. Francia. 1870–1874.*
1325. *XB. Correspondencia. Embajadas y Legaciones. Alemania. 1866–1870.*
1517. *XB. Correspondencia. Embajadas y Legaciones. Francia. 1869–1870.*
1366. *XB. Correspondencia. Embajadas y Legaciones. Austria. 1867–1870.*

The files *IIC. Sección histórica* were of a fairly high level of interest. The files *IIA. Política* and *XB. Correspondencia. Embajadas y Legaciones*, on the other hand, contained purely routine matters, and the fact that the sequence of documents shows here and there discontinuities in the numbering suggests that the more important documents concerned with policy-making were filed elsewhere. From a guide to the Madrid archives published by the Spanish Ministry for Education one could gather that the more important documents were filed under "Correspondencia General" (see *Archivos del Madrid*, p. 103. Madrid, 1952.)

[4] Even there some documents which one could have reasonably expected to discover were not to be found, for example the dispatch No. 44 mentioned below in Olozaga's report of 2 March 1870. Rancés' report of his interview with Bismarck in March 1869, when Bismarck, according to Pirala, mentioned the name of Leopold von Hohenzollern as a candidate, should also have been found in the archives of the Ministry for Foreign Affairs, unless Rancés reported to his Minister in a private letter which did not find its way into the official files.

have been carried on. Say so to your Chief and authorize Italian papers to state this.[1] . . .[2]

This Spanish *démenti*, however, is hard to reconcile with Pirala's declaration that Salazar, on his first visit to Germany in the autumn of 1869, had gone to see the father of Leopold of Hohenzollern on behalf of Prim.[3]

Nevertheless one can accept that in December 1869 the Spanish Government was concentrating on the candidature of the Duke of Genoa.[4] They were even anxious, for reasons of internal politics, to obtain a decision before 1 January 1870. The Italian King, however, refused to exert any pressure to disarm the objections of the candidate's family.[5] Consequently the Spanish Government abandoned the candidature of the Duke of Genoa and sent the following circular on 13 January 1870:

> By the circular of 17 December last Your Excellency was notified by the Ministry here of the ideas then held by the Government of His Highness the Regent with regard to the election of the Monarch. And Your Excellency will likewise have learned, though not through official channels, the outcome of the negotiations carried on with H.M. King Victor Emmanuel to obtain the acceptance of the crown of Spain by a nephew of his, the Duke of Genoa. The consequence thereof has been a Cabinet change of which under yesterday's date I have the honour to inform Your Excellency.
>
> Thus the conditions under which the question of the candidature for the throne of Spain was being proceeded with have essentially changed today; and one of the first things agreed upon by the present Government of His Highness has been to defer the solution of that question, carrying on the constitution of the country in the meantime under the organic laws framed to consolidate what has already been accomplished by the Cortes. Consequently Your Excellency should abstain from all action in the sense indicated

---

[1] At this point the difficult handwriting becomes impossible to decipher with certainty. The final phrase may be conjectured to contain the words "desmintiendo . . . suelto . . . Italia", and may thus mean: "contradicting . . . press report . . . Italy". [Tr.]

[2] Telegram No. 43, sent from Madrid on 21 December 1869 at 12 midnight (in bundle 2878: Telégramas).

[3] "This led to consideration being given in Spain to him (the Prince of Hohenzollern); an active part in those negotiations was taken by Sr. Salazar y Mazarredo; on behalf of Prim he approached the Prince's father, announcing in his credentials that he had full powers to carry his important mission to completion, and he left Madrid on 1 November accompanied by Don Juan Pablo Marina, a State Ministry Official.

"After Salazar y Mazarredo had successfully reached an understanding with the German Prince, fearing some hitch he returned to Spain to arrange all the details with Prim, and in this a direct part was taken by Ríos Rosas, Martos and Zorrilla, to whom alone Prim disclosed the news."

(Pirala, *Historia Contemporánea*, Vol. III, p. 392.)

[4] Telegrams Nos. 48 of 27.12.69 and 50 of 29.12.69 to Florence (in bundle 2878: Telégramas).

[5] Telegrams No. 49 of 28.12.69 and No. 54 of 1.1.70 (in bundle 2878: Telégramas) as well as the dispatch of 2.1.70 from Florence (in bundle 2878: Trono de España. Candidatura del Duque de Génova).

in the circular of 17 December or in any other in connexion with the election of the Monarch, about which the Government for the present defers all decision.[1]

By this circular the Spanish Government announced that they were giving up the candidature of the Italian prince, postponing for the time being any decision about the choice of a King. By 17 February, as the German documents show, Prim had made up his mind about the next candidate. It was Leopold von Hohenzollern. If Pirala is to be believed, the possibility of a Hohenzollern candidature had already been explored the preceding autumn by Salazar with the full backing of Prim, but this time Prim wrote directly, not only to Leopold, but also to Bismarck and to the Prussian King. Though still secret, this negotiation was fully official.

It seems from a dispatch of 31 January 1870 sent by Olozaga, the Spanish Ambassador in Paris, that the actual decision to turn to Leopold von Hohenzollern was taken in January, for Olozaga had been called to Madrid to attend conferences to which he refers in a mysteriously allusive way, adding that, for reasons he does not need to quote, prudence requires that the question of the candidates for the throne should not be mentioned at all:

No. 41   Paris, 31 January, 1870[2]

YOUR EXCELLENCY,
    I have received Your Excellency's dispatch of the 13th of this month cancelling the circular of 17 December last by which our representatives were instructed to prepare opinion in favour of the Duke of Genoa's candidature for the throne of Spain. The circular reached me when I had already received by telegraph the order to proceed to Madrid because, as it stated, to my great honour, the Government of His Highness the Regent of the Realm needed to confer with me. Hence I did not reply to the circular and, as regards the discussions which I had the honour to attend, I have nothing to tell Your Excellency who was present at them, taking the important part in them which was appropriate.
    I likewise do not dwell on the reasons for which, as Your Excellency knows, I regard as prudent and even necessary the instruction contained in your above-mentioned dispatch not for the present to raise the question of candidates for the throne of Spain, and Your Excellency may rest assured that no one will fulfil it more strictly or with greater satisfaction than myself.

God grant Your Excellency long life.
Paris, 31 January, 1870.
With most humble salutations
I am Your Excellency's
zealous and faithful servant.
SALUSTIANO DE OLOZAGA.[3]

[1] In bundle 2878.   [2] Received in Madrid on 2 January, 1870.
[3] In bundle 2878. If during these conversations of Olozaga in Madrid the Hohenzollern candidature was actually debated, the Marqués de Lema must be considered as ill-informed when he attributes Olozaga's attitude in July 1870 to his previous ignorance of the Hohenzollern candidature (De la Revolución á la Restauración, Vol. 1, p. 340. Madrid, 1927.

On the Spanish Government's reasons for choosing Leopold von Hohenzollern, the Spanish diplomatic archives also contain a document which suggests that the Spanish initiative of 17 February was preceded by a letter from the Prince of Rumania, Leopold's brother, to the Regent of Spain. It is a dispatch from the Spanish Ambassador in Paris, which I found almost accidentally in a file on France:

No. 93   Paris, 2 March, 1870

YOUR EXCELLENCY,

By the dispatch No. 44, dated the 24th of last month, which Your Excellency was so good as to send me I received a letter, addressed by His Highness the Regent of the Realm to His Highness the Prince of Rumania in reply to one from the latter.

I have the honour to inform Your Excellency that I have handed the letter in question to Sr. Don Juan Strat, the Agent of Rumania, in order that he may forward it to its destination.

> God grant Your Excellency long life.
> Paris, 2 March, 1870.
> With most humble salutations
> I am Your Excellency's
> zealous and humble servant
>
> SALUSTIANO DE OLOZAGA.[1]

Rumania had no diplomatic relations with Spain, and it seems improbable that the Prince of Rumania should have been writing on official matters concerning his country. The hypothesis that his letter dealt with the candidature of his brother cannot be discarded until we have found the dispatch No. 44 mentioned by Olozaga or the correspondence between the Rumanian Prince and the Spanish Regent. The files of the Spanish Ministry for External Affairs are supposed to contain neither of them. If the letter of the Prince of Rumania had been sent some time before 17 February, it could explain why Prim wrote so deliberately, and so officially, to Bismarck, to the Prussian King and to Leopold of Hohenzollern.

While it would be no surprise if the files of the Spanish Ministry for External Affairs contained no information on Salazar's activities in Germany (he was in direct contact with Prim),[2] it is to be hoped that the Spanish documents corresponding to the German ones here published will see the light in the near future.

---

[1] Bundle 1517: *XB. Correspondencia. Embajadas y Legaciones. Francia. 1869-1870*.

[2] The file *Hohenzollern Candidature* (bundle 2878) examined by Lord contained, however, two documents on the secret negotiation which he has reproduced in *The Origins of the War of 1870* (documents Nos. 256 and 257: letter of Prim of 17 February offering the crown of Spain to Leopold von Hohenzollern, and the latter's answer of 23 June accepting it). Incidentally, these documents are the only ones which, according to the Pirala document, Bismarck wanted the Spanish Government to publish: "Yo creo que el gobierno español hará mejor en no publicar más que la carta del general Prim del 17 de Febrero y la contestación de este" ["I think that the Spanish Government will do better not to publish more than General Prim's letter of 17 February and the reply to it."] (Pirala, *Historia Contemporánea*, Vol. III, p. 392). This coincidence would tend to prove the authenticity of the Pirala document.

LIST OF DOCUMENTS

Doc. No.	July, 1870	
264.	10	Count von Bismarck to Count von Solms, Prussian Chargé d'Affaires at Paris (Telegram, 9 a.m.).
265.		Count von Bismarck to Thile (Telegram, 10.15 a.m.).
266.		Count von Bismarck to Count von Bernstorff, Prussian Ambassador in London (Telegram, 10.15 a.m.).
267.		Count von Bismarck to General von Schweinitz, Prussian Minister at Vienna (Telegram, 11 a.m.).
268.		Abeken to Prince Karl Anton of Hohenzollern (Telegram, 12.10 p.m.).
269.		Count von Bismarck to the Prince of Reuss, Prussian Minister at St Petersburg (Telegram, 6.15 p.m.).
270.		Abeken to Count von Solms, Prussian Chargé d'Affaires at Paris (Telegram).
271.		Baron von Canitz, Prussian Minister at Madrid, to Salazar.
272.		Abeken to the Ministry for Foreign Affairs.
273.	11	Abeken to Prince Karl Anton of Hohenzollern (Telegram, 5.11 a.m.).
274.		Strantz to Abeken (Telegram, 10.35 a.m.).
275.		Salazar to Baron von Canitz, Prussian Minister at Madrid.
276.		Salazar to Baron von Canitz, Prussian Minister at Madrid.
277.		Thile to Bucher (Telegram, 3.32 p.m.).
278.		Count von Eulenburg to Count von Bismarck (Telegram, 4.7 p.m.).
279.		Prince Karl Anton of Hohenzollern to Abeken (Telegram, 5.25 p.m.).
280.		Count von Bismarck to Thile (Telegram, 6.30 p.m.).
281.		Count von Bismarck to Abeken (Telegram, 8 p.m.).
282.		Abeken to Prince Karl Anton of Hohenzollern (Telegram, 8.10 p.m.).
283.		Abeken to the King of Prussia.
284.		Count von Bismarck to the Prince of Reuss, Prussian Minister at St Petersburg (Telegram, 10.10 p.m.).
285.		Count von Bismarck to Thile (Telegram).
286.		Count von Bismarck to Thile (Telegram).
287.		Director General of Telegraph Office to Thile.
288.		Crown Prince Frederick William to Count von Bismarck.
289.		Prince Karl Anton of Hohenzollern to Abeken.
290.	12	Strantz to Abeken (Telegram, 3.15 p.m.).
291.		Prince Karl Anton of Hohenzollern to the King of Prussia (Telegram, 2.25 p.m.).
292.		Salazar to Baron von Canitz, Prussian Minister at Madrid.
293.		Crown Prince Frederick William to Count von Bismarck (Telegram, 9.20 p.m.).
294.		Count von Bismarck to Crown Prince Frederick William (Telegram, 10.50 p.m.).
295.		Prince Karl Anton of Hohenzollern to the King of Prussia.

DOCUMENTS

1. *Marshal Prim to the King of Prussia*[1]

(Copy) [French]   Madrid, 17 February, 1870

SIRE,

H.R.H. the Prince of Hohenzollern and Count von Bismarck will have informed Your Majesty of the confidential mission which, in my quality as President of the Council of Ministers of His Highness the Regent of the Kingdom of Spain, I have entrusted to M. Salazar y Mazarredo, member of the Constituent Cortes and Councillor of State.

If Your Majesty should desire to have more detailed and more first-hand particulars before taking a final decision on so weighty a question, M. de Salazar has instructions in so happy a circumstance to present this letter to Your Majesty and express to you the sincere good wishes of His Highness's Government for Your Majesty's happiness and the prosperity of Prussia.

I should be extremely flattered if I could venture to hope that Your Majesty would deign to accept the homage of deepest respect with which I have the honour to be,

Sire, Your Majesty's very humble and very obedient servant.

2. *Marshal Prim to Count von Bismarck*

(Original) [French]

Ministry for War   Madrid, 17 February, 1870

MONSIEUR LE COMTE,

Your Excellency will already have learnt before receiving this letter that in my quality as President of the Council of Ministers of His Highness the Regent of the Kingdom of Spain I have entrusted to M. de Salazar y Mazarredo, Councillor of State and Member of the Constituent Cortes, a confidential mission to H.R.H. Prince Leopold of Hohenzollern.

His Highness's Minister for Foreign Affairs might in this matter have opened direct negotiations with the Government of His Majesty the King of Prussia, but we deemed it more seemly and more expedient at the beginning to make an entirely confidential approach in order not to

[1] This document is preceded by an undated note the text of which is as follows: "Register note. The document, stitched, was handed to me on 13 May, 1870 by State Secretary von Thile for preservation in the Registry.

For this reason the papers of which it consists have been given no registry number and no *Praesentatum*[=submitted]. Roland."

awaken apprehensions which might be injurious to the success of our plans the sole aim of which is to serve the interests of Spain without pre-judicing the rights of all the other nations.

Europe will never have reason to mistake the honesty of our intentions but it is necessary also to take into account the hostile designs of political partisanship.

Spain desires to have a monarchic and liberal Government; she craves for tranquillity and progress, and in all the disturbances of which this country has been the arena since 1808 her aspiration has always been to found an order of things enabling the development of her great resources under the shelter and aegis of modern institutions.

The House of Bourbon has failed in this noble enterprise, and if in our long history there is a fact worthy of the meditation of great thinkers it is the example of a dynasty which in its blindness has left nothing undone that could alienate the heart of one of the most generous peoples of the whole human race.

However much the reactionary party may conspire, the cause of the Bourbons is destined to have in Spain the same fate as in England and France the Stuarts and the descendants of Louis XIV.

As for republican ideas the change which has taken place in the spirit of the populations is so considerable that the constituencies of Cadiz and Jerez, which even after the insurrection of these two cities had sent Federalist deputies to the Cortes, have just nominated Monarchist and Liberal candidates by a big majority.

To accomplish the task which the Government has in view in accord with the country, it is necessary for us to elect a sincerely constitutional king capable of representing tradition in its worthiest aspect and progress in its most lawful form.

M. de Salazar y Mazarredo is fully informed of the plans and ideas of His Highness's Government, and I beg you, *Monsieur le Comte*, to give full and entire credence to all that he will tell you relative to his mission.

Relations between Spain and Prussia have always been marked by such a spirit of cordiality that I venture to be confident that in you, *Monsieur le Comte*, I may find a reciprocity of sentiment which will be the best justification of the frankness with which I convey to you my impressions on this so weighty subject.

Should H.M. the King of Prussia desire to know more direct par-ticulars on this question I would beg you to be so good as to procure for M. Salazar y Mazarredo the opportunity to lay before H.M. the homage of his profound respect and a letter which I thought right to entrust to him in anticipation of this eventuality.

With the highest esteem I have the honour to be Your Excellency's very humble and obedient servant

COUNT DE REUS

3. *Marshal Prim to Prince Leopold of Hohenzollern*

(Copy)[1] [French]   Madrid, 17 February, 1870
                                      pr.[2] Berlin, 25 February, 1870

YOUR ROYAL HIGHNESS,

I take the liberty of addressing this letter to Your Royal Highness through M. de Salazar y Mazarredo, member of the Constituent Cortes of Spain, Councillor of State and my intimate friend. M. de Salazar is not unknown to Your Highness and your family, for a few months ago he had the honour at Weinburg of explaining to Your Highness the situation in Spain and the means of crowning the edifice of our political regeneration. At that time we had just overcome the Carlist insurrection but the Federalist Republicans were preparing to resort to arms in order to overturn the Government, and public opinion was desirous of putting an end to the uncontrolled passions of the extremist parties by the election of a King who could be the standard around which the immense majority of the nation would rally.

For that reason, Your Royal Highness, in September last there was no time to be lost and we had to take a definite decision as a matter of urgency.

Happily the revolt was easily repressed and since then the Government has found in its own spirit of initiative a strength which has enabled it to take stock of the situation and to study with more calmness the way to tighten the bonds which should unite all the liberal elements in modern Spain.

Last year we voted a constitution which has been accepted by the two big parties, the conservatives and the radicals. It remained for us to reach perfect agreement on all the important questions complementary to the fundamental code, and today the reports of commissions nominated to draft proposals for municipal, provincial and electoral laws and laws for the maintenance of public order offer fresh testimony of the patriotic feeling of all men who have at heart the strengthening of order and liberty.

Our task must be crowned by the election of a sincerely constitutional sovereign, and the conservative party, which was opposed to the Duke of Genoa as being a minor, will throw the weight of its influence in favour of a Prince who is of age and a Catholic and by his personal circumstances deserves to be elected by the Spanish nation.

[1] Marginal note: "Original sent to Prince of Hohenzollern on 8 May." From the Spanish diplomatic archives Lord has published a version of this letter differing considerably from the text sent to Berlin (cf. Lord, *The Origins of the War of 1870*, doc. No. 256).
[2] pr. is an abbreviation for *praesentatum* (=submitted).

You, Your Highness, unite all these desired qualities, and in my capacity as President of the Council of Ministers of His Highness the Regent of the Kingdom of Spain I approach with the plea that you will be good enough to give a favourable reply to the proposals which will be made to you in strict confidence by M. Salazar y Mazarredo.

A glorious era opens up before Your Highness. It is not exempt from difficulties, but a Prince of the Prussian Royal House can easily overcome all obstacles when assured of the support of a people rendered illustrious by centuries of honourable dealing, nobility of spirit and capacity for devotion.

I eagerly seize this opportunity to extend to Your Royal Highness the assurance of the deep respect with which I have the honour to be

Your Royal Highness's very humble and devoted servant

MARSHAL PRIM, COUNT DE REUS

4. *Prince Karl Anton of Hohenzollern to the King of Prussia*

(Original) [German]   Düsseldorf, 25 February, 1870

[The text of this letter has been published by Fester, *Letters*, No. 103, following Zingeler, *Karl Anton*, pp. 235-7. The Fester-Zingeler version contains, however, a variant from the original text. Their version runs:

"Should the interests of Prussian power be compatible [*vertragen*] with a solution of the question in the sense of acceptance, Your Majesty will be so good as to have this brought to my knowledge—if they are not thus compatible, our decision is already taken: it is for refusal."

The original text runs:

"Should the interests of Prussian power demand [*verlangen*] a solution of the question in the sense of acceptance, Your Majesty will be so good as to have this brought to my knowledge—if they do not demand it, our decision is already taken: it is for refusal."[1]]

---

[1] The reader will appreciate the import of this variant. The original text shows that Prince Karl Anton and his son will accept Salazar's proposals only if the interests of Prussia so demand. The substitution of *vertragen* (be compatible) for *verlangen* (demand) in Zingeler's text suggests that Prince Karl Anton is asking the King of Prussia whether from the point of view of Prussia there was no objection to Prince Leopold's acceptance of the Spanish crown. Zingeler's text thus tends to prove that Prussia was not called upon to play an active part in the affair of the candidature.

5. *Prince Karl Anton of Hohenzollern to Count von Bismarck*

(Original) [German]   Düsseldorf, 25 February, 1870

[The text of this letter, as published by Fester, *Briefe*, No. 104, follows that of Zingeler, *Karl Anton*, pp. 237-9. The Fester-Zingeler text is corrupt. We therefore think it needful to publish the original text *in extenso* italicizing the passages omitted from the Fester-Zingeler version.]

YOUR EXCELLENCY,

Circumstances render it necessary for me to make the present respectful and confidential communication.

The matter at issue is the candidature for the throne of Spain of my eldest son, the Hereditary Prince.

Were I unreservedly to obey my feelings and were I, moreover, permitted to voice the opinion of my son, the whole question would long since have been settled out of hand and it would not now be my duty to ask Your Excellency's wise and experienced advice in this matter.

But since the subject of my present communication is not solely our private concern and since higher interests of state may conflict with my own humble opinion I cannot do otherwise than appeal to the decision of His Majesty, the King.

Let me respectfully inform Your Excellency of the phases through which the matter has passed before coming in its present shape to the forum of a decision for acceptance or refusal.

It was in the month of September of last year that Don Salazar, a member of the Spanish Cortes, came to see me at my country seat, the Weinburg, in Switzerland. The object of his visit was to make the acquaintance of my son and myself in order to sound our feelings on the question of the candidature for the Spanish throne.

Both my son and I at that time absolutely declined to enter further into this idea though we objectively discussed existing chances of success in finding a suitable personality.

I dismissed on that occasion the not disinterested Don Salazar with the words: "If you prevail upon the Emperor Napoleon to address himself to my Royal Master and explain to him that the founding of a new Hohenzollern-Spanish dynasty would be a warranty of European peace and European tranquillity, and if my Royal Master were to express himself in a sense favourable to this solution of the question—then and then only would the moment have arrived for us to consider whether our family interests allow of acceptance or make it a duty to decline. ["]

With this categoric declaration Don Salazar then took his departure and until yesterday not a mortal word came to my ears of any further pursuance of the proposed idea.

Meanwhile the whole question of the candidature for the throne of Spain passed through the most various stages without arriving at any result. On all sides refusals and protests against possible pretensions to the throne. Almost the entire European press and right-minded public opinion spoke unanimously against Spain, whose fate it seemed to be to become involved more and more deeply in the vortex of revolution.

One could with an easy mind rejoice at having renounced ambitious hankerings in that direction.

Now all at once this Don Salazar again makes his appearance at my house and on a basis of plenary powers from the Spanish Government announces with the utmost emphasis the selection of the Hereditary Prince for the Spanish throne. All those enquiries which have been proceeding for months relative to placing princes of the House of Savoy, the Duc de Montpensier or Prince George of Saxony on the throne he describes as nothing but feints while all the time those with whom the decision rests have been keeping their eyes steadily fixed on a Catholic Hohenzoller.

Now, he declares, this latter question has come to a head and a decision has become urgent. Were the Hohenzollern plan to fail, a last endeavour before introducing a republican form of government would be to knock at the door of the House of Wittelsbach.

The above summarizes a conversation of yesterday between myself and Don Salazar. As he is also charged with letters from Prim to Your Excellency and my son, and also with one to H.M. the King, I could not prevent his going on to Berlin.

In Berlin he will avoid the Spanish Minister because, whatever happens, maintenance of secrecy is of the highest importance.

If he is to be successful in being received by Your Excellency it would be through Legation Counsellor von Keudell (to whom in this event I would send a note introducing Don Salazar) that this could suitably be arranged.

I now take the liberty to go on to a statement of my own impressions in connexion with this highly important decision.

Heart and feeling tell me that acceptance of this crown would be a risky venture. For success in such a task a character would be needed steeled by many-sided experience, of great self-control and thorough political training. So far my son has had no opportunity to give evidence of these qualities.

A Hohenzoller in Spain would give rise to a wild outcry in anti-Prussian Europe and either precipitate or defer the solution of many pending questions. This, however, is a consideration which lies outside the sphere of my judgement.

Acceptance of this crown would be on the one hand an event of world-wide historical importance, on the other, evidence of an uncommonly strong political consciousness of strength on the part of Prussia as a Power.

A dynasty which represents the centre of gravity of Central Europe and whose scions flourish by the Black Sea and beyond the Pyrenees—the one ruling over a nation of developing civilization, the other ruling over one whose civilization belongs to the past—a dynasty such as that has not been known to history since Charles V—on such a dynasty, therefore, rests the responsibility of a high mission willed by Providence and of a reputation for knowing how to rule over elements of the most heterogeneous kind.

These cursory remarks are but brief indications of the opinion which I hold that in this matter only His Majesty the King can say the decisive word—he alone knows the complexities of the present moment, the obstacles of the situation, the reasons which may speak in its favour, and has some insight into the shape of the future.

If, as is my duty, I am to speak frankly, I trust that His Majesty will command an unqualified refusal. I am altogether too free from the boundless ambition with which my peers already reproach me because of the Rumanian affair not to feel constrained from the depths of my heart to wish that His Majesty may spare me all that is necessarily inherent in an acceptance so pregnant with consequences.

But if the King *on higher grounds* commands the contrary I am too loyal a patriot not to stake everything on my son's proving ready and willing to take up this heavy burden.

I beg Your Excellency not to deny my son and me your experienced counsel and for the present to accept my most heartfelt thanks for the patience with which you will have perused this long epistle.

In the meantime, with feelings of the highest esteem I remain
Most respectfully
Your Excellency's most grateful and entirely devoted
PRINCE OF HOHENZOLLERN

6. *The King of Prussia to Count von Bismarck*

(Original) [German]   B[erlin,] 3.3.70

The Hereditary Prince of Hohenzollern knows nothing of his father's arrival tomorrow; we have however agreed to invite him to make the journey here immediately—this I have already telegraphed to him in words which will not arouse the suspicions even of the telegraphists. The Hereditary Prince remitted to me the enclosed, setting forth his reasons against acceptance, which please return to me.

WILLIAM

Annex: *Prince Leopold of Hohenzollern to the King of Prussia*

(Original) [German]   Berlin, 2 March, 1870

It is not reasons of personal convenience or those arising from a vague antipathy to an unknown and arduous future, but rather it is a deep repugnance which filled me as early as the September of last year, when for the first time the question arose of my candidature for the Spanish throne, and has only increased as a result of deeper reflection—and raises its voice in me against acceptance of a crown which, rendered vacant by revolution, is offered me by men of the revolution, while a series of descendants of the old legitimate reigning house, for example the Prince of Asturias, Don Carlos, the Duc de Montpensier, the Duke of Parma make justified claims, have to some extent adherents among the people and are, moreover, some of them closely related to my wife.

The standard of revolt was first raised by the army—whose duty above all else it is to be responsible for the safety of throne and government, and this fact offers no good guarantee of the support which a foreign ruling prince can expect from it, should the need arise. Conditions of disorder, partly of anarchy, have lasted now for more than a year and attempts have in vain been made to induce the most various candidates to accept the throne.

The clergy are mainly Carlist in sympathies or else in favour of Queen Isabella, they are fanatical and have an influence on the backward rural population which should not be underestimated.—The important commercial towns and their inhabitants were, and probably still are, predominantly in favour of a federal republic, the landed class is divided into adherents [*teilt sich in Anhänger*] of the expelled dynasty; individuals among them such as Marquis Abailda want a republic. There remain those who favour the establishment of a constitutional monarchy under a foreign prince—how much influence this party possesses, and how much power it has, I do not know; but the above-mentioned facts undeniably show that the task will be of great difficulty and one which will call for political understanding gained by long years of experience which I do not possess.

The men who for the past year have stood at the head of the government and who brought about the fall of the old Monarchy, feel that the present position is no longer tenable and that a solution of the question at issue is a pressing necessity—a foreign King, unfamiliar with the conditions, will at first be unable to dispense with these men, and how far they will renounce ambitious personal aims in order to ease his task, when that becomes necessary, I do not venture to decide. Moreover, I believe that in Spain, where national feeling is so sharply accentuated, it will be more difficult than in any other country for a foreigner to win full citizenship, and that renders it impossible for him to gain the support needed for the difficult task.

A final requisite for the fulfilment of such a task is personal ambition which, attracted by the lustre of a crown and lightly setting aside more conservative views, the verdict of public opinion, and many deeper and more tender emotions, keeps its eyes fixed on the one goal regardless whether the venture has an element of risk or not—whether the chances of success are great or small.

It would, therefore, be only with a heavy heart that I could take the decision to accept the offered position; I am to the innermost fibre of my heart a Prussian and a German, and the magnificent rise in our country's fortunes, to contribute to which in the measure of his modest powers must be the highest aim of every patriot, would render the sacrifice of expatriating myself only more grievous.

Accordingly I consider it my duty as a Hohenzoller, soldier and subject to submit to the expressed will of H.M. our King, accepting it as the guiding line of my conduct if higher political considerations and the expansion of the power and lustre of our House as a whole so demand.

7. Salazar to Count von Bismarck

(Original) [French]

Hotel Brandenbourg   [Berlin,] 3 March, [1870]

MR LE COMTE,

I came to the Ministry to say to Y.E. that, having only a few days at my disposal (because otherwise in the event of the non-success of my mission a long absence would be noticed in Madrid), I should desire to leave tomorrow, Friday, if the answer were not to be in the affirmative. If it were favourable I could not stay longer than Sunday.

H.R.H. the Hereditary Prince told me yesterday that his father is expected here tomorrow, Friday, and in that case I have hope that a decision will be taken which will enable me to return immediately, or to send a telegram to Marshal Prim. He has had no news from me since Sunday.

I should be very grateful to Y.E. if you would help me a little to find a way out of this situation which vitally concerns my country. As regards the matter itself, all the news I receive is extremely favourable to the success of the task which Spain desires to entrust to Prince Leopold.

Y.E.'s very humble servant

GAMA

8. *Salazar to Count von Bismarck*

(Original) [French]   [Berlin] 6 March, [1870]

MONSIEUR LE COMTE,

I went to take my leave of Y.E. at a quarter to five, after a long conference with the two Princes of Hohenzollern. The senior Prince had seen the King, and he thinks it will not be easy to overcome two objections raised by H.M.

The first is that it would be difficult for Prussia to aid the new king if he were threatened. This he could never be seriously enough for foreign support to be needed. The army is loyal under a stop-gap regime threatened on many sides; it would be still more so with a young and energetic prince at its head. Another factor must also be borne in mind, namely that today everybody is on the look-out to discover who is to be the new king elected by the Cortes. As long as that state lasts there will be uncertainty, for human nature ever tends to egoism and likes to face towards the rising sun.

As to the second objection I find it difficult to understand, since a people has the right to change dynasty when the weal of the nation requires it. Have not the Bourbons done enough for their rights to be prescribed? Their perjury, their conduct, is it not as worthy of reprobation as the behaviour of the House of Hanover?

As regards the Duc de Montpensier, he would be content to have a status in our country and to have his daughter wed the Hereditary Prince's brother. Both young ladies are very beautiful and charming.

Y.E.'s most humble and devoted servant

E. DE SALAZAR Y MAZARREDO

9. *Count von Bismarck to the King of Prussia*

(Original) [German]

> [Although already published by Thimme (*Bismarck. Die Gesammelten Werke*, Bd. VIb, No. 1521), this document is reproduced here because of the King of Prussia's marginal notes contained in the original but not known to Thimme.]

Berlin, 9 March, 1870

YOUR MAJESTY

Will, I trust, graciously permit me with my humble duty to summarize in writing the motives which in my modest opinion speak in favour of an acceptance of the Spanish Crown by His Serene Highness, the Hereditary Prince of Hohenzollern, now that I have already respect-fully intimated them by word of mouth.

I am of the opinion that it would serve Prussian and German state interests and bring indirect advantages if the acceptance takes place, and also that in the opposite case disadvantages and dangers are to be feared.

Acceptance of the Spanish Royal Crown by a Prince of Your Majesty's illustrious House would strengthen existing sympathies between two nations, which, exceptionally, are in the happy position of having no conflicting interests, not being neighbours, and whose friendly relations seem capable of considerable development.[1] The Spaniards would have a feeling of gratitude[2] towards Germany, if they are rescued from the state of anarchy into which a people predominantly monarchist in sentiment threatens to sink because it lacks a king.

For Germany it is desirable to have on the other side of France a country on whose sympathies[3] we can rely and with whose feelings France is obliged to reckon. If during a war between Germany and France condi-tions prevail such as those under Queen Isabella when there was a prospect of an alliance of the Latin Catholic Powers, and if on the other hand in such an eventuality one conceives of a Government in Spain sympathetic to Germany, the difference between the two situations in terms of the armed forces that France could put in the field against Germany may be estimated at not less than one to two French army corps.[4] In the former case it would even become possible for French forces to be relieved by Spanish and thus made available for use, in the latter case it would be necessary to keep at least one French Corps stationed on the Spanish frontier. French peaceableness towards Germany will always wax or wane in proportion to the dangers of a war with Germany. We have in the long run to look for the preservation of peace not to the good will of France but to the impression created by our position of strength.[5]

The prosperity of Spain and German trade with her would receive a powerful impetus under Hohenzollern rule. If even in Rumania the German dynasty has given a remarkable stimulus to trade relations be-tween that landlocked country and Germany, it is to be assumed in all probability that the renewal of friendly feelings towards Germany in Spain with her long coastline would provide new openings for the once so pros-perous German trade there.[6] It should not be forgotten that the political

[1] King of Prussia's marginal note: "Agreed."

[2] King of Prussia's marginal note: "This feeling, this sympathy, on the part of a nation which for the last forty years has wantonly proceeded from one revolution to another, seems to me highly problematic."

[3] King of Prussia's marginal note: "How long would these sympathies last?"

[4] King of Prussia's marginal note: "What potentate in Spain would be in a position to *guarantee* such a policy?"

[5] King of Prussia's marginal note: "Agreed."

[6] King of Prussia's marginal note: "I daresay that is possible."

attitude of Prussia towards Spain after the events of 1833 turned out disastrously for our trade, particularly for the Silesian linen industry; the opposite effect may be expected from a revival of our mutual political sympathies.[1] The repute of the Hohenzollern dynasty, the justifiable pride with which not only Prussia regards its Royal House but Germany too, tends more and more to glory in that name as a common national possession, a symbol of German fame and German prestige abroad; all this forms an important element in political self-confidence, the fostering and strengthening of which would be of benefit to national feeling in general and to monarchist sentiment in particular. It is therefore to Germany's political interest that the House of Hohenzollern should gain an esteem and an exalted position in the world such as does not find its analogy in the past record of the Hapsburgs since Charles V. This element of pride in the dynasty is not to be estimated lightly as a force operating in favour of the contentment of our people and the consolidation of conditions. Just as in Spain scant respect for the ruling house has paralysed the forces of the nation for centuries, so with us pride in an illustrious Dynasty has been a powerful moral impetus to the development of Prussia's power in Germany.[2] This impetus will make strong growth if the hitherto so imperfectly satisfied need of the Germans for recognition by other countries receives the incentive of a dynasty occupying an incomparable position in the world.

A rejection of the proffered crown would probably have undesirable consequences. It could not but highly offend the Spaniards[3] if a crown which in the past always occupied a high rank should not meet with acceptance and if a nation of 16 million souls, begging to be rescued from the anarchy into which it feels itself to be sinking, should suffer the rebuff of being refused the King of its choice.[4]

In the event of a rejection, the wishes of the Spaniards would probably turn to Bavaria. If Prince Adalbert's line or the Ducal line there accepted the offer, Spain would have a ruling house which looked for support to France and Rome, maintaining contact with anti-national elements in Germany and affording them a secure if remote rallying point. The same

[1] King of Prussia's marginal note: "Are great sympathies for Spain noticeable or existent in Prussia?"

[2] King of Prussia's marginal note: "This appreciation of Prussian conditions, spirited, highly creditable and true, would however be profoundly shaken and damaged if the Hohenzollern Dynasty in Spain were to meet *the same* fate as the dynasty which reigned there for over a century."

[3] King of Prussia's marginal note: "The rejection of the Spanish crown by the House of Savoy has caused no offence, although after all *these same* arguments must have appealed to Florence too."

[4] King of Prussia's marginal note: "Would this choice be any more certain than three months ago? when the Cortes rejected the Cabinet's proposal of the Italian prince?"

tendency to enter into relations with Rome, France and Austria[1] with the approval of native ultramontane reactionaries would take place in Spain under Carlist rule. We should then consistently have to regard her as belonging to the ranks of our adversaries.

Failing the Bavarian and the Carlist possibilities Spain would in the first instance probably lapse into a republic. The repercussions of a Spanish republic would most immediately make themselves felt in France and Italy. How easily revolutionary movements spread from Spain to Italy is in our memories since the beginning of the twenties. In France the now repressed party of Rochefort and Co. would draw fresh strength from a Spanish Republic[2] and whether then the increased dangers of a republic in France would impel the Emperor to a breach of the peace is a possibility which at least cannot be ruled out. For all lack of concord in Spain, for all the dangers with which a Spanish republic would threaten Europe, public opinion in Germany—since the present proceedings can scarcely remain secret in the long run—would hold those responsible from whom emanated the rejection of the Spanish crown.[3]

Acceptance would lead to a development of the Spanish question free from hazard.[4] For France it would be of great value if both the Orleanist candidature and the republic in Spain were to seem definitely eliminated.[5]

According to information given, the election of the Hereditary Prince would result by a majority of over $\frac{3}{4}$ of all the votes.[6] For centuries it has only happened twice in history that a great nation like the Spanish has appointed its ruler by such a majority bordering on unanimity: in England at the election of the present ruling house in place of the expelled Stuarts, and in Russia at the election of the Romanov dynasty. The legitimacy of the right by which these dynasties rule in England and Russia is uncontested. The same can hardly be maintained of the rights of the Bourbons in Spain, since this dynasty was forced upon the country

[1] King of Prussia's marginal note: "These hypotheses are possible, but equally possible is their non-occurrence."

[2] King of Prussia's marginal note: "These *possibilities* cannot be denied, but the pros and cons seem to be equally balanced."

[3] King of Prussia's marginal note: "The responsibility whether for *rejection* or for *acceptance* of the Spanish crown by a foreign prince seems to me equally great, as would be the resultant sequelae and consequences, which after all can be only of a purely hypothetical nature."

[4] King of Prussia's marginal note: "A development free from hazard is hardly to be anticipated when there exist more candidates with valid claims to the throne than those in France."

[5] King of Prussia's marginal note: "True."

[6] King of Prussia's marginal note: "The same proportion of votes was promised to the candidature of the Prince of Savoy but was reversed at the ballot. So who can now undertake to guarantee that things will not go again in the same way? Could one wish the Hohenzollerns a result like this?—Is it permissible to expose that House to such an affront?"

by foreign arms at the beginning of last century to the prejudice of the hereditary Hapsburg dynasty, and since 1808 a succession of revolutions and outrages have called every claim to the throne in question.

A reappearance of Queen Isabella on the throne would seem to me a danger to all monarchic interests in the whole of Europe.[1] The English would never have tolerated even for a year a Queen of such habits of conduct. It says much for the rigorously monarchical feeling of the Spaniards that after all the upheavals since 1808 and all the misgovernment of the last hundred years they have borne the rule of Queens Christina and Isabella for 35 years.

No danger to the person of the Hereditary Prince need be anticipated. In all the revolutions which have convulsed Spain the idea of an outrage against the person of the Monarch has never arisen, no threat has ever been uttered.[2] The forces of the present Spanish army have displayed great valour and extraordinary devotion to the monarchic principle[3] in fighting the republican insurgents in the towns; they will provide a reliable support[4] to the future Monarch whose rewarding task it will be to develop anew the rich resources of the country by benevolent rule.

I can therefore only respectfully commend to Your Royal Majesty that You should graciously prevent the rejection of the Spanish crown unless there exists invincible repugnance on the part of the Hereditary Prince.

In view of the need for absolute secrecy in regard to all the relevant negotiations I do not venture to recommend a discussion of them by the Ministry of State,[5] but I venture the respectful proposal to admit the Minister for War, von Roon, the General of Infantry, von Moltke, and perhaps also the Minister Delbrück, into the secret,[6] and, at a full discussion of the matter in the presence of His Royal Highness the Crown Prince, who is against acceptance, and of His Royal Highness the Prince of Hohenzollern, to be graciously willing to hear the advice of these loyal and judicious servants of Your Royal Majesty. If I am not mistaken they know Spain from personal experience; this is also the case with the Minister, Major-General von Schweinitz, whose inclusion in this important discussion would likewise seem to me open to no objection.[7]

---

[1] King of Prussia's marginal note: "Undoubtedly."

[2] King of Prussia's marginal note: "But the *expulsion of the dynasty* did take place."

[3] King of Prussia's marginal note: "It seems to be not so much monarchic principle for which the troops fight well as for the preservation of the rulers whom they support in a revolutionary spirit in order to get into power."

[4] King of Prussia's marginal note: "Reliable support from an army which has made all the revolutions for the last 40 years is hardly to be expected!"

[5] King of Prussia's marginal note: "Agreed."

[6] King of Prussia's marginal note: "and Minister von Schleinitz; and State Secretary von Thile. W."

[7] King of Prussia's marginal note: "Do not recall. W."

I feel a personal need to make it plain by the present humble memo-randum that if the outcome is a refusal the responsibility will not lie at my door, especially if in a near or more remote future historians and public opinion were to investigate into the grounds which have led to rejection.[1]

v. BISMARCK[2]

10. *Salazar to Count von Bismarck*

(Original) [French]   [undated]

MONSIEUR LE COMTE,

His Highness the Hereditary Prince has this instant informed me that to his great regret his father has not yet arrived.

As my position is becoming extremely difficult I beg Y.E. to grant me a moment's hearing in the course of the day, for I foresee an unfortunate result and I should be compromising my Government if I outstepped its instructions.

I have the honour to be Y.E.'s most humble and devoted servant

E. DE SALAZAR

My address is: Mr Erquelines, Hôtel de Saxe, Burgstrasse.

11. *Prince Karl Anton of Hohenzollern to Count von Bismarck*

(Original) [German]   B[erlin,] 10.3.70

YOUR EXCELLENCY

I lose no time in respectfully informing you that today the Portuguese Minister Count Rilvas talked to me about the Spanish matter as one in full possession of the facts.

---

[1] King of Prussia's marginal note: "The above marginal notes make it clear that I have strong scruples against the acceptance of the Spanish crown by the Hereditary Prince of Hohenzollern and would only consent to his acceptance of it if his own conviction told him it was his duty to mount the Spanish throne, in other words, that he regarded this act as a definite vocation. In these circumstances I am unable to advise the Hereditary Prince to such an act. William."

[2] King of Prussia's marginal note: "At the discussion which took place on . . . March in my presence and that of the Crown Prince, the Prince, and Hereditary Prince of Hohenzollern, the Minister-President Ct. Bismarck and the persons mentioned above (p. 14) all reasons pro and contra were taken under consideration and the majority gave adherence to the view put forward by the Minister-President, namely to acceptance of the Spanish crown by the Hereditary P. of H.

Since however the latter upheld his verbal and written declaration that he could only decide on acceptance at my command and I from conviction am unable to give this command, the discussion was thereby brought to an end. William."

As in speaking with him I could not do otherwise than take the standpoint of denial—my request may not seem unjustified that you will be so good as to bring about a definite decision as soon as possible.

Most respectfully

HOHENZOLLERN

12. Bernhardi to Count von Bismarck

(Copy) [German]   Madrid, 11 March, 1870
Extract A 1021
pr. 31 March, 1870

In the general weariness, the hopelessness of present conditions, of the present situation, the whole of Spain—except for the Republicans who alone definitely know what they want—sighs for a King. The political parties, the Carlists, Isabelinos, Alfonsists and Montpensierists have each of course definite personalities in view: not the masses, however, they only ask in general for a King—even if every minute they thereby fall into the self-contradiction that their national pride rebels against the idea of a foreign King. They are, withal, dominated by a rather hazy, unfounded, untenable notion that everything will surely turn out all right as though by fairy-tale magic if only an end is made of the present insufferable provisional situation and a King proclaimed.

De Martino, the First Secretary of the Italian Legation, whispered to me that the Duc de Montpensier had spent a lot of money to bring about the failure of the negotiations with the Royal Family and the candidature of the Italian prince—he had by money induced the Headmaster of Harrow School, in whose house the Duke of Genoa was, to advise the young prince emphatically against acceptance of the Spanish crown,—to expatiate on the precariousness of conditions here, the impermanence of the proffered position—in short spare no effort to inspire the young prince with mistrust and antipathy towards Spain.

This—he went on to say—was successful—and in addition Montpensier had contrived to buy over this and that man of influence in the King of Italy's own personal entourage—and thus create a resistance within the Royal Family itself on which the plan would suffer shipwreck. De Martino was not willing to name anyone else than the Duchess of Genoa's Consort, Marquis Rapallo.

During the Christmas holidays General Prim had arranged a hunting party on his estates outside Toledo to which Unionists and Progressists were equally invited, and in addition the French Ambassador, Baron Mercier, and Baron Saurma from the Royal Prussian Legation.

74

At a party of this composition there was, of course, as if by formal agreement, no mention of politics; but early one morning General Prim found himself obliged to receive in the garden—in the presence of Baron Saurma, while waiting for the rest of the hunting party—a deputation of country folk from the neighbourhood. These people expressed a desire for a definite organization of the Government, the wish to see a King elected—and wanted to know whether the present interim situation would last much longer.

General Prim answered very pleasantly and fully—warning them against both the Carlists and the Republicans, telling them not to be led astray by either of them, since the former would lead to reaction and the latter to anarchy. For the rest he invited them to have patience and confidence, saying that in a short time he would bring the country a King. He would be a foreign prince—it is true—that could not be avoided, but he would be a young prince who would complete his education in the country, would adopt the customs and outlook of the country, in a word would be able to turn into a Spaniard.

The active elements are above all the Carlists and Republicans. Both are manifestly preparing for new risings. The Carlists have undoubtedly won considerable ground in the last few months so that it has now become possible to form Carlist committees even in Andalusia where that would have been impossible as recently as last year. The Republicans have correspondingly lost ground, undoubtedly by their own fault. The innumerable crimes, murder, arson, pillage, rape, with which the Republicans marked the first stage of their rising in October, have caused widespread terror and still more perhaps the foolhardy theories of socialism which were at the outset proclaimed as the future law of Spain.

For all this, however, and much as the situation may have changed in this respect, the Carlists are far and away less powerful and dangerous than the Republicans. They have no support in the army and nothing can make up to them for the lack of the influence of the monasteries. The Republicans on the other hand are constantly aided by the wild impulses of the mob, particularly that of the town population, and in addition they can count on assistance from abroad, especially from the Association Internationale. To be sure, their success does not always equal their expectations, for, as is always the case with party blindness, they overestimate both their own resources and even more still the strength of that cosmopolitan revolutionary Association. During the disturbances led by Rochefort in Paris the Republicans here were in a state of the tensest excitement, expecting from one hour to another the news that the republic had been proclaimed in France. The Association had held out the prospect of no more and no less than that.

signed VON BERNHARDI

13. *Count von Bismarck to the King of Prussia*

(Original) [German]   Berlin, 14 March, 1870[1]

I submit the enclosed[2] to Your Majesty with the respectful enquiry whether I may fulfil the wish expressed therein.

Provided that the secrecy promised to us is maintained I have no objections to make to it. The hitherto existing transcription is written with his own hand by Privy Counsellor von Keudell and any further copy would also have to be written out by him since no other official of the Ministry beside himself has any knowledge of the matter.[3]

v. BISMARCK

14. *Crown Prince Frederick William to Count von Bismarck*

(Original) [German]   14.3.70

Will you have the kindness to provide me with a copy of your memorandum which was laid before H.M. about my cousin Leopold Hohenzollern's candidature for the throne of Spain?

The immense importance of the burning question to which you are devoting weighty and sympathetic attention has caused me to give it mature consideration. I can, however, only order my thoughts if I have the things lying before me.

Your devoted

FREDERICK WILLIAM

15. *The King of Prussia to Count von Bismarck*

(Original) [German]   15.3.70

To the dinner and the Spanish discussion I have further invited the House Minister, von Schleinitz, who was always consulted by the Prince of H[o]h[en]z[o]ll[ern] a[nd] also in the Rumanian question,—and in addition the Secretary of State, von Thile, who has more claim than Delbrück to be heard.   W.

[1] King of Prussia's marginal note: "Agreed. W. 14.3.70."
[2] See Document No. 14.
[3] Bismarck's marginal note: "I request Herr von Keudell to be so kind as to make the copy for H.R.H. and deliver it to me. v. B[ismarck]."

16. *Baron von Keudell to Count von Bismarck*

(Original) [German]   15.3.[70]

Marshal Prim's letter has not been before me nor do I possess relevant papers other than the draft of the report laid before His Majesty.

KEUDELL

17. *Baron von Keudell to Count von Bismarck*

(Original) [German]   Berlin, 15 March, 1870

On account of a slight inflammation of the eyes I am forbidden by my doctor to go out today.

Three answers have been agreed on to be dispatched as cipher telegrams:

Anastasio Alonso
     34 Hortaleza

[French] (1) Loan arranged, details soon.[1] ERQUELINES

(2) Loan to be arranged tomorrow, details soon.

ERQUELINES

[German] This latter will mean that everything has been arranged not for the original candidate but for the brother.

[French] (3) Loan cannot be arranged. ERQUELINES

[German] For communications other than these three decisions nothing has been concerted. Time limit: 20th of the present month.

KEUDELL

18. *Count von Bismarck to Baron von Canitz,*
Prussian Minister at Madrid

(Telegram—Draft for cipher in Bismarck's hand)[2] [German]
[15 March, 1870]

Communicate unobtrusively the following to Anastasio Alonso, 34 Hortaleza:

[1] Bismarck's marginal note: "l'armement?"

[2] Hesselbarth (*Drei psychologische Fragen*, p. 28) publishes part of this document in French, giving it as a telegram to Salazar.

[French] The bankers interested are to meet this evening to discuss the loan in my presence. I will inform you of the result. ERQUELIN.[1]

19. *Baron von Canitz, Prussian Minister at Madrid,*
to Count von Bismarck

(Telegram. Decipher) [French]   Madrid, 16 March, 1870

The last ten numbers of today's telegram[2] "er quatre vingt liens fondé? un nom. u.v." make no sense by our cipher.   CANITZ[3]

20. *Baron von Canitz, Prussian Minister at Madrid,*
to Count von Bismarck

(Telegram. Decipher)[4] [German]
                    Madrid, 17 March, [1870.] 12 o'clock

On account of the situation in the country the interested bankers should in all circumstances be advised against the proposed loan, the terms of which, it is true, I can only conjecture; the lenders would lose everything and the recipients gain nothing. The need is for Spanish money, foreign money will yield no profit.   v. CANITZ

21. *Count von Bismarck to Count von Bernstorff,*
Prussian Ambassador in London

(Telegram. Draft for cipher in Bismarck's hand)[5] [German]
                    [17 March, 1870. 2 o'clock]

Since telegrams to Madrid via France are being garbled I beg you to telegraph the following, direct if possible, to Canitz Madrid:

---

[1] Bucher's marginal note: "Enciphered with Ciphers No. 265 and 1189. Sent to telegraph office 15 March, 12.45 noon. Bucher."

[2] Cf. Doc. No. 18.

[3] The following is the text of the draft of this document for cipher: "Chancellor of the Confederation. Berlin. The ten last numbers of today's telegram '2090. 4570, 3340. 62. 2391. 55. 36. 3835. 40. 5848' make no sense with our cipher. CANITZ."
Berlin replied on 17 March: "The last three groups of the telegram of the 15th are the stop and two dummies. The three which precede: 'er que lien' make a proper name."

[4] It would seem to be an abstract of this telegram which was published by Hesselbarth: [French] "17 March to Bismarck. Do not arrange the loan; in Spain Spanish money is needed, not foreign. CANITZ." (*Drei psychologische Fragen,* p. 28.)

[5] Hesselbarth gives the text of the message to Salazar: [French]
"(5) 18 March to Salazar. At the conference of bankers the two big houses raised and maintained their opposition; they are disposed to consent to the loan being arranged if their travelling companion [*compagnon de voyage*] agrees to the share assigned to him. BISMARCK." (*Drei psychologische Fragen,* p. 28.)

[French] 1189. Deliver the following to Anastasio Alonso, 34 Hortaleza:[1]

At the conference of the bankers the two big houses have maintained their opposition, but they are disposed to consent to the loan being arranged tomorrow if their associate, today on travel [*compagnon aujourd'hui en voyage*], agrees to the share assigned by him.

ERQUELIN [2, 3]

22. *Salazar to Baron von Canitz, Prussian Minister at Madrid*

[Original] [French] Thursday, 17.3.70

MONSIEUR LE BARON

I should be most obliged to you if you would be so kind as to send to Count Bismarck by cipher telegram the words which you will find written on the next page. Herr von Keudell will receive them since it is he who opens everything relating to his chief, to whom he will have spoken about the matter. I shall drop in on you between 2 and 3 o'clock today.

If you return the envelope of this letter to the person who will give it to you, that will prove to me that the telegram is going to be dispatched.

I beg you to pardon my giving you so much trouble and to rest assured of all my feelings of gratitude and high esteem.

E. DE SALAZAR Y MAZARREDO

★ ★ ★

The municipal council of the town and all the classes interested in its credit will greet with great joy the immediate effectuation of the loan.

Signed. ALONSO

23. *Baron von Canitz, Prussian Minister at Madrid, to Count von Bismarck*

(Telegram. Decipher)[4] [French] Madrid, 17 March. 2.20

The Municipal Council of the city and all classes interested in its

---

[1] From this point the text is in Bismarck's hand, the first lines being in Bucher's hand.

[2] Bucher's marginal note: "Enciphered and taken to telegraph office 17 March, 2 p.m. B[uche]r."

[3] The Madrid decipher bears in the margin the following note: "N.B. Communicated to M. Anastasio Alonso on 18th March at 7 in the evening."

[4] Hesselbarth's text: [French] "(2) 17 March to Bismarck. The Municipal Council of the city and all the classes interested in its credit will view the immediate effectuation of the loan with great joy. SALAZAR." (*Drei psychologische Fragen*, p. 28.)

credit will view the immediate effectuation of the loan with great joy.

Signed: ALONSO

Alonso occult[1] begs me to send the above telegram to Your Excellency.

CANITZ

24. Count von Bismarck to Baron von Canitz, Prussian Minister at Madrid

(Telegram. Draft for cipher in Bismarck's hand[2]) [German]

[17 March, 1870. 10 p.m.]

Telegram relative to the loan received. As I assume that up to the present[3] our cipher is not compromised will Y.E. kindly formulate more clearly.

[BISMARCK][4]

25. Prince Karl Anton of Hohenzollern to the King of Prussia

(Original)[5] [German]   Berlin, 17 March, 1870

TO HIS MAJESTY THE KING.

Most humbly adverting to the conversation which Your Majesty was graciously pleased to have with me yesterday I would most respectfully beg Your Majesty's most gracious permission to fix it in writing.

The Hereditary Prince's personal aversion to acceptance of the Spanish crown is probably strengthened by two considerations, one of a political, the other of an emotional nature.

From the political standpoint what takes the highest place is the reflection that the Spanish Government may possibly have it in mind to bring about Iberian union or may be forced by circumstances to do so. To an Infanta of Portugal, having mounted the Spanish throne, such a thought would seem monstrous. How could she silence her conscience if she were to remain a mute and passive spectator of an occurrence which would be aimed directly against her family and the land of her birth? How dimmed would be the lustre of the crown and how difficult for her to appreciate the blessings of her position if her consort were faced with the command to carry out a national Spanish policy in this sense bowing

---

[1] The word "occult" does not occur in the Madrid draft for cipher.

[2] Bucher's marginal note: "enciphered with Cipher No. 265 and taken to the telegraph office 17 March 10 p.m. B[ucher]."

[3] In the Madrid decipher the word "bisher" [up to the present] is lacking.

[4] The decipher in Madrid bears the signature of Bismarck.

[5] King of Prussia's marginal note: "For Minister, Count Bismarck. W. 17.3.70."

to a relentless necessity which would lead to the fall of the House of Braganza?

In the second place family considerations give rise to the conviction that separation from a thriving and promising young family of children and grandchildren would be an unassuaged and lasting sorrow to his mother and would prove a mortal blow to her delicate health.

I must, however, once again most solemnly repeat that these considerations, weighty though they be, are not of a nature to shake our attitude if the higher interests of the state demand the sacrifice. My House serves above everything King and country, and private feelings remain always subordinated to these great and highest duties.

As, however, the problem as a whole concerns not an individual person but a member of the Catholic House of Hohenzollern I have come to the view that it might perhaps be my youngest son, Prince Frederick, on whom might devolve this great, if thorny, mission. What he lacks is neither force of character nor natural intelligence but only that wide experience of the world which the Hereditary Prince to a certain degree undeniably possesses.

Although I have no knowledge of my youngest son's intentions I am sure that my paternal influence will be strong enough to incline him to acceptance of the crown. What he lacks in experience and practical training would be compensated by strict observance of the letter of the constitution. His sense of honour would afford the necessary guarantee for the future, and his not unpleasing exterior would produce on the Spaniards the impression of a young man who is the scion of a vigorous German stock.

By this proposal, however, I do not mean to convey that the Spanish royal crown for a member of our family is the goal of my hopes and wishes—quite the contrary—only that I think that I may put forward this idea under two aspects—not as a *pis aller*—but as an ultimate solution.

In the first place the crown would fall to a Hohenzoller, which according to the discussions which have taken place is recognized as a Prussian state interest.

Secondly the Heir Apparent's rejection would be softened and the worst impressions in Spain rendered less acute. Prussia could no longer be held responsible for the consequences of the refusal since we should have resisted the nomination only of one certain member, not that of all members of the House.

This form of solution may further be opportune because for several weeks the appeal of the Spanish Government, the organ of the proudest people on earth, has been left unanswered.

I do not think it would be advisable to give a written reply containing a reference to Prince Frederick—for Europe must never learn of any other than a Spanish initiative—but the confidential emissary whose task it would be to carry the Hereditary Prince's letter of rejection to Madrid might verbally convey the suggestions in question.

Further steps would then have to be awaited in complete passivity and our conduct regulated accordingly.

At all events one great object would be attained, namely not to have inflicted a contemptuous slight on the Spanish Government, and for this object I am ready for any sacrifice.

Your most humble servant and subject,

F. OF HOHENZOLLERN

26. *The King of Prussia to Count von Bismarck*

(Original) [German]   Berlin, 17.3.70

Yesterday evening the Prince of Hohenzollern was with me to give me his and his son's impressions of the reception of two days ago. On both of them it made a very strong impression, but they are both more determined than ever not to accept the offer to the Hereditary Prince unless I very definitely command it. The Hereditary Prince cannot make up his mind to renounce his position as a German, Prussian and Hohenzoller in exchange for so utterly insecure an existence.

I, too, must confess that I should regard it as highly undesirable to see the disappearance of the name and family from Prussia and Germany as they would remain only in 2 castles if Rumania and Spain carried off 4 castles, thus leaving only the youngest Prince of Hohenzollern remaining, not yet married, whereas the Hereditary Prince already has two sons. To create a *secunda genitur* for the second of these sons would be a mortal blow to the parents since this son would have to come as early as possible to Germany. The Hereditary Princess has again expressed herself with the utmost decision to the effect she would regard it as impossible to enter upon a station in life which would necessarily bring her into the most lamentable conflict with near relatives, especially if the Iberian question were to crop up again, perhaps even seeking, precisely on her account, the union of the Spanish and Portuguese crowns which would be made possible only by the expulsion of her father and brothers.

The Prince therefore reverted to the idea suggested to me and to yourself of putting forward his youngest son in place of his eldest to show that no opposition exists to the choice of a Hohenzoller for the Spanish crown. This of course could not take place without the consent and cooperation of Prince Frederick of Hohenzollern; but since his return will take place in a fortnight, it would be necessary to await it. His brother, the Rumanian, was only in command of a cavalry squadron when he received the call to Bucharest; Pr. F. is said to have ability so that the risk with him would be no greater than was that in the East!

My view of the question being what it is I do not feel in a position to give the Hereditary Prince the required command.

The rest by word of mouth!

WILLIAM

27. *Count von Bismarck to Prince Karl Anton of Hohenzollern*

(Draft in Bucher's hand. The passages deleted by Bismarck are placed within round brackets) [German]

Berlin, [17] March, 1870

MOST SERENE HIGHNESS!

MOST GRACIOUS PRINCE!

In taking the liberty of placing before Y.R.H. the enclosed letter of today's date from H.M. the King with the most humble request for its return, I am convinced that I am not acting contrary to His Majesty's intentions (I deplore the decision arrived at by the Hereditary Prince because from the point of view of personality and family connexions I regard him as pre-eminently suitable, but I believe that the political aims, on account of which I advised in favour of acceding to the wishes of the Cortes, can be fulfilled in another way. For this, however, the presence of His Highness Prince Frederick would be indispensable. If action is to be taken at all it must be taken quickly. For in view of the number of persons who have necessarily come into possession of knowledge it is practically impossible that nothing will transpire, and if that were to happen one could but expect interference from the intrigues of rival claimants which would increase the already existing difficulties). If therefore Your Royal Highness, (inspired by what I know to be your feelings for our country and the dynasty) is, as I do not doubt, willing to render further service in this important matter, the first need would seem to be to recall Prince Frederick immediately under some pretext in order to enable me to return a definite reply to Madrid. (With feelings of the highest esteem I sign myself as Your Royal Highness's)

28. *Crown Prince Frederick William to the King of Prussia*

(Original) [German]

18.3.70

Enclosed, dear Papa, is a copy of my mother-in-law's reply which has just come in the form of a short memorandum for me.

Your FRITZ[1]

[1] King of Prussia's marginal note: "To Prince Hohenzollern. Count Bismarck. Circular. W." Marginal note by Prince Karl Anton of Hohenzollern: "Read. Prince v. Hohenzollern."

Annex: *Queen Victoria to Crown Prince Frederick William*

(Copy in the Crown Prince's hand)[1] [German]
Windsor Castle, 16 March, 1870

About the letters from General Prim to the Prince of Hohenzollern I have spoken *quite* confidentially to Lord Clarendon and we Both agree that *I* can express *no* opinion—either in favour or against, as it is a matter on which only the Prince and his son must come to a decision on which *I* would *not* care to exercise the least influence.   Signed V.R.

29. *Baron von Canitz, Prussian Minister at Madrid, to Count von Bismarck*

(Telegram. Decipher)[2] [German]   Madrid, 18 March [1870]. 12.10
pr. 18 March

I take it to be a question not of a financial project of the city of Bilbao but of the candidature of the Hereditary Prince or of a prince of the Royal House for the Spanish throne. Acceptance of this would in my opinion be a misfortune for the Prince, the Royal House and for Prussia without being of help to Spain. The foreign King would have a weaker party in his favour than Don Carlos, than the Prince of Asturias, than Queen Isabella, than the Duc de Montpensier, than the republic: he would be the acknowledged King only of a section of the Unionists and Progressists in the Cortes and, even though elected by a majority of the Cortes, would have the country against him and no prospect of founding a new dynasty. The inevitable consequence of his proclamation as King would be nothing else than civil war which would undoubtedly end in his disfavour. A German Prince by his acceptance would only serve the momentary supposed interests of one party in the Cortes.   v. CANITZ

30. *Prince Karl Anton of Hohenzollern to Count von Bismarck*

(Original) [German]   Berlin, 18 March, 1870

YOUR EXCELLENCY,

Pray accept my most devoted thanks for the confidential communication of His Majesty's personal letter, which I return herewith.[3]

---

[1] The text of this document was published by Zingeler. See on this subject Fester, *Briefe*, No. 115.

[2] It is, apparently, a summary of this telegram that Hesselbarth published: "(4) 18th March to Bismarck. In the event of the loan being made civil war is inevitable sooner or later. CANITZ." (*Drei psychologische Fragen*, p. 28.)   [3] Probably Doc. No. 26.

As to the present whereabouts of my youngest son I have no information—he is probably somewhere between Marseilles and Paris. In Paris he will probably stay at the Hôtel Bristol.

Your Excellency might perhaps be so kind as to have enquiries made through the Embassy whether rooms have been taken for him or whether he is not already there. In any case, as he wants to avoid the Imperial Court, he will not engage rooms under his real name. However he is known at the hotel, as the proprietor is a native of Hohenzollern.

As soon as the reply comes in, I would call my son back from Paris immediately.

Most respectfully
PRINCE OF HOHENZOLLERN

31. *Count von Bernstorff, Prussian Ambassador in London, to Count von Bismarck*

(Telegram. Decipher) [German]   London, 18 March, 1870
pr. 18 March

Yesterday's telegram for Baron von Canitz only received today.[1] No direct line to Madrid, hence I have had to telegraph via Hâvre and Bordeaux. An unciphered English private telegram which I received yesterday from Madrid by this route arrived quite intact, although it is maintained that Spanish telegraphists are very unreliable whereas German and French ones are highly praised.

BERNSTORFF

32. *Count von Bismarck to Baron von Werther, Prussian Ambassador in Paris*

(Telegram. Draft for cipher in Bismarck's hand) [German]
Berlin, 18.3.70

The Prince of Hohenzollern desires to know whether his son, Prince Frederick, who was to be travelling from Marseilles to Paris, has arrived or had rooms engaged for him there. At the Hôtel Bristol, the proprietor of which is a native of Hohenzollern, this information could be discreetly obtained. The Prince will be staying on here for another few days and would like to have a talk here with his son, hence desires his speedy arrival.   [BISMARCK][2]

---

[1] See Doc. No. 21.
[2] Marginal note: "To telegraph office 18/3 10.20 p.m."

33. *Baron von Werther, Prussian Ambassador in Paris, to Count von Bismarck*

(Telegram. Decipher) [German]   Paris, 19 March, 1870. 3.55 p.m.
arrived 5.57 p.m.

Prince Frederick of Hohenzollern not yet arrived here. Rooms not engaged at Hôtel Bristol. Arrangement has been made to receive immediate announcement of his arrival.   Signed VON WERTHER[1, 2]

34. *Count von Bismarck to Count von Bernstorff, Prussian Ambassador in London*

(Telegram. Draft for cipher)[3] [German]   Berlin, 20 March, 1870

Please telegraph the following to Baron von Canitz at Madrid:

I do not share your opinion and am of the opposite opinion on most of the points brought forward by you; in particular I believe that a lawfully elected King would be at least as strong as the present Government which, as experience has shown, has proved itself equal to all the elements described by you as being stronger. The matter must be kept strictly secret; if anything practical comes of it Your [Excellency][4] will in good time receive written notice thereof. V. BISMARCK.[5]   V. BISMARCK[6]

35. *Salazar to Baron von Canitz, Prussian Minister at Madrid*

(Original) [French]   Monday, 21 [March,] 1870

MY DEAR BARON,

I beg you to send Count von Bismarck as urgent the telegram written on the next page.

[1] Bismarck's marginal note: "Content to be communicated to H.R.H. the Prince of Hoh[enzollern] in the 3rd person without signature."

[2] Service note: "done 19/3 p.m. H."

[3] Marginal note by Bucher: "According to information from H.E."

[4] The abbreviation here used is "p.p." which means "etc."

[5] It seems to be a summary of this telegram which Hesselbarth published: "I do not share your view and am of another opinion on several points. A caballero well and lawfully elected is at least as strong as the chevaliers who hold their own at present in spite of the opposition put up against them on all sides. BISMARCK." (*Drei psychologische Fragen*, pp. 28-9.)

[6] Marginal note by Bucher: "enciphered and taken to telegraph office 20 March 2 o'clock. B[uche]r."

I will call in on you this afternoon but do not know at what time. It will be before 4 o'clock.

I have the honour to salute you most cordially

E. DE SALAZAR Y MAZARREDO

*   *   *

Urgently wish to know approximately on what day M. Gama will be able to meet travelling companion. ALONSO.

36. *Baron von Canitz, Prussian Minister at Madrid, to Count von Bismarck*

(Telegram. Decipher)[1] [French]   Madrid, 21 March, 1870
pr. 21 March

Urgently wish to know approximately on what day M. Gama would be able to meet the companion for after [sic][2] journey [*le compagnon d'après voyage*]. ALONSO.

M. Alonso asks me to send the above telegram to Your Excellency.

CANITZ

37. *Count von Bismarck to Hasse, Director of the Head Post Office at Aix-la-Chapelle*

(Draft) [German]   Berlin, 21 March, 1870

TO THE DIRECTOR OF THE HEAD POST OFFICE, HERR HASSE.
In the case of his absence to his deputy at Aix-la-Chapelle.

I request you to have the enclosed telegram sent off as soon as possible prepaid from Liége by someone not known there whom you will kindly send for that purpose, reporting in writing to me personally that the order has been carried out.

signature of H.E.
on the fair copy[3]

---

[1] Hesselbarth publishes the following version of the document: "21 March, to Bismarck. Urgently wish to know approximately on what day M. Gama will be able to meet the travelling companion. SALAZAR."

[2] The draft for cipher has: "le compagnon de voyage" and not "le compagnon d'après voyage".

[3] Marginal notes: "B[uche]r. 21.—Written with his own hand and signed by H.E."
[Annex:] "Telegram as per draft of H.E.—fair copy made 21.3. and taken to Post Office. B[ucher]."

Annex: *Count von Bismarck to Salazar*

(Telegram. Draft in Bismarck's hand) [French]   21 March, 1870

Anastasio Alonso
   34 Hortaleza
     Madrid.

I will reply as soon as I know myself. No information at present as to traveller's whereabouts and address. Enquiries in progress.

ERQUELINES.

38. *Count von Bismarck to Baron von Werther, Prussian Ambassador in Paris*

(Telegram. Draft for cipher) [German]   Berlin, 23 March, 1870

I have notified the arrival of Prince Frederick in Paris to his father and requested instructions. Immediate departure for here is in my opinion of urgent importance.

fair copy signed by H.E.[1]

39. *Salazar to Baron von Canitz, Prussian Minister at Madrid*

(Original) [French]   [Madrid] Wednesday. [23 March, 1870]

MY DEAR BARON,

I beg you as a matter of urgency to have the following telegram dispatched as soon as possible.

Most cordially
E. DE SALAZAR Y MAZARREDO

Telegram

Complete agreement on basis loan. Urgently request frank reply today: (1) what is to be understood about Friday's traveller; (2) whether loan is accepted or declined; (3) whether verbal explanations by Gama can still be useful. Urgent.

ALONSO

---

[1] Bucher's marginal note: "As directed by H.E. Enciphered 1086 and taken to Telegraph Office same day. 5 o'clock. B[uche]r."

40. *Baron von Canitz, Prussian Minister at Madrid,*
to Count von Bismarck

(Telegram. Decipher)[1] [French]   Madrid, 23 March, 1870
                                          arr. 23 March

Complete agreement on basis loan.

Urgently request frank reply today: Firstly, what is to be understood about Friday's . . .,[2] secondly, whether loan is accepted or declined, thirdly, could verbal explanations by Gama still be useful? Urgent. ALONSO.

Alonso asks me to send the above telegram to Y.E.[3]   CANITZ

41. *Baron von Werther, Prussian Ambassador in Paris,*
to Count von Bismarck

(Telegram. Decipher) [German]   Paris, 23 March, 1870
                                       12.55 p.m.
                                       arrived 3.2 p.m.

Prince Frederick of Hohenzollern arrived here yesterday evening, content of telegram relating to him communicated to him, he desires to remain here for several days and to travel via Brussels to Düsseldorf, he enquires whether there is any objection to this plan or whether his presence in Berlin is urgently necessary and how long his father will be staying in Berlin.

                                       (signed) WERTHER[4]

42. *Prince Karl Anton of Hohenzollern to Count von Bismarck*

(Original) [German]   B[erlin], 23 March, 1870

YOUR EXCELLENCY,

Most respectfully I thank you for the very obliging communication.[5] With His Majesty the King I have agreed that my son Fritz is to arrive

---

[1] The text published by Hesselbarth runs: "(8) 23 March to Bismarck. Complete agreement on basis of loan. Urgently request frank reply today. (1) What is to be understood about Friday's traveller, (2) whether loan is accepted or declined, (3) whether verbal explanations can be useful. SALAZAR." (*Drei psychologische Fragen*, p. 29.)

[2] Marginal note by Bucher: "the group in question is a fill-in. At any rate what is referred to is the telegram via London which speaks of the companion."
The missing word here is "voyageur" according to the Madrid draft for cipher.

[3] Marginal note by Bucher: "this is the third cipher telegram which Herr von Canitz has ended with the same groups."

[4] Bucher's marginal note: "Put on file. B[uche]r 27/3."

[5] See Doc. No. 33, note.

here on Sunday evening or Monday morning travelling via Metz-Frankfort so that he will not be delayed either in Brussels or Düsseldorf.

Your Excellency would do me a great favour by having this message forwarded and delivered to him by word of mouth by a member of the Embassy staff because a telegram addressed to my son would make his presence in Paris known to the Emperor, a thing to be avoided for the moment.

In highest esteem

PRINCE OF HOHENZOLLERN

43. *Bernhardi to Count von Bismarck*

(Copy) [German]   Madrid, 23 March, 1870. Extract from A 1023
received 31 March, 1870

A longish conversation with the French Ambassador, Baron Mercier, has left me with the impression that, now that France has become parliamentarian again and thinks she has reconciled the Orleanists with the dynasty of Napoleonic lineage, there is perhaps less opposition than formerly to the accession of the Duc de Montpensier to the throne of Spain. At the Tuileries at least any monarchic solution without exception would be preferred to a republic.

Baron Mercier has left me in no doubt whatever that the French Government fears the proclamation of a republic here in Spain because it believes itself to be endangered thereby in France.

He, like me, expressed the conviction that no system, no Government which might be set up here now would be able to maintain itself; he conceded that in these circumstances it might possibly be most fortunate for Spain herself if in the first place a republic were proclaimed and in consequence the republic would wear itself down amid all the uncertainties and so render itself impossible for the subsequent period. But for Europe he thought this would have great drawbacks. The proclamation of a Spanish republic would constitute a real danger to Europe.

The Republicans here state every day as loudly as possible that their plans are not limited only to Spain. Castelar declares in the Cortes that armies have become superfluous because in four years there will be not a throne left in Europe and the great republic of the "United States of Europe" will stand fulfilled.

signed VON BERNHARDI

44. *Count von Bismarck to Baron von Werther, Prussian Ambassador in Paris*

(Telegram. Draft for cipher in Bismarck's hand) [German]

Berlin, 24 March, 1870

No. 8

Will Y.E. immediately inform the Prince of Hohenzollern that his father requests him to come here via Metz and Frankfort without stay or delay. His Majesty the King expects the Prince's arrival by Sunday evening at the latest.

[BISMARCK][1]

45. *Count von Bismarck to Baron von Canitz, Prussian Minister at Madrid*

(Telegram. Draft for cipher)[2] [German]

Berlin, 24 March, 1870
[Dispatched at 12.40 p.m.]

Your telegram of yesterday[3] is the third ending with practically the same groups. Such a thing will compromise the cipher.

fair copy signed by H.E.

B[UCHER]24

46. *Count von Bismarck to Count von Bernstorff, Prussian Ambassador in London*

(Telegram. Draft for cipher in Bismarck's hand)[4] [German]

Bernstorff, London. Request you to telegraph the following to Canitz, Madrid:

[French] For Alonso: It seems that in 4 or 5 days I shall be able to give you definite and satisfactory information in the sense of the second alternative of the programme. ERQUELINES.

[BISMARCK] [24 March, 1870. 1 p.m.]

---

[1] Marginal notes: "enciphered 1086 R. Riese.—No. 533. Taken to telegraph office the 24th at 11.50 a.m."

[2] Bucher's marginal note: "dictated by H.E."

[3] See Doc. No. 40.

[4] The following is the text published by Hesselbarth: "24 March to Salazar. It seems that in 4 or 5 days I shall be able to give definite information in the sense of the second alternative of the programme. BISMARCK." (*Drei psychologische Fragen*, p. 29.)

47. *Baron von Werther, Prussian Ambassador in Paris, to Count von Bismarck*

(Telegram. Decipher)[1] [German]   Paris, 24 March, 1870
                                                          3.25 p.m.
No. 13   arrived 5.52 p.m.

Today's telegram No. 8[2] communicated to the Prince [Frederick] of Hohenzollern. He will this evening take the prescribed route for the journey to Berlin.

signed WERTHER

48. *Salazar to Baron von Canitz, Prussian Minister at Madrid*

(Original)[3] [French]   [24 March, 1870]

MONSIEUR LE BARON,

I have received the telegram, and I beg you to send off the words below this evening or tomorrow morning, as you think best.

Very affectionately

E. DE SALAZAR Y MAZARREDO

I will tomorrow send you a letter for Herr von Keudell who lives in the street given in the telegram below. I received yesterday evening a telegram from Liége which conflicts with the one you have just sent me. The telegraph service is very subject to error.

*   *   *

Kindly await letter which will go off to Victoriastrasse on Friday 25th.

ALONSO

49. *Hasse, Director in Chief, Post Office at Aix-la-Chapelle, to Count von Bismarck*

(Original)[4] [German]   Aix-la-Chapelle, 24 March, 1870

YOUR EXCELLENCY,

I hasten most respectfully to inform you that I personally at 3.15 p.m. on the 23 inst. dispatched from Liége the telegram received that same day.

---

[1] Bismarck's marginal note: "Send message to H.R.H. Prince Karl Anton: H[is] S[erene Highness] P[rince] Fr[ederick] will leave for Berlin via Metz this evening." This minute is followed by the note: "dispatched 24/3.70. 9.30 p.m."

[2] See Doc. No. 44.

[3] Marginal note [in German] :"On 26 March the letter in question to Baron von Keudell was dispatched by the agency of Count Bernstorff to the Royal Embassy in Paris to be forwarded on by a quick and sure route. A[lexander] K[leefeld]."

[4] Bucher's marginal note: "Put in the files. B[ucher] 26/3."

Will Your Excellency graciously accept the renewed assurance of the high esteem and respect with which I remain Your Excellency's
most obedient

HASSE,
Director of Head Post Office

50. *Baron von Canitz, Prussian Minister at Madrid, to Count von Bismarck*

(Telegram. Decipher) [French]   Madrid, 25 March, 1870

Please expect letter which will go off Friday fifth for Victoriastrasse. ALONSO.

CANITZ

51. *Count von Bernstorff, Prussian Ambassador in London, to Count von Bismarck*

(Telegram. Decipher) [German]   London, 25 March, 1870
pr. 27 March, 1870

As I have no direct cipher communication with the Royal Legation in Madrid, the three telegrams sent by Your Excellency for dispatch thither have had to go from here with Your Excellency's signature.[1] As thereby the attention of the French Government might be drawn to this correspondence in a manner not desired by Your Excellency, I deferentially suggest that I might be given powers to forward any more such telegrams from here to Baron von Canitz over my own signature after due announcement to him by yourself.

Yesterday's telegram[2] was dispatched from here at 3 p.m., arriving in Madrid at 7.20 p.m.

BERNSTORFF

[1] Bucher's marginal note: "There was no reason for this. The telegrams were worded as follows: (In the cipher for London) 'I request Y.E. to telegraph the following to Herr v. Canitz in Madrid.' What followed in the cipher for Madrid ended with the name of Bismarck, also in cipher."

[2] Bucher's marginal note in French: "It seems that in 4 or 5 days from now", etc. (See Doc. No. 46.)

52. *Salazar to Baron von Keudell*

(Original) [French]

Madrid, 25 March, 1870
pr. 31.3
1 annex

MY DEAR HERR VON KEUDELL,

Telegraphic errors and the use of ambiguous language have given rise to one of the most curious and serious incidents which could happen in politics. On Friday, 18th, the telegram from London was understood to mean that the King and the Heir Apparent of H[ohenzollern], who had maintained their opposition at the Tuesday conference, had later consented on condition that Spain accepted terms which were brought by an emissary leaving Berlin that same Friday.

As these terms would probably be two-thirds of the votes or even $\frac{3}{4}$, which might at a pinch have been agreed to, the affair seemed to be on the right road and it became necessary to prepare the ground here for a resounding success. M. Topete, the Navy Minister, who alone among the Ministers was pledged to the Duc de Montpensier, had decided to resign from the Cabinet temporarily as soon as another candidature was accepted to save his dignity, as he had done at the time of the Duke of Genoa. He would then have given his support to the vote of the majority and could thereupon return to office later, just as two months ago; but that experience had shown that a candidature would lose its force if at the moment it was officially announced it led to the resignation of so considerable a figure.

It was then agreed to simulate a weakening of the agreement between the two parties, radical and conservative, which form the coalition by making a political issue of an amendment to a bill of the Finance Minister. The ensuing vote was to have served M. Topete as a pretext for resigning on an internal and relatively minor disagreement. Besides that, M. Topete being rather conservative, his temporary disappearance from the Cabinet would have facilitated the passing of two laws which are a logical consequence of freedom of worship: civil marriage and a reform of the clergy. These are measures which only a united Cabinet can propose and it was going to be much better for the new dynasty that these changes should have been introduced before its installation to prevent its incurring the animosity of the aggrieved interests. On the contrary it would be able to soothe susceptibilities.

M. Topete's resignation would of course lead to that of several high officials belonging to his party and more intimately bound to him, and by this means great prominence would be given to the proclamation of the new king, since disagreement on a secondary issue would have to cease pending the election of the monarch. Agreement on this capital issue is complete among 250 deputies as against 80 or 82. They will all vote for the Government candidate if he is a prince of a foreign royal family, of age and a Catholic.

In this way the proclamation was going to take place under the best auspices, and after that a coalition government would have been formed. The comedy was carried to the point of my offering my resignation in order not to awaken the suspicions of those who might have noticed my three weeks' absence. And in fact the voting took place on the 19th at midnight and the enclosed Gazette will show you the decrees.

Now by the telegram received from London I see that it is a question of the second alternative on the programme, i.e. that Friday's traveller is Prince Frederick and that he has not yet made up his mind.

The situation will be exceedingly grave if a refusal comes to complicate it, because if there is an avowal of what has happened, the ridicule will be tremendous, and if nothing is said, the breach will be final, because M. Topete has declared he will not continue to be minister under a provisional regime and no one can foresee the consequences. So long as the provisional regime lasts his agreement with the two Marshals is a force of the first magnitude. If the provisional regime ceases, it would still be possible to put forward a patriotic explanation for what has happened.

I, therefore, beg you to place this letter before the eyes of Count Bismarck in order that the difficult position may be understood in which we have been placed by the telegraphic error.

If Prince Leopold does not make up his mind, his brother also might save us and instead of a Portuguese Queen who would be very popular we should have a Spaniard, even though a Bourbon.

The situation in the country improves every day; the Carlist party recognizes its impotence, especially after the Council's follies, and lies low, the Republicans have lost ground enormously among the Liberal and Catholic classes because of their atheist excesses. Nobody any longer thinks of the Duc de Montpensier, especially after his misfortune, and the prestige of the Paris exiles has altogether evaporated. All who have something to lose desire the ending of the provisional regime at any price, and Prince Alfonso who is only twelve would be the worst and most unpopular of the interim[1] proposals.

All the provinces are perfectly quiet. Business is looking up. The Cuban insurrection is reduced to a handful of brigand bands, and, a crowning good fortune, last year's harvest which was good is by all accounts going to be followed in 1870 by the best since 1817 for cereals, wines and oils. The fallen dynasty on top of all its faults had the misfortune to see 4 bad harvests in 1865, 66, 67 and 68.

The good sense shown by this people in these 18 months of provisional regime is the best augury of the prosperity it might attain under a sincerely

[1] Salazar uses the word "intérinité" for "interim".

95

constitutional prince. I do not know a nation which would have come through such a crisis with greater calmness and good behaviour after the fall of a dynasty lasting 168 years.

The army is in good shape and conscription was voted yesterday in the Cortes by a huge majority as usual.

I today sent off the telegram[1] asking you to expect this letter. The three persons who are in the secret with me do not doubt that after the above explanations a favourable solution will come to end the uncertainties of the present and the dangers of the future.

The misunderstanding on the part of the telegraph service or of our interpretation is so great that I have for three days in succession gone to the railway station to welcome you or Herr Bucher. Having left Berlin on Friday the emissary ought to have arrived here by Tuesday, or Wednesday at the latest, and when the envoy failed to put in an appearance I was made to telegraph twice to find out how matters stood: what an anxiety!!!

I salute you most cordially

E. SALAZAR Y MAZARREDO

[Annex]

I am asked to request Count von Bismarck to make a last effort with the Heir Apparent. As head of an honoured and numerous family he would more *amply* than anyone else fill the physical and moral void created at the Palace by the fall of the former dynasty.

Beg him also to forgive the urgency of the telegrams. Our military chiefs imagine that in diplomacy one can carry out operations as expeditiously as on the battlefield; on the other hand one must do justice to them and their good faith; 18 months of a never ending provisional situation is enough to try the patience of Job.

How many sleepless watches these last few days!

53. Baron von Canitz, Prussian Minister at Madrid, to Count von Bismarck

(Telegram. Decipher) [German]   Madrid, 26 March, 1870. 3 p.m.
arr. 8.50 p.m.

Count Bernstorff leaves here today for Paris with two communications[2] from Alonso and a report[3] from me.

CANITZ

[1] See Docs. Nos. 48 and 50.
[2] See Docs. Nos. 52 and 54.
[3] See Doc. No. 55.

54. *Salazar to Baron von Keudell*

(Original) [French]   Madrid, 26 March, 1870
                                       pr. 31/3
                                       1 annex

I wrote you yesterday, but as the person who is to bear the letter is perfectly trustworthy I am going to add a few lines today.

First of all I will say that the word *frankly* in the telegram referred to Herr von Canitz, because although I have spoken to him of a loan which a large city wants to raise with German bankers, friends of Herr von Keudell, he will not believe a word of it.

In confirmation of what I said yesterday I will add that the new Navy Minister is entirely devoted to M. Topete and is *proposed by him* to take his place.

As regards the country, the progress in its political education is so great that there are several nephews of Queen Isabella in the army and nobody thinks this surprising. Among them is Don Enrique's eldest son.

Two years and less of constitutional government with a good prince would be enough to obliterate memories of all the claimants. This is the general opinion *without distinction of class*, for everyone is tired of the scandals among the Paris exiles and the duellists. What is needed are good princes like yours to uphold the prestige of the monarchic principle; those like the Prince of Wales and Prince Pierre Bonaparte would do well to be more steady going.

I am instructed to say to Count von Bismarck that in the event of acceptance by Prince Frederick the reply ought to speak only of him and it would be he who would reply in place of his brother.

If publication were to become necessary these letters would be brought into harmony with those of which M. Gama was the bearer.

The question will perhaps be asked in the Chamber why the invitation was not addressed to the Hereditary Prince, and the answer might be that after the blunt refusal from Don Fernando prudence made it advisable not to approach his son-in-law and that if it were regrettable not to have a Portuguese Queen and the succession assured one would have the compensating advantage of being able to bring off some political good stroke in connexion with the new King's marriage.

In order that there may be no more misunderstandings in the telegrams we will call the King Article I of the loan. Article II will be the Crown Prince; Article III the Prince of Hohenzollern; Article IV the Heir Apparent; Article V the Princess, and Article VI Prince Frederick.

Examples

Article IV (or VI) is accepted . . . will mean that Prince Leopold (or his brother) is not opposed to being the Cortes' candidate.

Articles IV and VI cannot be accepted . . . will mean that they both decline.

An interview with M. Gama will take place (on such and such a day) . . . will mean that the emissary bearing the replies will arrive in Madrid on such and such a day or thereabouts.

The journey from here to Berlin takes three and a half days, stopping off 23 hours in Paris.

I have told Herr von Canitz that a M. Gama is the bankers' intermediary with the Municipal Council of the city.

It is impossible to depict the dismay caused in the conclave of us four who hold the threads of this affair by the telegram from London of the day before yesterday, 24th. On Saturday evening we anticipated a disastrous end to the *so-well-acted* comedy, unless our efforts were crowned with success.

Pray accept the assurance of my sentiments of cordiality and esteem.

E. DE SALAZAR Y MAZARRADO

A quite good and *well situated* hotel here is the Hôtel des Ambassadeurs, Calle de la Victoria.

---

55. *Baron von Canitz, Prussian Minister at Madrid, to Count von Bismarck*

(Original)[1] [German]   Madrid, 26 March, 1870

Confidential

No. 14

I beg Your Excellency's gracious permission to add a few fresh remarks —the conveyance of which I can safely entrust to Count Bernstorff, who leaves here today for Berlin—to my cipher telegrams of the 17th and 18th inst. in which I regarded it as my duty respectfully to advise against acceptance of the candidature for the Spanish throne on behalf of the Hereditary Prince of Hohenzollern.

In the present state of the country a foreign prince may be regarded as a lawfully elected King of Spain if he were to be elected by plebiscite or by a more or less big majority of the constituent Cortes.

Of the first alternative there can be absolutely no question, since such an election, in so far as it was to be free and express the will of the people

---

[1] Cf. Hesselbarth, *Drei psychologische Fragen*, p. 29: "(10) 26 March to Bismarck. The whole affair seems to me hazardous in the extreme. CANITZ."

—which alone would give weight to the election—cannot possibly be expected of a people which in overwhelming majority has never heard the name of Hohenzollern even uttered and barely that of the Prussian Monarchy.

It can, thus, only be a question of the King's election by the constituent Cortes called for that purpose under the terms of the Constitution drawn up by themselves. In the trouble and perplexity which reigns in Cortes and Government, the Government and part of the Cortes would regard the election of a foreign prince as in the highest degree desirable as a means of prolonging their own existence and, as was seen on the occasion of the Duke of Genoa's candidature for the throne, could without great difficulty bring it about—but the election would have little significance because Cortes and Government have themselves long since lost the moral influence and authority which in the first months after the revolution they enjoyed both with their own party members and with their at that moment intimidated opponents.

The present Government, as no attentive observer of conditions here can fail to notice, is hastening towards its dissolution in party warfare. Yet another step in this direction in the last few days has been the ending of the unnatural alliance between Progressists and Unionists and the resignation of the more important of the latter from all Government posts; the present Government is not only not strong but grows every day more incapable of governing;—if in outward appearance order has till now been maintained or restored where it had been unsettled, and in this way the Government has remained in power, this is due more to the peculiar character of the Spanish people than to the Government's ability and strength.

The crisis will come for the Government over the election of the King, if not earlier: it will survive the crisis in the first instance if the army remains on its side. But neither Prim nor any other General can confidently count on the army in all circumstances; the army is in favour of monarchy, and it can be assumed that it will always be ready to fight the Republicans and also the Carlists against whom an old military feud dating from the past has still survived; but it is more than hazardous to place permanent reliance on the army as the support of a foreign prince, however constitutionally elected, against the Prince of Asturias and his standard. Perhaps the most characteristic trait of the Spanish people is its aversion for everything foreign, its disdain of all that is not Spanish. This trait of the Spanish national character will unite all parties hostile to the present Government in the struggle against the foreign candidate for the throne as soon as his election has taken place. The Government of the foreign King will thus be in a worse position than the present Government, and weaker, because many who in present circumstances, while awaiting the unknown future, adhered to it to keep it in being, will desert as soon as they see that a foreigner is to be thrust upon them as their King.

In these observations on the situation I have entirely left aside the difficulties, already in themselves seemingly unsurmountable, which any new King, were he even a Spaniard, would encounter in taking over the legacy of the present Government: the utterly disordered finances of the country, the disorganization of the army brought about by the officers forced upon it by Prim, the lack of statesmen, the corruption and incapacity of the official class, the apathy of the masses, all of this points to the prospect that the new conditions needed by Spain will be attainable only in a distant future and only after many upheavals.

The secret of the negotiations relating to the candidature of the Hereditary Prince of Hohenzollern has till now been strictly kept—since the failure of the Duke of Genoa's candidature the Prince's name has never been mentioned in the daily press.

Eusebio de Salazar y Mazarredo is a valued spokesman of the *Union Liberal* in the Cortes but is without great influence. He acquitted himself faithfully if not conspicuously well of his role to create the illusion in me that the negotiations with Prussia were merely for a loan. He thinks the happiness and welfare of Spain only attainable through the *Union Liberal* and therefore his party interests, which require the speedy election of a King, take precedence with him above all else. The prospects of success in this direction are very slight and it seems to me advisable not in any way to link the interests of Prussia in this respect with those of Spain, but rather to leave it to the Spaniards themselves to recover their lost equilibrium.

CANITZ

56. Count von Bismarck to Count von Bernstorff, Prussian Ambassador in London

(Telegram. Draft for cipher)[1] [German]   Berlin, 27 March, 1870

According to Y.E.'s cipher report of 25th inst.[2] the telegrams sent you for transmission to Herr v. Canitz must have been dispatched from London over my signature. I beg that Y.E. will kindly inform me wherein lay the necessity for this procedure, unforeseen and undesired by me as being of a nature to endanger the success of the affairs in question. In my telegram of 17th inst.[3] as the reason for the circuitous route I had given the circumstance that telegrams from here to Madrid were, as experience has shown, being apparently intentionally garbled and rendered illegible in France and I had therefore requested Y.E. to telegraph the cipher message for Madrid, which already bore my

---

[1] Marginal notes by Bucher: "For next report. By today's courier."
[2] See Doc. No. 51.   [3] See Doc. No. 21.

signature in cipher, if possible direct to Madrid. Even after Y.E. kindly informed me on 18th[1] that the cable from Falmouth to San Sebastian, of which there was once word in the newspapers, had never material-ized, and in spite of the lesser skill of the Spanish telegraphists in com-parison with the German and French, I have continued to direct my communications to Herr von Canitz via London, lest my signature should attract the attention of the French Government and on the assumption that telegrams to Herr von Canitz with Y.E.'s signature would not be singled out for garbling by the French telegraphists. The transmission of telegrams with my signature via London may well have only sharpened the attention of the French authorities and I shall be compelled to see whether I can manage to get telegrams to Madrid safely delivered to their destination via Florence.

fair copy signed by H.E.[2]

57. *Prince Karl Anton of Hohenzollern to the King of Prussia*

(Original) [German]   Berlin, 28 March, 1870

I most humbly inform Your Royal Majesty that I have had a talk with my son, Prince Frederick, about the question of the Spanish throne in all its extreme seriousness.

My son was deeply moved by disclosure made to him but not so surprised as I had expected.

The idea of his possible candidature for the throne had during his stay in Florence been several times touched upon by the accredited Spanish Minister there, and each time firmly discountenanced by him.

But now today when he is immediately brought up against this eventuality he realizes the full seriousness of the situation.

As I know my son I was not surprised by his answer, coming, as it did, from his inmost heart—it was first and foremost a rejection without any prospect of further reconsideration. The first impression was so over-whelming, so touching to the heart and spirit that he needed to collect his thoughts before further discussion of the matter was possible.

No one is less filled with ambitious dreams than my son, and no one is further removed than he from all overestimation of himself.

Up to the present all his effort has been concentrated on the firm determination to fulfil his duty to the utmost as an officer and, because he is the last born of our sons, we have for that reason thought it right in his whole training and education to avoid awakening hopes and wishes in him which would not be in harmony with his later position in life.

---

[1] See Doc. No. 31.
[2] The document bears the initials of Bismarck, Thile and Bucher.

Hence nothing is more natural than that Prince Frederick should feel reluctance for a station for which he does not feel fitted.

But as on grounds of experience I ascribe greater capacities to him than he does to himself, I placed the further dynastic and political points of view before him and they have made him see the position in its more objective and less subjective aspect.

It behoves an officer to fulfil the tasks of his profession not only in the sphere of his service, he must in addition to this be ready to sacrifice himself utterly and unreservedly for King and country anywhere and at any time.

To these latter considerations and only to them Prince Frederick will oppose no further resistance.

In complete self abnegation and subordination of his personal convenience and solemnly disclaiming all imputation of vain or ambitious motives, Prince Frederick after a severe struggle places himself absolutely at Your Majesty's disposal and will dutifully act according as Your Majesty's will and reasons of state shall command.[1]

PRINCE OF HOHENZOLLERN

58. *Count von Bernstorff, Prussian Ambassador in London, to Count von Bismarck*

(Telegram. Decipher)[2] [German]

No. 80

London, 29 March, 1870
arrived 31 March

In reply to Your Excellency's dispatch No. 163 of 27th inst.[3] I have the honour to report as follows:

---

[1] Marginal note by the King of Prussia: "My attitude towards the candidature of Prince Frederick of Hohenzollern for the Spanish throne is exactly the same as I have adopted towards that of his eldest brother, the Hereditary Prince of Hohenzollern. The situation in Spain since the expulsion of the Royal Dynasty, especially in the last half century, is such that I cannot persuade or advise anyone to accept the Spanish crown unless (as was the case of Prince Charles of Hohenzollern with the Rumanian Candidature, which I also opposed) he has taken it upon his shoulders as a vocation, with the conviction that acceptance is both an inward call and a duty. Since, according to this letter from the Prince of Hohenzollern, this is as little the case with Prince Frederick as with the Hereditary Prince, both being only ready to submit to my command and will, while I according to my present views cannot with conviction and an easy conscience pronounce such a command or expression of my will—I must leave it to Prince Frederick to make his final decision.   Berlin, 2.4.1870. William."

[2] Marginal note by Bismarck: "Bu[cher], seen."
[3] See Doc. No. 56.

Your Excellency's first telegram for Madrid of 17 March[1] only contained the following introduction addressed to me:

"Since telegrams to Madrid via France are being garbled I beg you to telegraph the following, direct if possible, to Baron von Canitz Madrid."

As Your Excellency will kindly note from this, I could not with certainty conclude that telegrams from Berlin to Madrid were rendered illegible with evident intention in France nor that the telegram to Baron von Canitz already bore Your Excellency's signature in cipher. And as the telegram to Madrid had to bear a signature outwardly and I, without possessing a cipher for Madrid, could not preface it by an intimation that it had been sent to me for further transmission, I do not think I may regard myself as empowered to append my signature without further ado, thereby possibly making the source of the communication doubtful to the recipient, and therefore in my report of 25th inst. I suggested to Your Excellency that this authority should be given me for future cases. If Your Excellency desires to send me further telegrams for Madrid I will henceforth transmit them over my signature, and the punctuality with which the ones hitherto transmitted by this route seem to have been delivered makes me hope that these have not been mutilated on the way.

(signed) BERNSTORFF[2]

59. *Baron von Werther, Prussian Ambassador in Paris, to Count von Bismarck*

(By King's Messenger. Original) [German]   Paris, 29 March, 1870

The Minister of the North German Confederation in Madrid, Baron von Canitz, has sent me by a trustworthy bearer, arriving yesterday morning, the enclosed dispatch with the request to have it forwarded by a safe and quick route to Berlin.

As the dispatch[3] in question is sealed and its contents therefore unknown to me, I judged it necessary in the absence of an immediate sure occasion to forward it by a King's Messenger sent off to Aix-la-Chapelle today for that purpose.

WERTHER

[1] See Doc. No. 21.
[2] Marginal note by Bucher: "For the files. B[uche]r. 1.4."
[3] i.e. Canitz's dispatch of 26 March, 1870 (Doc. No. 55).

60. Count von Bismarck to Baron von Werther,
Prussian Ambassador in Paris

(Telegram. Draft for cipher in Bismarck's hand) [German]

No. 9   Berlin, 30 March, 1870

Has Count Bernstorff brought a letter[1] for me from Madrid, and is it coming with the messenger who is on his way here?

v. B[ISMARCK][2]

61. Roland to Baron von Keudell

(Original) [German]   30.3.[1870] 10.15 p.m.

DEAR SIR,

In forwarding Herr von Bernhardi's letters I am instructed to ask you whether in them or directly you have received a letter from Madrid which His Excellency our Chief finds missing from the official packet.

ROLAND[3]

62. Baron von Keudell to Count von Bismarck

(Original) [German]   Berlin, 31 March, 1870

According to the content of the annexes[4] just received,—apparently in consequence of an erroneous interpretation of the telegrams—Madrid regards the question as still open and asks for one more final effort to be made to get the Hereditary Prince, failing that, "his brother also might save us".

On p. 2 of the second letter a new cipher is proposed.

When the decision has been made Madrid expects a courier with a written reply.

KEUDELL

---

[1] The reference is to Canitz's dispatch of 26 March, 1870 (Doc. No. 55) which Canitz had announced by telegram the same day (Doc. No. 53).

[2] Marginal note: "Enciphered with 1086 Kohler and Willisch No. 593 to the telegraph office 30/3. 7.20 p.m."

[3] Marginal note by Keudell: "returned. In a sealed envelope in the annex. K[eudell]."

[4] The annexes mentioned by Keudell are Salazar's letters of 25 and 26 March (see Docs. Nos. 52 and 54). The letters were addressed to Keudell or, more exactly, according to the wording of the address on the envelopes, to "Madame, Mme de Keudell, 32 Victoriastrasse, Berlin."

63. *Salazar to Baron von Canitz, Prussian Minister at Madrid*

(Original) [French] [Madrid] Thursday 31[.3.1870]

MY DEAR BARON,

I should be greatly obliged if you would be so good as to tell me what you know about the letters of the other day. Did they get to Paris on Monday morning? Did they get sent on that evening or the following morning?

I remain always your grateful and humble servant

E. DE SALAZAR Y MZRDO.

64. *Prince Karl Anton of Hohenzollern to Count von Bismarck*

(Original) [German] Berlin, 1 April, 1870

I hasten very deferentially to inform Your Excellency that on the 28th inst. I made a humble statement to His Majesty the King about the question of the Spanish throne with reference to my son, Prince Frederick.[1]

The statement bases itself on the fact that my son has no ambition for his own candidature and does not in any way feel equipped for that great task either by his tastes or by his whole previous training. Nevertheless he is, in this case as in all others, the more ready to bow to His Majesty's definitely expressed will, as he has only to reckon with his own feelings and is not prevented, by ties of relationship or descent, from subordinating his personal convenience to a great historic task. Your Excellency doubtless shares my humble opinion that it is high time to bring about a final settlement of this long pending matter, and therefore I take the liberty of making the proposal that Your Excellency should respectfully suggest to His Majesty the King a brief discussion to which perhaps I, as representative of my son and on my own behalf, could be invited.

With highest esteem

PRINCE V. HOHENZOLLERN

65. *The King of Prussia to Count von Bismarck*

(Original) [German] Berlin, 2.4.1870

Enclosed I am sending you the Prince of Hohenzollern's letter of 28 ult.[2] on the outcome of his talks with his son, Prince Frederick, about the

---

[1] See Doc. No. 57. [2] See Doc. No. 57.

candidature for the Spanish throne. The outcome of this talk is entirely similar to that of the one at which the Hereditary Prince decided to refuse the crown unless I gave him the command to accept. Unable as I felt myself to give such a command in the Hereditary Prince's case, I am no less unable to do so in the case of Prince Frederick and have appended this opinion to the Prince's letter. Accordingly I have sent Prince Frederick a paper which formed a basis of our conference at that time in order that he may once again by himself go over all the pros and cons set forth in black and white.

WILLIAM

Will you, accordingly, send the enclosed to the Prince of Hohenzollern, who departs on the evening of the day after tomorrow, the 4.4.

W.

66. *The King of Prussia to Count von Bismarck*

(Original) [German]   B.[erlin] 3.4.70

Although since dinner I have just been discussing the matter at issue with Prince [Karl Anton] and Prince Frederick.—The latter persists in his refusal, as I am not in a position to exercise persuasion on him in favour of acceptance, I wish after all to have another word with you—and therefore request you to come to me tomorrow, Monday, at 1 o'clock when you will meet Prince [Karl Anton].[1]

WILLIAM

67. *The Crown Prince of Prussia to Count von Bismarck*

(Original) [German]   3.4.70. Evening

The King has just kept the Prince of Hohenzollern and Prince Frederick behind with him after dinner, asking me to be present at the conversation. Prince Frederick reiterated his declaration of refusal, whereupon the King on his side said he could not give a command in such a question to any member of the family, since he did not recognize it as our House's historic task.

This as an appendix to our yesterday's talk.

Your

most devoted

FREDERICK WILLIAM HOHENZOLLERN

---

[1] Punctuation as in original. [Tr.]

68. *Prince Karl Anton of Hohenzollern to Count von Bismarck*

(Original) [German]   Berlin, 4 April, 1870

I herewith return the annexes to Your Excellency with most sincere thanks.[1]

Yesterday after dinner H.M. the King in the presence of H.R.H. the Crown Prince invited me with my son to his apartments to discuss the matter once again.

H.M. was unable to decide to attach importance to the question as one coming within the interests of the Prussian State—on the contrary his words gave the impression that he clearly did not desire the proposal to be entertained. My son was able to motivate his disinclination still more strongly with full justification in view of His Majesty's concurring advice against the proposition, while I repeated to His Majesty my opinion that if His Majesty were to regard acceptance as a Prussian state interest, my son would enter upon the new position.

With highest esteem

PRINCE VON HOHENZOLLERN

69. *The Crown Prince of Prussia to Count von Bismarck*

(Original) [German]   4.4.70

As things actually are and in view of the father's[2] impending departure at 12 o'clock it would in my opinion be important that His Majesty should reach *no final* decision *today*.

Since you have spoken to me of sending a confidential emissary or observer, I would suggest that General von Moltke, who is in the secret, should be asked to send a trustworthy officer under some non-committal pretext to Spain. I think this expedient will result in yet another *respite*!

Your

FREDERICK WILLIAM Hz.

70. *Count von Bismarck to the Crown Prince of Prussia*

(Copy)[3] [German]   Berlin, 4 April, 1870

I humbly inform Y.R.H. that H.M. the King has today commanded that an officer to be designated by General von Moltke be sent to Spain

[1] The annexes are probably Salazar's letters of 25 and 26 March (Docs. Nos. 52 and 54).   [2] Karl Anton.

[3] The draft of this document has been published by Thimme, *Bismarck. Ges. Werke*, VIb, No. 1548.

and that with His Majesty's approval Legation Counsellor Bucher shall depart for Madrid within the next 3 days in order to deliver to the Spanish Prime Minister my provisional reply to the letter he has addressed to me. This reply would seek to postpone the decision by making it dependent on three questions:

(1) Is there an assured majority of $\frac{3}{4}$ or $\frac{2}{3}$ in favour of the election?

(2) Are the finances in such a state that the newly elected King will not be obliged from his own resources to take measures which would damage his reputation at home or abroad?

(3) Does the development of the religious situation lend support to the apprehension that the Monarch by acceptance of the crown would be exposed to papal excommunication?

It would be the task of the Foreign Ministry's emissary to obtain such clarification on these points as is feasible. The army officer, to be designated by Herr v. Moltke, would with introductions from Bernhardi have to gather information on army conditions, the two reports being mutually complementary. I should deeply deplore it if, after a final rejection of the desires expressed by Spain, the subsequent development of events should give occasion for seeking the causes of undesired consequences resulting in one or in many European countries in the fact that monarchic Europe failed to make a timely resolve to take up the battle against republican Europe.

signed V. BISMARCK

71. Count von Bismarck to Baron von Canitz, Prussian Minister at Madrid

(Telegram. Draft for cipher)[1] [French]   Berlin, 5 April, 1870[2]

For Anastasio Alonso: An interview with M. Gama will take place one of the first days of next week. Signed ERQUELINES.   BISMARCK[3]

72. The Crown Prince of Prussia to Count von Bismarck

(Original) [German]   5.4.70

In returning many thanks for your letter I beg to be enabled to have a word with Bucher before his departure. In the next few days except

[1] Cf. Hesselbarth, *Drei psychologische Fragen*, p. 29: "(11) 5 April to Salazar. An interview with Salazar will take place one of first days of next week. BISMARCK."

[2] Marginal note by Bucher: "enciphered with No. 1189 and taken to telegraph office 5/4. 2.15 p.m. Br."

[3] The Madrid decipher bears the following remark: "communicated to the person concerned on 6 April at 11.30 a.m.!"

between the hours of 1.30 and 3 p.m. I shall be at home, because knee trouble prevents my taking exercise.

Your

devoted

FREDERICK WILLIAM HZ.

73. Baron von Canitz, Prussian Minister at Madrid, to Count von Bismarck

(Telegram. Madrid original draft)[1] [French]

Madrid, 6 April, 1870. 5.40 p.m.

Minister for Overseas Territories today read to the Cortes a telegram of yesterday from Havana. General Caballero says the insurrection may be regarded as over. The last of its leaders have taken ship. He is forming companies of volunteers [who have] offered to pursue fugitives. Conscription of 40 thousand men has proceeded quietly everywhere save around Barcelona; Captain-General hopes to have the situation under control today or tomorrow.

74. Baron von Canitz, Prussian Minister at Madrid, to Count von Bismarck

(Telegram. Decipher) [German]

Madrid, 6 April, 1870
5.45 p.m. arr. 11 p.m.

I am addressing my telegram *en clair* of today to Y.E. at the wish of An as *wrong group* io Alonso in the form in which it was delivered by him to me.

CANITZ[2]

75. The Crown Prince of Prussia to Count von Bismarck

(Original) [German]

6.4.70

The enclosed[3] will no doubt be of great interest to father and son,[4] and as up till their departure from here the contents were known to

---

[1] The copy in the files of the *Auswärtiges Amt* is corrupt and is here replaced by the Madrid original.

[2] The Madrid original draft has the text as follows: "I am directing my telegram *en clair* of today to Y.E. at wish of Anastasio Alonso and in the form in which he delivered it to me. CANITZ."

[3] The enclosure is a draft of a Spanish constitution accompanied by a translation. See Doc. No. 77.

[4] "Father and son" here mean Prince Karl Anton of Hohenzollern and his son Leopold.

nobody, I return the papers to you recommending that they be given to Bucher to take with him, as he is to break his journey in order to see them. If this is not the case I would ask for the enclosed to be returned to me.

FREDERICK WILLIAM Hz.

76. *Bucher to Count von Bismarck*

(Original) [German]   Berlin, 8 April, 1870

A printed copy of the Spanish Constitution was yesterday sent to H.R.H. the Crown Prince, and in accordance with the enclosed letter[1] one has today been addressed to the Prince of Hohenzollern.

B[UCHE]R

77. *Count von Bismarck to Prince Karl Anton of Hohenzollern*

(Draft) [German]   Berlin, 8 April, 1870

YOUR SERENE HIGHNESS,

At the command of H.R.H. the Crown Prince I have the honour to send Y.R.H. for your information the enclosed draft of the Spanish Constitution, adopted without substantial changes, together with a translation, with the humble request that these papers may be handed over to the person who will present himself on Sunday morning for that purpose.

[Final message to be added by H.E.]

v. B[ISMARCK][2]

78. *Bucher to Count von Bismarck*

(Original) [German]   Düsseldorf, 10 April, 1870

I have the honour briefly to report with my respects to Your Excellency on my audience today with the Prince of Hohenzollern lasting exactly three quarters of an hour. The Prince first of all discussed the three points in the following order.

On the *religious* matter he said he himself had no personal feelings and he did not touch upon the existence of such feelings in other quarters, merely stating that "the position of his House, as a Catholic one, would become very unpleasant in Germany" were it to be placed under an

---

[1] See Doc. No. 75.
[2] Marginal notes: "B[uche]r.—Sent registered.—fair copy made and taken to post office same day."

interdict. It would be essential that "the religious houses and all the other excrescences should be abolished *beforehand*".

As regards the *financial situation* the possibility of state bankruptcy greatly perturbed him but he had been following attentively the Finance Minister's latest plans not without hopefulness, and said one could see that people were bestirring themselves to remedy the evil. I did not regard myself as authorized to make any allusion to Cuba.

The three-quarters or at the least two-thirds majority he only briefly mentioned without dwelling on its reason or otherwise laying stress on it.

He then went on to speak of the aptitudes of the two Princes. The Hereditary Prince, he said, would have been the more developed and the more affable one; for that reason it was a fortunate circumstance that the Constitution assigned a limited sphere of activities to the King, hence a limited burden of responsibility. He clearly regarded it as settled that there was no longer question of anyone else than Prince Frederick. The latter, he continued, would have to marry as soon as possible if he becomes King of Spain, and in His Highness's opinion only one of the following Princesses (in the order given below) could come under consideration:

1. a Princess Coburg-Cohary of Vienna,
2. a daughter of the Duc de Montpensier, to whom he would give the preference on political grounds on account of the probability of an Orleanist restoration in France,
3. Princess Margaret, daughter of the Duc de Nemours,
4. a daughter of Prince Luitpold of Bavaria, perhaps to be recommended in order to conciliate the father.

I am to talk the matter over with Salazar. He then went on to a detailed discussion of the way in which the official announcement is to be made, the reception of the deputation, the Prince's journey to Spain, whether via France or via Leghorn, to what Spanish seaport and with what ceremony. Of all this I only single out the fact that to his enquiry as to how I thought things should be done I answered that I had little experience of ceremonial matters, but that, if I might be allowed to give a lawyer's point of view, I would say that the Royal ceremonial could not begin until the traveller had set his foot on Spanish soil.

Finally he spoke of the necessity for making another appointment to the Madrid Legation and for preparing for a big press war, since there would be a loud outcry about Prussian intrigue. I remarked that everything that happened anywhere in the world and displeased the enemies of Prussia was set down as the work of Prussian intrigue and that was very flattering. A man's greatness can be measured by his enemies. We should be well able to carry on our own defence in the press. He thought it would be very desirable to influence the *Kölnische Zeitung* and *Indépendance* in good time, if that were possible.

Even from this brief outline there emerges the impression with which the conversation filled me that the Prince in his thoughts already sees his son Frederick as King of Spain. In accordance with Your Excellency's instructions I will turn this success of the endeavours made up to the present to good account in Madrid.

BUCHER

79. *Count von Bismarck to Marshal Prim*

(Copy)[1] [French]   Berlin, 11 April, 1870

MONSIEUR LE COMTE,

Y.E. will doubtless have heard from M. de Salazar that I have received the overtures which you were kind enough to make with the prompt sympathy of my own personal conviction which entirely harmonizes with the attitude of public opinion in Germany. I have unhesitatingly given my loyal support to your projects, *M. le Comte*, but I have found the ground unprepared. Prince Frederick was travelling incognito in Italy and it was only later in Paris that contact was established in a manner enabling him to be summoned to Berlin.

In royal families decisions of great importance are neither more nor less easily arrived at than with private people like ourselves. One has to be prepared for delays and doubts when it is a question of inducing a young prince to take upon himself the responsibility of a historic mission which till that moment has been foreign to his thoughts and the difficulties of which are perhaps magnified by the anxieties aroused in his parents by the prospect of life-long separation and an uncertain future. The Prince, it is true, is of age, but morally he remains obliged to respect the decision of his parents, with whom he is at present staying, and I have not yet succeeded in calming all the apprehensions or overcoming all the scruples arising from a mother's feelings rather than from political reasoning. I should, *M. le Comte*, have desired to reply not otherwise to your letter than with the announcement that the fulfilment of our projects was assured, and I feel convinced that with a little patience we shall still see that moment come; but it seemed to me urgent to place you in possession of the situation and let you know what questions occupy the chief place in the minds of the persons concerned. I have entrusted the matter to Herr Bucher, who knows what my ideas are, and if you will kindly allow it, will explain them to you with complete frankness. I was unable to take advantage of his departure to write a letter to Y.E. and crave your pardon for the delay to which my reply has been subjected by the course of events;

[1] Marginal note by Thile: "The original went off to Madrid with Major von Versen on 13 April. For his own and Herr Bucher's information he has also taken a copy of the copy. v. Th[ile]."

I have been suffering for some time from such a violent attack of rheumatism that all work has been forbidden me and it is only with difficulty today that I am able to pen these lines. It has been my most pressing, and at the same time most agreeable duty as soon as my strength has made it possible. Desirous of avoiding the attention which the dispatch of one of our official couriers would have attracted, I have asked Herr von Versen, one of my personal friends, to take charge of this letter for the delivery of which into Y.E.'s hands he will ask the advice of M. de Salazar.

Accept, *M. le Comte*, the expression of the very high esteem with which I have the honour to be

Y.E.'s most humble and obedient servant

signed BISMARCK

80. *Thile to Eichmann, Prussian Minister at Dresden*

(Telegram. Draft for cipher) [German]   Berlin, 12 April, 1870

Inform Major von Versen of the General Staff, staying at present at the Hotel Stadt Berlin, Dresden, that Count Bismarck requests him to come here as quickly as possible and report to me.

TH[ILE] 12.4.70[1]

81. *Bucher to Thile*

(Original) [German]   Madrid, 14 April, 1870

I have taken the liberty of putting Your Excellency's name so to speak as an emergency address on the enclosed report[2] because there was word that H.E. the Chancellor was to be away on a journey. I respectfully propose for consideration whether, if Count Bismarck is not in Berlin, the report should be at once laid before His Majesty. In my humble opinion acceptance on behalf of one Prince or refusal on behalf of both should be declared before the matter becomes public knowledge here or in Paris. Unless this is done success would be imperilled in the event of acceptance, and in the event of refusal the impression would be given of a capitulation.

If there is still time I beg both urgently and deferentially that Herr v. Versen shall be instructed to behave for the present simply as a tourist, and stay only in Madrid.

BUCHER

[1] Marginal note: "enciphered with 265. Willisch—taken to the telegraph office 12.4. 7.45 p.m."
[2] See Doc. No. 82.

If need arises to telegraph to Herr v. Canitz something destined for me, the message should be addressed: For M. Alonso, and end: signed Erquelines, without mention of my name.

82. *Bucher to Count von Bismarck*

(Original) [French]   Madrid, 14 April, 1870

I am under the necessity of addressing this report to Your Excellency before Herr von Versen has even reached here and I take the responsibility of sending it off today at 2 o'clock in the afternoon by a trustworthy man whom I am sending at my own expense to Aix-la-Chapelle.

Having arrived here yesterday in the morning I had several times in the course of the day uninterrupted talks with M. de Salazar, talks which were prolonged up to midnight. Today early in the morning I saw Marshal Prim, who gave me a gracious reception although to his first question: "What are you bringing me?" I had to reply that I am the herald of a letter from Count von Bismarck. He was obviously informed of all I said yesterday to M. de Salazar, for without formulating the three points he set about elucidating them. The language of the two men was in perfect concordance save that what M. de Salazar had discussed at greater length the Marshal repeated in a more condensed and sententious form. There is not the time to go over separately what was said by each. I will make a joint report of it, and in order to render their words as faithfully as possible am writing in French, craving Your Excellency's indulgence towards both the wording and the handwriting.

The situation. Parliament will reopen on Tuesday 19th inst. and by that or the following day news of acceptance must have been received by telegraph. If not, all the negotiations will be in jeopardy. Everything may be sent to Baron von Canitz. It is through him that Your Excellency will receive General Prim's reply. The French Government is already on the alert. This has become known through indiscretions of its Minister here, M. Mercier, and the day before yesterday the Regent said that if France took a hand she would contrive to make an international question of what is an affair of private or municipal policy. He added that France cannot complain because the first to be approached were Portugal and Italy and because the new dynasty is based not on a Prussian interest but only on a Spanish interest which cannot be otherwise than useful to Spain's neighbours. These latter could not contemplate with indifference the establishment of anarchy or of a republic in Spain.

"In spite of all the maintenance of secrecy, as daily the pressure to end the provisional situation grows stronger and stronger, one has all the time to be giving intimate friends with whom one has to put up a certain show of confidence some sort of an answer to the question: What are your ideas? What are you doing?" These are Marshal Prim's actual words to me.

The two Marshals in every respect prefer the Hereditary Prince to Prince Frederick because of his age, the existence of a Prince of Asturias, and also because he would spare them the difficulties about a marriage. Of the four Princesses who come in question three are Bourbons and Prince Luitpold's daughter would not be popular in Spain; Prince Adalbert of Bavaria is married to a cousin of Queen Isabella's. One might also consider the Duke of Alba's younger daughter (the elder is almost mentally deficient); but there is a fear that this marriage would place them too much under Bonaparte protection.

Religious question. The question of church property was long ago settled by the two Concordats of 1851 and 1859, the latter signed by Don Antonio de los Rios y Rosas, the present leader of the Unionist party in the Cortes. See enclosed extracts.[1] As regards the reductions to be made in the credits for the clergy these will be in the same ratio as for all the other services in order at the end of several years to bring expenditure down to the total of revenue. The Government will grant the Church all sorts of freedom by abolishing the Crown *regalias,* i.e. all the restrictions which since King Charles III and his predecessors have hampered the clergy's freedom of action, in other words by abolishing the "Gallican liberties" of Spain. The Conservative party, far from crying out against the Government in the interests of the Church, regards the proposed concessions to the clergy as excessive, especially the abolition of the *placet.* It would be, they say, the subject State within the free Church.

Great reserve is maintained over freedom of worship. The Constitution, which I have before me, says, Article 21:

"The exercise public or private of any form of worship other than that of the Catholic Church is guaranteed to all foreigners domiciled in Spain without other limits than those of morality and law.

If any Spaniards profess a religion other than the Catholic religion all the provisions of the preceding paragraph shall apply to them also."

The Archbishop of Toledo, the Primate of Spain, has just taken the oath to the Constitution.

"El arzobispo de Toledo, como habiamos annunciado, ha prestado ya su juramento a la Constitucion."[2]

The new King will be able to abolish all obligation on the part of the clergy to take the oath to the Constitution and render himself very popular by granting a full amnesty to all who have not taken it, not only priests but also Carlists, republicans, etc., and by saying that he wishes for no other moral obligation to sustain him than the welcome his people will give to his eagerness to be of use to the country.

[1] See Annex.   [2] Quotation from a Spanish newspaper.

The suppression of certain archbishoprics, decreed in principle, will be carried out only by degrees as vacancies are caused by death.

All these reforms will be carried out in the interval between the election and the arrival. The King will not be involved in them at all.

Financial question. In ordinary times revenue totals 2600 million reals (1 real=2 silver groschen). Within three or four years expenditure could be brought down to that sum by introducing economies in all the services on the one hand, while on the other the collection of taxes would improve as soon as there was a stable Government. Sound policy brings sound finance. This would then render possible a reduction of the deficit which according to the report of M. Vignerola, Minister of Finance, this year totals 6000 million reals, or 143 million francs. The Finance Minister and the Minister for the Colonies stated in the Cortes, amid general applause, that Spain will always meet the claims of her creditors, as she has done hitherto, and that they adopted as their own the noble words spoken by General Grant at the time of the payment in gold of the interest on greenbacks. Spain has paid all her English and French debts and the London and Paris stock exchanges have been open for the last three years. At present they are suffering from the enormous expenditure and work on the construction of railways (over which I have just travelled and which rise to as much as 1359 metres above sea-level). At the present moment the country suffers from stagnation of commerce and enterprise caused by the temporary nature of the regime, as always happens in such conditions. Government stock is taxed only 10% whereas in Austria it is 25 or 20%.

Majority. There would be more than $\frac{2}{3}$ of the votes, there would even be $\frac{3}{4}$ if all the absentees were called up. In any case, as the monarchic principle has been voted by 214 votes to 36, this figure would certainly be exceeded after the new elections, in other words the Monarch's person will command more votes than the article of the Constitution sanctioning the monarchic idea.

Army. "The army", said Marshal Prim to me, "will go off like a cannon ball from the cannon's mouth whichever way I direct it. At the time of the Carlist and republican revolts old army pensioners reported to their regiments to take part in the fight".

The last words were: "the longer the affair drags on the more we must expect to see men who today are monarchists slipping towards a republic from anxiety and uncertainty".

[Spanish] "It seems that one of these days the merchants of this capital are going to call a meeting for the purpose of reaching an agreement to address a statement to the Cortes appealing for a speedy settlement of the constitution of the country in view of the serious damage to their interests they have suffered in recent months."[1]

---

[1] Quotation from a Spanish newspaper.

Annexes: *Extracts from the Concordats with Spain*

Annex (Original)

[Only the German translation of the Spanish text given by Bucher is here translated]

I

Isabella II, by God's grace and in virtue of the Constitution of the Spanish Monarchy Queen of Spain, proclaims to all who can see or hear these presents: that I, applying the powers to proceed to a general regulation of the Clergy and to the settlement of ecclesiastical questions conferred on my Government by the Law of 8 May, 1849, in agreement with the Holy See, Do command that as the law of the realm there shall be published and observed the Concordat concluded with the Holy See on 16 March and ratified on the 1 and 23 April of the present year, the text of which runs as follows:

Concordat

concluded between H.H. Pope Pius IX and H.M. Queen Isabella II of Spain

Article 41

Henceforth the Church shall have the right to acquire new possessions by any lawful title and its possession of all it now owns or shall in future acquire is solemnly declared inviolable. In future as regards ecclesiastical foundations both old and new no abolition or amalgamation may take place without the participation of the authority of the Holy See save in virtue of the powers granted to the bishops by the Council of Trent.

Article 42

With this premise and in consideration of the usefulness which this convention will have for the cause of religion, the Pope at the request of H.M. and for the preservation of the public peace, resolves and declares that those who under earlier conditions in the Catholic Kingdom and in virtue of the civil laws of the time have purchased ecclesiastical properties and entered into possession thereof and the successors to the possessions of such purchasers shall at no time be in any way molested, either by him, the Pope, or by his successors, and that rather the ownership, revenues and benefits of these properties may securely and in peace appertain to themselves and to their successors.

Signed at the Royal Palace on 17 October, 1851. I, the Queen. The Minister of Justice, Ventura Gonzalez Romero.

II

Concordat

of 25 August, 1859, likewise published as law of the Realm
on 4 April, 1860

Article 4

In view of the dilapidated condition of the majority of the properties
which have not yet been sold, the difficulties of their administration and
the various contradictory and inaccurate estimates of their yield, in view
of these circumstances which have hitherto made the endowment of the
clergy uncertain and inapplicable, H.M.'s Government has proposed to
the Holy See the change that the bishops should be given powers in
consultation with their chapters to settle the price of the church properties
situated in their dioceses, and that in exchange for all of these same and
for their surrender to the State, which is still to be made operative, the
Government offers as many non-transferable bonds of the 3% stock of the
National debt as are requisite to cover the full value of the said properties.

Article 5

In the desire that without delay a fixed, secure and independent endowment of public worship and of the clergy shall be brought into being, the
Holy See, after hearing the views of the Spanish Bishops and recognizing
the greater advantage to the Church both in the present case and in these
conditions taken as a whole, has found no objection to the putting into
effect of the above mentioned change in the following way:

Articles 6-19. Regulations for execution.

Article 20

In consideration of the advantages conferred on the Church by this
new agreement, the Holy See, in compliance with the repeated requests of
H.M. the Queen, has found itself called upon hereby to extend the gracious
permission contained in Art. 42 of the Concordat (of 16 March 1851) to
the Church lands alienated pursuant to the Law of 1 May, 1855.*

 * This law orders the sale of all properties in mortmain.

From the above Concordats it can be seen

1. that the question which so long cast a shadow over the relations
   between the two Courts *was thoroughly cleared up* under the
   previous Government;
2. that the *clergy are now dependent on the Treasury*;
3. that by the sale of church lands in small lots a peasant class has
   come into being which is as firmly attached to the new order as
   were earlier the purchasers of state lands in France.

B[UCHE]R

83. *Salazar to Prince Karl Anton of Hohenzollern*

(Copy)[1] [French]   Madrid, 17 April, 1870
                                                          pr. 18 April

YOUR ROYAL HIGHNESS,

I was going to write a very long letter to Y.R.H., but Herr Bucher is in such haste to send the person who is the bearer of his dispatches[2] this very day as far as Aix-la-Chapelle, that I beg Y.H. to excuse me if time obliges me to lay before you the few pages I have just written to Count von Bismarck.[3]

In this way Y.H. will receive the letter for the Count on Saturday evening and Herr von Bismarck will be able to have cognizance of it on Sunday.

The Regent and Marshal Prim on whose behalf I speak beg Y.H. to be so good as to go to Berlin immediately on receiving this letter in order that the family council may meet on Monday or Tuesday.

Marshal Prim will at once communicate by telegraph his reply to the letter addressed to him by Herr von Bismarck which is to be delivered to him the day after tomorrow.

The Cortes will meet again on Tuesday, the 19th, the clamour in favour of the crowning of the edifice will gain new strength after Holy Week and the Easter holidays and longer delay will *jeopardize the whole thing.*

Next week all the merchants, shopkeepers, etc., of Madrid are to lay before the Cortes a petition with more than 20,000 signatures, asking for a solution to be found of the interim situation [*sic*: the expression *interinité* means interim], and the position of the two Marshals will become very difficult, *very difficult.*

I am greatly pleased by the very coincidence of dates: it is exactly six years ago today that as Minister at Lima I with Admiral Pinzon took possession of the Guano islands to force Peru to pay an old debt to Spain. I succeeded in my mission and returned safe and sound to Europe in spite of the ambush laid for me at Panama. If we had contented ourselves with the three million dollars paid to us by Peru at that time we should not have needed to bombard Le Callao in 1866, but the Queen, who thought she could keep the wealth of those islands, did not know that in politics grasp all is lose all. In personal matters she paid dearly her inordinate appetite in certain directions.

Herr Bucher writes me that all is ready and I end these lines by asking Y.R.H. to accept the respectful homage of my entire devotion.

                                             E. DE SALAZAR Y MAZARREDO

---

[1] Marginal note by Bucher [in German]: "Original sent to the Prince of Hohen-zollern on 9. May."

[2] Cf. Docs. Nos. 81 and 82.   [3] See Doc. No. 84.

The bomb which will burst here when the result becomes known will have a considerable influence in determining the number of votes in the French plebiscite.

The two Marshals desire to have large photographs of the Hereditary Prince and Princess.

84. *Salazar to Count von Bismarck*

(Original) [French]   Madrid, 14 April, 1870

Herr Bucher's arrival has produced the most favourable impression on the Regent and Marshal Prim. I have just introduced him to the latter and I think he must be satisfied with the explanations given him by Count de Reus about the finances, the army, the clergy and all the political questions of the day.

The Marshal laid stress on the need for taking a decision as soon as possible, for he is harassed on all sides, accused of having neither plan nor system, of keeping the country in this interim state which is causing the paralysis of trade and industry, and of doing nothing to crown the constitutional edifice. As he can tell nobody what is in the wind his position like that of the Regent is becoming untenable and they are suspected of prolonging the interim regime indefinitely. If those who accuse him only knew the secret anguish which I witness!!!

The two Marshals commission me to tell you that the new dynasty will establish itself much more easily with the Hereditary Prince than with his brother. The latter's marriage would cause considerable difficulties. If Prince Frederick has been mentioned in the second place it is because it has been understood from the telegrams that Prince Leopold had definitely declined.

There would be only 4 marriages possible: 3 would be with Bourbon princesses, and as regards the Bavarian princess the Bavarians are not too popular in Spain since Prince Adalbert's last visits.

An alliance with the Alba family would rouse the jealousy of the Grandees and would place us at the mercy of our neighbour. On the other hand the Conservative party in the Chamber has pledged itself to vote for a prince who is of age, a Catholic, and a member of a *royal family*. This requirement would be extended of course also to the Queen, and in spite of the ambitions of the Duke of Berwick and Alba his relationship with the Stuarts is now antiquated even if it were legitimate.

The Hereditary Prince, say the Marshals, would be the solution of a host of questions, all very important: his sons, the high repute of his family, his suitable age, the goodwill of the Portuguese, etc.

Delay of a definite solution may jeopardize the whole thing. M. Mercier, the French Ambassador, suspects something, and though the *Regent* in his ebullient way says that Napoleon's open opposition would help rather than harm the undertaking it will be more prudent to have the candidate elected by a Cortes majority in secret session without previously giving the alert. Once the vote has been taken, satisfactory explanations can be given to France since the issue is one of Spanish not of Prussian interests; and we cannot be reproached with seeking to defy France after the démarches which have been made at Lisbon and Florence.

The press is full of nothing else—and the public likewise—than the urgent need of ending the interim situation; by further delay we shall lose certain votes of impatient men who are ready to leave the Cortes and never to return in view of the stagnation of the situation.

As Marshal Prim told Herr Bucher yesterday we have no serious questions at issue with the Pope. The ecclesiastical lands were sold with his authorization under the Concordats of 1851 and 1860, and the retrenchment we shall have to make in certain endowments is connected with a plan for balancing the budget which will equally affect all the other administrative services. Present incumbents will remain in office and certain sees, etc., will only be suppressed on the death of the present beneficiaries. There are some sees which have only 7 or 8 thousand souls, as there are certain judges, etc., for populations of 3 to 4 thousand inhabitants while others amount to more than 100 thousand. All this is being done without noise and with general approval.

As regards the Church we in return give it full and entire freedom without concerning ourselves with the Council; the *exequatur* is being abolished together with the jurisdictional privileges of the military orders, the royal precincts, the army, etc. All prerogatives disappear and the bishops see their influence considerably strengthened, for under the old regime a great proportion of the territory was dependent on the King and not on Ordinaries nominated by the Pope.

The scheme is so favourable to them that it has been attacked by a Conservative paper as reactionary because it will make the State subject under a Church that is free. The latter can acquire property, etc., and in spite of this the State undertakes to pay it 40 million francs annually, much more than is granted to the clergy of the whole of France with a population of 38 millions.

As for the form of oath to the Constitution it is a formality which is about to be abolished for all classes in order not to cause trouble over futilities.

In conclusion I would add that once the Prince was here many of the difficulties would be smoothed away by his very presence. When the master is absent petty formalism always tends to gain the upper hand over matters of basic importance.

I have the honour to be Y. Excellency's most devoted servant and colleague in this great undertaking.   E. DE SALAZAR Y MAZARREDO

85. *Prince Karl Anton of Hohenzollern to the Ministry for Foreign Affairs*

(Telegram en clair) [German]   Düsseldorf, 17 April, 1870
dispatched at 11.10 a.m.

When does Count Bismarck return from Varzin?
PRINCE OF HOHENZOLLERN

86. *Thile to Prince Karl Anton of Hohenzollern*

(Copy) [German]   Berlin, 17 April, 1870. 1 p.m.

Health permitting, Count Bismarck intended to be back here for the opening of the Customs Parliament.   signed v. THILE

87. *Thile to Count von Bismarck*

(Original) [German]   B[erlin], Sunday, 17.4.1870

HONOURED CHIEF,
Just now, 30 minutes before the departure of the Stettin train, I have received the enclosed, which must no doubt be read in the first place by Your Excellency before it can be laid before His Majesty as proposed by Lothar.
In extreme haste
Your most obedient   THILE

Thus Prince Hohenzollern enquires by telegraph when you return. I am replying: "probably for the 26th".

88. *Count von Bismarck to Thile*

(Telegram en clair) [German]   Varzin, 18 April, 1870 [9.55 a.m.]

Telegrams received and immediately sent back to His Majesty. I am seriously ill in bed unable to attend to business. My opinion in the matter is known and remains unchanged. My return quite undecided, impossible in the next week in any case.   v. BISMARCK

89. *Thile to Prince Karl Anton of Hohenzollern*

(Telegram en clair) [German]   18.4.70. 12.10 p.m.

While in the act of forwarding your communication to Varzin I have just received by telegraph the announcement from Count Bismarck that he is seriously ill in bed and absolutely unable to attend to business, and that his return to Berlin is quite undecided and certainly impossible for a week. I have therefore regarded it as my duty to lay Your Royal Highness's communication immediately before His Majesty.

TH[ILE]

90. *Thile to the King of Prussia*

(Original) [German]   Berlin, 18 April, 1870

I humbly beg to inform Your Majesty of the following.

Yesterday at noon I received a letter from Legation Counsellor Bucher, on a mission in Madrid, addressed to the Minister-President with the note that in case of the latter's absence it was to be opened by me. It contained a very detailed report from Bucher about his first moves and impressions in Madrid. I perceived at once from a cursory glance over the contents that Count Bismarck would wish to make a report to Your Majesty on this highly important matter immediately on his return (perhaps as early as the day after tomorrow, when we expected him back), and, in order to give him time to gather further information, sent the whole of Bucher's communication by express messenger to Varzin. Time was so short that I was not even able to keep notes of the contents.

Now *this morning* I receive the enclosed documents[1] from His Royal Highness the Prince of Hohenzollern (who yesterday had enquired by telegraph when the Prime Minister was returning). In obedience to His Royal Highness's wish I was about to send these papers, too, to the Minister and was just in the act of dispatching a second express messenger to Varzin when I received the Minister's telegram[2] of today, which I respectfully enclose. The telegram shows:

1. That Count Bismarck immediately dispatched Bucher's consignment directly to Your Majesty, who will doubtless receive it this evening or tomorrow morning;

2. that for the time being the Minister is "absolutely unable to attend to business".

In these regrettable circumstances I could not do otherwise than lay

---

[1] See Docs. Nos. 83, 84 91, 92.   [2] See Doc. No. 88.

the Prince's communication, too, directly before Your Majesty instead of sending it to Varzin, humbly awaiting Your Majesty's further commands—perhaps after the Bucher reports have come back from Varzin.

In the meantime I am telegraphing the Minister's illness to the Prince of Hohenzollern.

v. THILE

91. *Prince Karl Anton of Hohenzollern to Count von Bismarck*

(Original) [German]   Düsseldorf, 18[1] April, 1870

YOUR EXCELLENCY, my Lord Chancellor of the North German Confederation,

From Don Salazar, Counsellor of State, I have just received a letter beginning as follows:

> "I was going to write to Y.R.H., but Herr Bucher is in such haste to send the person who is the bearer of his dispatches this very day as far as Aix-la-Chapelle that I beg Y.H. to excuse me if time obliges me to lay before you the few pages I have just written to Count von Bismarck."

I conclude from this that the open letter to Your Excellency enclosed with the one to me must be the original, which I therefore hereby enclose.[2] I also have the honour to add for your information Don Salazar's letter[3] to me s.p.r.[4] [i.e. requesting its return]. Its assumption that the Hereditary Prince might in the end let himself be persuaded to accept the throne is incorrect—already during our visit to Berlin the Hereditary Prince returned a definite refusal and his decision was approved by His Majesty on grounds of his aversion for the solution of the Iberian question and further in consideration of the problem of the inheritance and of the retention within Prussia of the immense entailed possessions of the Hohenzollerns.

Hence the only candidature that could come into question would be that of Prince Frederick, and he alone can be considered for it, although he lacks all inward urge and has received no encouragement from His Majesty the King to shoulder a task that is no less great than onerous.

In my humble opinion Madrid should again be told definitely by telegraph that they must give up all hope of the better and more desirable alternative, namely the Hereditary Prince's willingness, leaving it to their

---

[1] Marginal note: "17?"
[2] See Doc. No. 84.
[3] See Doc. No. 83.
[4] s.p.r.="sub petitione remissionis."

judgement whether they will make themselves responsible for the election of Prince Frederick and take vigorous action.

In all circumstances there should be a warning against precipitate moves such as are being foreshadowed. Having waited for months they can wait for another few days.

If H.M. the King and Your Excellency again command and desire my presence in Berlin, regarding it as in the interests of a general clearing up of the matter, a brief hint is all I ask.[1]

The particulars given by Don Salazar about questions of relations between Church and State seem to be quite reassuring and satisfactory.

I hope Your Excellency will excuse the only too evident haste of these hurried lines and believe me ever with feelings of highest esteem

Your devoted

PRINCE OF HOHENZOLLERN

92. *Prince Karl Anton of Hohenzollern to Thile*

(Original) [German]   Düsseldorf, 18 April, 1870

YOUR EXCELLENCY,

Many thanks for your kind information about Count von Bismarck's return.

As the subject of my communication is one of extreme urgency and every effort must be made at all costs to avoid *precipitancy* I cannot see what else I can do in the circumstances than place the letter[2] I have written to the Chancellor *unsealed* in Your Excellency's hands.

I trust that this may make it considerably easier for the Chancellor to send you instructions as he is doubtless doing,[3] since Count Bismarck will find it less trying to correspond with you by telegraph than by letter through the post.

From the contents of my and Don Salazar's letters Your Excellency will easily gather all the necessary information and I therefore refrain from a detailed discussion.

Furthermore exhaustive information will have come in from Legation Counsellor Bucher. This morning's post brought me the letters posted at Aix-la-Chapelle.

I regret having to intrude upon Your Excellency's Easter repose—but events often outstrip one's ideas, therefore apologies.

It is with the highest esteem that I remain

Ever Your Excellency's devoted

PRINCE OF HOHENZOLLERN

[1] Marginal note by Bismarck: "Yes!"   [2] See Doc. No. 91.
[3] Marginal note by Thile: "not now, of course."

93. *Prince Karl Anton of Hohenzollern to the King of Prussia*

(Telegram en clair) [German]   Düsseldorf, 19.4.1870. 7.50 a.m.

arrived 8.15 a.m.

Arriving Thursday morning.

Prince of Hohenzollern

94. *Baron von Canitz, Prussian Minister at Madrid,*
to Count von Bismarck

(Telegram. Decipher)[1] [French]   Madrid, 19 April, 1870. 1.40 a.m.

arrived 20 April 8 a.m.

Salazar brings me the following for Your Excellency:
"Your letter received by the Marshal. He upholds the declarations made to Herr Bucher on the present state of affairs intended to avoid foreign complications and retain considerable number of votes."
Bucher asks whether he may return, since a long stay here would awaken suspicions.[2]

signed: Canitz

95. *Thile to the King of Prussia*

(Original) [German]   Berlin, 19 April, 1870

I humbly present to Your Majesty in the enclosure the communications[3] from Bucher which the Chancellery porter, just back from Varzin, has brought me addressed *to me*. The statement in Count Bismarck's telegram[4] that he had sent the dispatches at once back to Your Majesty was thus in that respect inaccurate.

In order not further to delay your receiving these documents I enclose a translation of the (not important) annexes in Spanish which Your Majesty will perhaps graciously permit me to translate orally when I report, as commanded, today at 4 o'clock.

Thile

---

[1] Cf. Hesselbarth, *Drei psychologische Fragen*, p. 29: "(12) 19 April to Bismarck. Chevalier Prim received letter cordially. He upholds declaration made to Bucher (that caballero has come to Madrid incognito) as to the home and foreign situation in order to avoid complications and retain good number of votes. Salazar."

[2] Marginal note by King of Prussia: "I think he should! W. 20.4.70."

[3] Cf. Doc. No. 82; cf. also Doc. No. 81.

[4] Cf. Doc. No. 88.

96. *Thile to the King of Prussia*

(Original) [German]   Berlin, 19 April, 1870

In sending Your Majesty the draft telegram as commanded I most humbly beg to say that Legation Counsellor Bucher specially requested this form (to Herr von Canitz, for M. Alonso).[1]

THILE

Annex

Draft of cipher telegram

[French] Count Bismarck seriously ill at Varzin and incapable of attending to business. Hereditary Prince unfortunately unable to accept. Prince Frederick and his father are summoned to Berlin, where all will be done to speed up a final decision.[2]

97. *Versen to Count von Bismarck*

(Original)[3] [German]   Madrid, 19 April, 1870

DEAR COUNT,

Honoured Chancellor of the Confederation
Minister-President and Major-General!

Having just presented your letter[4] to Marshal Prim I hasten obediently to report:

The Marshal read the letter and then asked whether I was charged with any further instructions? I answered: No others than to tighten (*estrechar*) the bonds between himself and Your Excellency, since Herr Bucher was entrusted with the negotiations.

Prim: How long do you mean to stay here?

Myself: I intend to make a short excursion to the South so that if my mission were to become known I could say I had come here as a tourist.

Prim: Tell me what information you are looking for, say about the army or the country or anything else. I am entirely at your service and will provide you with all you need to form an opinion.

Myself: Your Excellency will understand from my official mission

---

[1] Marginal note by King of Prussia: "Approved. W."

[2] Marginal note by Bismarck: "Transposed, see next page." Cf. Doc. No. 98.

[3] Marginal note by Thile written on the envelope: "Opened by me at H.M.'s command. Thile. 28.4.70."

[4] See Doc. No. 79.

that I have no other minor commissions. I would gladly learn more about the excellent military institutions and organization but my short leave renders this impossible, unfortunately. I can only confine myself to a short excursion.

Prim: Where do you want to go?

Myself: I was thinking of Cadiz, Seville, Cordova, Malaga, and have not yet made up my mind whether, according as time permits, to return via Genoa or by the main southern railway via Saragossa. (As I had been told by Herr Bucher that it is believed here that Berlin is carrying on espionage all over the place, I purposely did not mention Barcelona, though meaning to have a look at it.)

Prim: Are you thinking of going to Barcelona?

Myself: If occasion permits, otherwise not.

Here Salazar interrupted: "That makes a tour of over a month." Seeing from their faces that they were not pleased at this, I dropped it at once and said: "Then my time would not stretch to it. I should therefore not go near it." (The newspapers of all parties have printed such a lot about Catalonian conditions in connexion with the suppressed disturbances at Barcelona that I am fully informed in that respect.)

Prim: Then you had best return via Madrid and I will give you a letter for Count Bismarck. You can then see Saragossa on the return journey. How did you come?

Myself: Via Burgos.

Prim: Would you like to see anything here? The troops are the same here as everywhere.

Myself: That will give me great pleasure.

He gave the order that I am to be treated as an English officer and in the company of an adjutant visit all the barracks and view the exercises of one division of every arm of the service.

To Salazar he said that Herr Bucher was authorized to negotiate, and to me that the matter was urgent and could brook no further delay. To this I remarked that Your Excellency had been acting with all energy but that Berlin, when I left, had no idea of the urgent turn taken by events here. I said Your Excellency was endeavouring to speed matters up but would need at least another fortnight to overcome all obstacles, as you would undoubtedly do.

He did not say a word about my talk with M. Salazar of the previous day though he certainly knew all about it. As it was carried on in Spanish, I take the liberty of giving here the gist of it, which Herr Bucher, who was also present, will also have gathered approximately. I respectfully remark in advance that it was not at all in my intention to exercise any sort of influence, having no instructions to do so. But since I was invited to do so, I trust that in view of the slowness of communications with Berlin I have acted in accordance with Your Excellency's views in embarking cautiously on a discussion with Salazar. It was confined to two points. Firstly, that both he and Marshal Prim definitely[1] reckoned on Prince Leopold's acceptance of the crown, and, secondly, that relying on the courier dispatched a few days ago they expected the acceptance by Thursday, 21st inst. at the latest. I did not flatly contradict the first point, but only said that as far as my information went there was little prospect of Prince Leopold's acceptance, that on the other hand Prince Frederick felt much inclined and was receiving support from high quarters. As regards the second point, the time factor, they could not count on receiving an answer in less than a fortnight; I could not say, to be sure, what would be the effect of news reaching Berlin after I left and it might possibly be that the decision was speeded up thereby.

The conversation lasted a good half hour during which he particularly wanted to know what difficulties were causing this long delay. Without touching on personalities and in order to combat Spanish mistrust a little I merely remarked that our Royal Family lived on such happy terms with the Hohenzollern Princely House that it had not seized (*agarraban*) the offer, flattering as it was, out of hand, that only the "ladies" had some hesitations not known to me which it would take Your Excellency no great time to overcome. Your Excellency, I added, had recently been ill, Holy Week and Easter also came in between, and in view of the slowness of communications at least a fortnight would be needed. At the time of my departure nobody in Berlin had any idea that the matter was as urgent as I had found it here.

Your Excellency will have learnt from Herr Bucher how much all parties press for a speedy settlement of this question by the Cortes when they reassemble after Easter. M. Salazar stressed in particular the importance of the votes lost by the impending departure of the members for Porto Rico and the Balearics, and also the expectation of bribery by the French as soon as they learn of the secret, which can hardly be kept much longer.

As Salazar very rightly remarked that Prince Leopold with his Princess and three sons would receive a much more enthusiastic welcome I took the liberty of commending Prince Frederick, who is now the same age as was Prince Carol when he accepted election in Rumania. Without exactly extolling his energy I went to the length of saying that he would devote himself perhaps with greater intensity to the new task in life than an older man. As I took my departure M. Salazar asked me "Will you come back again tomorrow?" I answered: "That would be remarked in Berlin, where my journey will in any case soon become known, and that was why I was combining it with a little tour." Marshal Prim, as I have already said, touched only on this matter of the tour apart from a few

[1] Marginal note by Bucher: "They did not say that to me; only that they *hoped*."

other trivial matters, but was extremely friendly. I am not to call upon the three Spanish General Staff officers whom I know, and as I assured the Marshal that I was not in any contact with Herr von Bernhardi and only knew his name as a military writer, I shall actually not call upon him, especially as there is plenty of opportunity to see and hear enough to form an unbiased opinion.

Madrid, 20 April, 1870

As Your Excellency may be interested to hear the impression I have so far received of the army after five days in Spain, I can only express my astonishment that after such crises an army has been able to preserve such normal discipline and bearing. I have inspected here the barracks of the infantry, riflemen, cavalry, artillery and engineers, some troops of which have been here only for a few weeks, since infantry and cavalry constantly change garrison. Also in Burgos I saw the troops, and daily listened to officers' private conversations in coffee-houses, trains, etc. The troops much remind one of the French in composition and quality, go in for a lot of hard duelling at every opportunity and appear to be kept out of all party intrigues by their garrison life. Only the senior officers above regimental rank seem to take part in politics, and General Prim knows how to keep these in order. With the help of the well-planned network of railways he can speedily concentrate adequate forces wherever unrest breaks out, and although 40,000 men have been dispatched to Cuba he keeps all the larger towns garrisoned with more than sufficient troops. In addition there exists a Gendarmerie Corps of 15,000 men, called Guardia Civil, organized on military lines and recruited from men who have served their term in the army, which if there were a King would be sufficient to maintain peace. It seems to me that a King, if he would only devote some care to the troops, could be sure of their loyalty and devotion, which till now only the political Generals have troubled about.

Not until I have understood more of conditions and seen the big cities of the South shall I be able to furnish a faithful picture and do not now presume to do more than offer these first impressions. As I can see that I must get through my task as speedily as possible I will make my return in about 11 days unless I receive a telegram from Herr Bucher to Saragossa telling me I can stay longer. I have arranged with Herr Bucher on this point.

With highest esteem I have the honour to remain

Your Excellency's most obedient

VON VERSEN

Major, General Staff

5th Army Corps.

98. *Thile to Baron von Canitz, Prussian Minister at Madrid*

(Telegram. Draft for cipher)[1] [French]   B.[erlin] 20.4.70

For M. Alonso.

Count von Bismarck seriously ill at Varzin and unable to attend to business. The fourth clause of the loan unfortunately cannot be accepted. The sixth will be discussed today; everything will be done to expedite a definite decision. Erquelines

Th[ile]

99. *Bucher to Count von Bismarck*

(Original) [German]   Madrid, 20 April, 1870
received 27 April

Before reporting to Your Excellency about my second talk with Marshal Prim, Count Reus, which took place today, I venture to advert to the circumstances which enable me to hope for a merciful judgement on the grave imperfection of my humble report of the 14th inst.[2] I had not been out of my clothes for 5 days and 4 nights and was in a state bordering on fever when I arrived here on the 13th. I at once got in touch with M. Salazar, who came to see me a few minutes later and with brief interruptions did not leave me till midnight. On the following morning he made the proposal, which I unhesitatingly accepted, to present me to Marshal Prim even before Your Excellency's letter arrived. As Marshal Prim confirmed all that Salazar had told me, especially that longer delay would be dangerous in view of the pressure from the Cortes and the population on the one hand and the awakening of French suspicions on the other, my resolve came to a head to dispatch that same day a messenger whom at my request Salazar had in the meantime engaged for me. The man had to be sent off by 2 p.m. in order not to miss the train and thus cause a delay of 24 hours. It was 11.30 a.m. before I could set to work on writing my report, reading through and making extracts from the Concordat of 1859 drawn up in Italian and Spanish; the earlier one I had read through the previous night, making the necessary extracts. Although I have no practice in French, have no works of reference and no time for reflection, I thought it better to write in that language; a careful rendering

---

[1] Cf. Hesselbarth, *Drei psychologische Fragen*, pp. 29-30: "(13) 20 April. Chief Bismarck ill at Varzin. The fourth clause of the loan unfortunately cannot be accepted. For the present there is to be a discussion today. Everything will be done to expedite a definite decision. Thile."

[2] See Doc. No. 82.

of what the two men had said and which I to a great extent remembered word for word would have slowed me up and a hasty one would have blurred the colour effect which I trust remains to some extent recognizable even in my imperfect performance. I said to myself that what was at issue here was not French grammar but the Spanish crown. I humbly beg Your Excellency to take these facts into consideration and use them also to excuse me with His Majesty the King if my report of the 14th has been laid before him.

After Major von Versen's arrival on the 18th, his presentation by me to M. Salazar, and by M. Salazar to Marshal Prim on the 19th for the purpose of delivering Your Excellency's letter, the Marshal today sent for me. He began by reading Your Excellency's letter slowly out loud, expressing his pleasure at the flattering things it contained about himself and declaring his readiness to provide Your Excellency through me with all the information in his possession. He then begged me to tell him all I know about the grounds and circumstances of the hesitation in Berlin. I exposed to him the three points concerning relations with the Holy See, the financial situation, and the majority which could be reckoned on, informing him that I had already on the 14th reported what I had had the honour to hear from his lips and what I had found in the Concordats.

After a friendly allusion to M. Salazar's activity in Berlin and my own here he answered my three questions on the same lines as on the 14th, only more directly and fully. I take the liberty of letting him speak for himself, adding at the appropriate place certain utterances which he had made on the 14th and which dropped out of my earlier report.

"With the Holy See we have no difficult problems of any kind. The affair of the estates belonging to the clergy is, as you know, settled by the Concordat. How we have settled freedom of worship is shown in the Constitution, the relevant clauses of which have been in full application since its publication (June, 1869) without giving rise to any complaints. Our attitude towards the Council is known to your Government. It is not to be anticipated that in the matter of civil marriage and on certain other points where Church and State come into contact the Holy Father should not grant us what he has granted to so many other countries.

"When in October, 1868, the new Finance Minister made his preliminary survey he told me with an expression of despair that he had found an apparently bottomless pit; the Treasury was empty; claims falling due [des échéances] would be hailing down on him from France, England, Belgium; and a large proportion of the most urgent debts had been contracted not at all for the benefit of the country but for personal needs of the ruling family. I told him: keep your courage up! pay all debts honourably! we shall be our country's saviours even financially! And our confidence has not been unfounded. At the last Cabinet meeting the Finance Minister had the pleasure of showing us that we had paid everything owing and that our financial position had nevertheless considerably improved in the last 18 months, although conditions were very unfavourable. For, in the first place, we are suffering from the stagnation of trade which follows every political upheaval and accompanies every stop-gap Government, and secondly we found ourselves with the troubles in Cuba on our hands. I myself can hardly understand how my colleagues have achieved it all. Just think that we have sent 42,000 men and a big fleet to Cuba and that every soldier who lands there has cost us 40 piastres (1 piastre= 5 francs 25 centimes). Add to that the enormous mass of material. Without fuss we have done more than France with the Mexican expedition. That proves that Spain has good stuff in her and that Spaniards and other people know it. How else could we have raised the needful resources? In this year's budget we have reduced expenditure by 300 million reals; next year we shall do the same, and by the fourth, if not by the third, year the budget will be balanced. The great railway main lines have cost enormous sums but are paying high dividends; the smaller lines will have to wait. Since the tariff reform which we introduced customs revenues have risen by 20 millions compared with the same period in the previous years. In the market reports you will see that our government stock is rising. Tell Count Bismarck he may regard Spain as a man who has come in for a big inheritance, one with ample resources but badly mismanaged, and who must go very carefully for a time. (See Annex.)

"We are sure of a more than two-third majority but every further day threatens to lose us votes. Many of the members are returning home to their businesses; others, positively despairing of a monarchic solution, are inclining towards the Republicans. Today is the 20 April; by 20 May when the hot weather sets in the whole business must be settled, in other words, the secret election of the King must have taken place, his official acceptance have been received, and the law passed for the establishment of the dynasty as laid down in the 'Transitional Regulations' of Article I of the Constitution. It is not possible for us to maintain any longer the secrecy we have till now so successfully preserved. We have friends in the Cortes from whom we cannot entirely keep things hidden. We are threatened with a hail of addresses from the country and parliamentary questions in the Cortes. Admiral Topete said to me yesterday with his characteristic impetuosity: 'if you people don't do something about it soon, I'll make a hell of a row [esclandre]'. Our press is in part open to influence, as is doubtless not unheard of elsewhere; there are newspapers with a weakness for gold even if coming from France."

The Marshal came in conclusion to the subject of the Regent: "The Regent and I, he said, are of the same mind and, even if in this connexion it seems like blowing my own trumpet, I do not hesitate to add: He is a man of integrity, generous and caring only for the welfare of his country."

He did not this time touch upon the army. On the 14th he had been led to do so by the remark, made by M. Salazar, who was present, that Berlin did not feel quite sure about its discipline. He must have brought this knowledge back from Berlin; I at least never said a word to him of such a thing.

The Marshal signified to me as I took my leave that I was to be the bearer of a letter of reply from him.

I must finally add that Salazar in the interval spoke to me about the unexpected incident of the question in the English House of Commons about an alleged English request to Spain. I had read of this shortly before I left Berlin in the English newspapers. Salazar said that during the fighting against the Carlists England had furnished the Christinos with war material, giving the impression that this was a gift and saying not a word about it for nearly 30 years. But when a few years ago Spain went to war with Morocco and was about to launch the expedition against Tangiers, the English, who did not approve of the enterprise, trotted out a doubtful claim dating from that time, threw it in our faces, as he expressed himself, in order to paralyse operations. The claim was met and the expedition carried out all the same. It was remarkable, he added, that at the present moment another much weaker claim complicated by questions of compensation was being put forward dating from the time of the civil war. He did not say in so many words but obviously thought that London may have somehow got wind of the present negotiations and was wanting to stop or thwart them.

I have not attempted to make enquiries of my own about the finances and the state of the parties. For the former purpose more time would be needful and a knowledge of finance which I do not possess. The latter could only be attained by making personal contacts which would at once have attracted attention to me. Even as things are, I have had difficulty in escaping observation. Madrid has, to be sure, only about 400,000 inhabitants but they live crowded together in tall houses and narrow streets, and throngs concentrate on Puerta del Sol Square where eight streets meet. Foreigners are few except for English tourists, who are only numerous in the autumn. The press of all parties is active and vigilant.

BUCHER

Annex: *Article 104 of the Spanish Constitution*

Annex

Appendix to the report of 20 April, 1870.

Article 104 of the Constitution runs:

"La Deuda pública està bajo la salvaguardia especial de la Nacion", which means:

The Public Debt is under the special protection of the nation.

100. *Thile to Baron von Canitz, Prussian Minister at Madrid*

(Telegram. Draft for cipher)[1] [French]

Berlin, 22 April, 1870. 5.30 p.m.

For M. Alonso. I hasten to inform you that, the fourth clause of the contract for the loan having been definitely ruled out, *insurmountable* obstacles likewise stand in the way of the sixth clause. Thus the whole loan unfortunately falls through. We most deeply regret this outcome of such lengthy negotiations. Tell Herr Bucher to return to Berlin. signed (in cipher) ERQUELINES.

signed (en clair) THILE[2]

101. *Prince Karl Anton of Hohenzollern to Thile*

(Original) [German]   22.4.70

At His Majesty's command I am to have a word with Your Excellency today since I am intending to travel back this evening—I would have come to see you, but fear that this would rouse more attention than the other way round—I therefore ask you for any time before 1 o'clock or between 2 and 4 p.m. at your own convenience.

With highest esteem

PRINCE V. HOHENZOLLERN

102. *Marshal Prim to Count von Bismarck*[3]

(Original) [French]

Ministerio de la Guerra   Madrid, 24 April, 70

TO HIS EXCELLENCY COUNT VON BISMARCK.

I have the honour to receive the letter which Y.E. has kindly sent me through the medium of Herr von Versen and I am greatly touched by the sympathetic reception accorded by Y.E. to mine of 17 February.

---

[1] Cf. Hesselbarth, *Drei psychologische Fragen*, p. 30: "(14) 22 April to Salazar. I hasten to inform you that, the fourth clause of the contract for the loan having been definitely ruled out, insurmountable obstacles likewise stand in the way of the sixth; thus the whole loan unfortunately falls through. We exceedingly regret this outcome of lengthy negotiations. Tell Bucher to return here. THILE."

[2] Marginal note by Thile: "Read to H.M. and approved by him. Th[ile]."

[3] The envelope bears the marginal note: "Opened by me at H.M.'s command. Thile. 28.4.70."

I well understand the delays which have arisen over the solution of our projects and am ready to do everything to enable Y.E. to dispel the apprehensions still in the way of the desired success. But as I had the honour more than once to deplore to Herr Bucher, the situation through which Spain is passing at the present moment does not admit of too long a delay.

From all sides I receive eager enquiries about the subject on which depends the future of the Spanish people, and the reserve I am obliged to maintain places me in an equivocal position towards the country and the statesmen to whom I owe the most consideration.

Herr Bucher will be able to inform Y.E. of all the details of this so difficult situation and I would ask you, *M. le Comte*, to be so good as to take into consideration the arguments which he will lay before Y.E. in order to bring about a solution during the first fortnight of the coming month of May.

I deeply regret that Y.E.'s health has been affected these last few days, and with good wishes for your recovery I have the honour to be

Your Excellency's humble servant

COUNT DE REUS

103. *Bucher to Count von Bismarck*

(Original) [German] Madrid, 24 April, 1870
received 27 April

After the arrival of the telegram[1] of refusal from Berlin M. Salazar asked me in deep depression if I saw no further way out. I replied that if for the time being the telegram were regarded as *non avenu* and Marshal Prim were to hasten the delivery to me of the promised letter[2] for Your Excellency, Your Excellency would perhaps still find it possible to bring about a further discussion of the matter. Salazar seized upon this idea with alacrity, declaring he would take the responsibility of keeping the telegram secret and asking that if all hope vanishes another telegram should be sent him in the form used hitherto, running as follows:

[French] It is deeply regretted that the loan cannot be arranged.

I do not actually believe that he has kept the telegram from the Marshal's knowledge. The latter sent for me early today, and handed me the enclosed letter[3] for Your Excellency, saying:

"I have expressed in it the wish to receive Count Bismarck's final answer in the first fortnight of the month of May. In the letter I felt obliged to use this somewhat loose expression; to this I add verbally that I cannot wait for an answer longer than ten or twelve days counting from the day of your return, therefore until the 7 or 9 May; after that my

[1] See Doc. No. 100. [2] See Doc. No. 102. [3] See Doc. No. 102.

position will be untenable. Tell them in Berlin that if one means to found a dynasty one must take some risks [*un peu courir l'aventure*]. You yourself, moreover, can bear witness that the country is peaceful. In the mountains a few shots are fired here and there, but they will die away when we have a King. The King will find people here who know how to keep order."

He concluded with sincere greetings to Your Excellency.

I did not fail to represent to M. Salazar that if on the 13th and 14th something of the patience had been shown to which they have now resigned themselves the matter would have taken a quieter and more promising course. He answered that the wish to afford Your Excellency the opportunity to give further attention to the matter takes precedence over all other considerations. Moreover the situation has changed since those days in one respect. At that time it was feared that the revolt in Barcelona might still show signs of life during the Easter days; and the public felt an apprehension, not shared by the Government, of a Carlist rising. But Easter had passed without disturbance, and as I must have read, Cabreza had resigned from the Committee and Count Chambord had declared he would not give any more money. This was in fact published in the Spanish newspapers.

Salazar expressed the wish that I would let him know at once by a telegram en clair to a third person, for which he gave me the cipher, whether the "insurmountable obstacles" referred only to the person of Prince Frederick or to French counteraction. I replied that I could not send him telegrams without authorization. With regard to the misgivings about France I must mention that Salazar told me on the morning of the 17 inst. that the Spanish Minister in Paris had announced by telegraph that the Emperor Napoleon had made a communication to him on the subject of the choice for the Spanish throne; he was sending a report by courier. Later Salazar did not say anything more about it to me and was evasive when I again touched on the subject. This morning he told me the French Minister here had given a big dinner a few days ago at which he had inveighed against the Duc de Montpensier's candidature, and later, when the guests were in an excited mood, speaking to groups of members of the Cortes majority and minority, had let fall the words: "As for Prussia she will not dare to challenge us on this question." The Generals present had afterwards said: "That is the best way to make Montpensier popular. If Bonaparte interferes in the matter we shall stir up the nation against him."

I take the liberty of enclosing today's *Gaceta de Madrid*[1] containing a detailed law about the powers granted to the authorities when a district is placed under a state of emergency. Also a copy of the Constitution.[1]

BUCHER

---

[1] Not reproduced here.

Note to Report of 24th.

The telegram
[French] it is deeply regretted, etc.
is to go ciphered via Herr v. Canitz, addressed to Anastasio Alonso, without street or number; signed: Erquelines.

104. *Bucher to Count von Bismarck*

(Original) [German]   Berlin, 27 April, 1870

If the Hohenzollern candidature is looked at from the standpoint of Prussian state interest an important factor seems to be the feeling of the Spanish people against France. I therefore have the honour respectfully to report to Your Excellency certain observations which prove that memories of the embittered struggle against Napoleon are still alive and will long remain so.

After Napoleon had lured King Charles IV, his Consort, and the Prince of Asturias to Bayonne, Murat on his orders demanded that the members of the Royal Family still remaining in Madrid should also be taken there. On the day appointed for their departure, 2 May, 1808, the population rose in revolt, resisted the removal of the Royal Children, cut down individual Frenchmen in the streets, and drove the garrison, two battalions with their artillery, out of the city. Murat returned with rein-forcements, recaptured the city, and the same evening had sixty people, many of whom are said to have taken no part in the fighting, shot on a sand-hill outside the Puerta de Alcalà. Napoleon's saying that this incident set him for ever at enmity with the vengeful Spanish nation proved to be true. In the National Museum in the room containing the best pictures of Murillo, Velasquez and other masters of the Spanish School there hangs in a conspicuous place an almost life-sized painting by Goya depicting this execution in a manner harrowing to the feelings even of one who is not a Spaniard. On the sand-hill stands a huge obelisk surrounded by cypresses, and at this monument, the central point of the great Prado promenade, a mass for the dead is said every year on 2 May, attended by a large congregation. A society founded in remembrance, the Orden humanitario del dos de Mayo, still flourishes, combining its good works with the memory of that tragic day.

After the expulsion of the French the city authorities of Madrid in 1813 decided to replace the old Puerto de Toledo, leading to Andalusia, by a ceremonial edifice and prescribed at the same time what inscription the new gate was to bear. The completion of the building was delayed until 1827; but in spite of what had happened in the interval, and although the division of the Duke of Angoulême's army stationed in Andalusia had not yet passed through Madrid on its return march to France, the inscription was put up as composed in 1813. It runs:

A Fernando VII el deseado, padre de la patria, restituido a sus pueblos, esterminada la usurpación francesa, el ayuntamiento de Madrid consagró esto monumento de fidelidad, de triunfo, de alegría—Año D. 1827.

It means:

To Ferdinand VII, the beloved, father of his country, restored to his peoples after the expulsion of the French usurper, the municipality of Madrid consecrated this monument of its fidelity, triumph and rejoicing.

That French division arrived in Madrid the day after the inaugural ceremony at the gate and either had to pass through it or make a détour to avoid it. Which of the two things happened I have not been able to find out.

BUCHER

105. Note by Bucher

(Original) [German]   Berlin, 27 April [1870]

Major v. Versen, who intends to be back in Madrid today from Andalusia, asks for a telegram to be sent him:

Monsieur Charles Müller
    Madrid
        Hôtel des Princes.

either:

[French] Buy x hogsheads of Malaga.
    i.e. You can still spend x days exploring.

or:

[French] Buy no more.
    i.e. Come back.

to be signed: NIKET.

106. Bucher to Count von Bismarck

(Original) [German]   Berlin, 27 April, 1870[1]

EXCELLENCY,

Having left Madrid on the 24th inst. and arrived here today I still have to make a connected report to Your Excellency about my reasons for writing and immediately dispatching my account of the 14th inst,[2]

---

[1] Marginal note by Bucher: "I delivered this account only on the twelfth of May. B[uche]r."   [2] See Doc. No. 82.

although I realized that it would set things going on lines not corresponding to Your Excellency's expectations.

The immediate reason was the urgency of the situation in Madrid. What M. de Salazar said to me immediately on my arrival about not feeling sure a day longer of the matter being kept secret from the Cortes and France was reaffirmed to me by Marshal Prim verbally[1] on the following day and again on the 20th, and as I later learnt, on the 19th to Your Excellency by telegraph.[2] On what was for me completely unfamiliar ground I was not able to form an opinion. Even assuming that the danger was being exaggerated in order to hasten a decision, I could not indefinitely keep to myself such definite assurances from the two people to whom I had been directed.

A second reason was that the difficulties connected with finding a wife for Prince Frederick only became clear to me in Madrid. On this point I was able at once to form an independent judgement. In the first few days Salazar brought the conversation round to this subject in the following way. His Government, he said, had had its attention drawn to a notice in a French newspaper that a marriage was being arranged between the daughter of the Duke of Theba and a Prince of Hohenzollern; this it regarded as a feeler put out by some quarter or other. Pausing a moment he gave me a searching look and added: "It is thought to have been by Your Excellency." I answered with undisguised astonishment that I neither had any knowledge of it nor could imagine how such a conjecture, at variance with all the facts of the case, could have been made as to its origin. It is believed, he replied, that there are other indications that just at this moment Prussia is seeking intimacy with the Tuileries; the newspapers had been reporting that Herr v. Werther had been making very friendly declarations. I remarked in the first place that it looked as if undeserved importance were being attached here to the newspapers. I knew nothing of recent declarations of this kind by the Ambassador. That he should on suitable occasions speak pacific and friendly words was perfectly natural; we wanted to live in peace and amity with all our neighbours; on the other hand I could not for the life of me see any reason why my Government should be seeking the intimacy of the Paris Court at this precise moment. I would like to set one newspaper off against another and refer him to a semi-official article in the *Norddeutsche Allgemeine Zeitung* about §5 of the Treaty of Prague. He knew the article and agreed that it was incompatible with his conjecture. Reverting to the young Duchess of Theba he further explained, with what seemed to me still a remnant of suspicion, that the lady could not possibly become Queen of Spain. The other Grandees of the country would grow jealous. The population would never tolerate Countess Montijo as Queen Mother and the relationship with the French Imperial family. In addition, the Duke of Theba was not

[1] See Doc. No. 99.   [2] See Doc. No. 94.

respected and was so deeply in debt that he was living on an allowance made him by his son. I repeated that nobody in Berlin contemplated such a match. H.R.H. the Prince of Hohenzollern had already considered the question of marriage and had told me that only a Princess of Coburg-Cohary of Vienna, Princess Marie Amelie de Montpensier, one of the Duc de Nemour's daughters, and the daughter of Prince Luitpold of Bavaria could be considered. M. Salazar had already compiled the same list and made the comments on the four ladies which are contained in my humble report of the 14th:[1] namely that the first ones are Bourbons and the fourth would be unpopular because of her relationship to Prince Adalbert of Bavaria, who is married to a cousin of Queen Isabella's. The question of the marriage would thus cause a certain amount of trouble. Therewith M. de Salazar brought the conversation round again to the subject we had discussed in the first days, namely whether, when the in his opinion completely satisfactory information as regards the three doubtful points (cf. my humble reports of the 14th and 20th)[2] reached Berlin, the candidature of H. Highness the Hereditary Prince could not once more be considered. The question undeniably had its justification. But I neither had authority to express an opinion in the matter nor could I in view of its extremely personal nature form a judgement on it; I therefore confined myself to repeating what had been said to me about the refusal of the candidature by those in the secret with whom I had had the honour to talk. One point, which must have been just as present in M. de Salazar's mind during this whole conversation as it was in my own, received not a word of mention, namely that the future King of Spain must have the *consent of the Cortes* to his marriage *embodied in a law*. Remembering that the battle-cry of the revolution had been "Down with the Bourbons", as can still be seen written on houses and churches, for example, in the busiest street, the Calle de Alcalá, I could not but translate Salazar's words that the princesses in question were Bourbons into the thought of his heart: we do not know which of them or if any of them would be passed by the Cortes. For while a Prince of Hohenzollern would command a big majority just because he excluded all Bourbon candidatures, the votes would group themselves quite differently if he were to ask consent for a match with a Bourbon princess. I therefore thought I ought not to refuse my co-operation in a last attempt to ask for the Hereditary Prince's consent.

I did not judge it expedient to show that I knew and remembered that article of the Constitution; I should not have achieved anything else than to be the recipient of soothing assurances, perhaps not shared even by their giver. I thought it preferable merely to enquire, as H.R.H. the Prince of Hohenzollern had asked me to do, which of the four princesses Salazar would regard as the most desirable, and otherwise maintain a waiting attitude.

[1] See Doc. No. 82.   [2] See Docs. Nos. 82 and 99.

The result has strengthened my opinion of the inopportuneness of this subject. Salazar did not give an answer to my question immediately but only a few days later, and to the effect that Princess Amalie of Coburg-Cohary would be the most acceptable. Only on the 22nd, when I was asking for certain technical explanations on other articles of the Constitution, did I casually remark that, as I understood the Constitution, the King needed a law to enable him to marry. Salazar answered with a brief: Yes, and immediately passed on to something else. On the 24th, a few hours before my departure, he said without prompting on my part and in contradiction with his remark above: "If the Prince's choice fell on a Montpensier Princess then the affair could go through as an act of reconciliation."

If in conclusion Your Excellency will permit me to express my humble opinion on the whole Hohenzollern candidature it is that the Hereditary Prince's dynasty would soon strike deep roots. The stirrings of the dynastic parties in the Cortes would very soon die away before the rejoicings of the people over the restoration of stable conditions under the iron hand of Marshal Prim and thanks to the loyal support of Marshal Serrano, who impatiently awaits the moment when he can exchange the Royal Palace for the simple country house he has already leased. Of a threat to the royal person I can think of no example in recent Spanish history. By entrusting the legislative authority entirely to the Cortes the Constitution relieves the King of the heaviest responsibilities, leaving him wide scope for useful activity in the field of administration.

How great the value of intimacy between the two courts would be for Prussian policy without imposing any sacrifice or representing any danger to her became more and more clear to me the more convinced I grew that people here go to the newspapers for information on international affairs and have no conception of the respective weights, relations and mutual dealings of the Great Powers.

If I am correctly informed it is chiefly on two counts that the Hereditary Prince's refusal is based, namely the Iberian idea and the Hohenzollern entail.

On a basis not of my short visit to Madrid but of many years of activity as a publicist I venture to express the conviction that the Iberian idea has no broad foundation and no future, hence would cause no disharmony in the relations between the Courts of Madrid and Lisbon so long as Madrid lends it no support. I regard it as still more unsubstantial than the idea of Scandinavian union. Popular feeling in Portugal is dead against it; in Spain it has a few doctrinaire adherents and is occasionally exploited by certain politicians for their own ends. The happiness of the two peoples seems to depend on their remaining separate. A subjugated Portugal would be not an additional strength to Spain but a source of mortal weakness.

I leave it to Your Excellency's wise judgement to decide how the second objection could be removed. Perhaps by the renunciation of Prince Leopold for the period during which he occupied the Spanish throne of the receipt of revenues from the entail in favour of other members of the family. If then in the foreseeable distant future Prince William were to mount the Spanish throne conditions would have become so well consolidated that there would be no difficulty in getting the order of succession to the entail changed by a family decision in favour of a cadet line of the princely House.

How much less favourable the chances of Prince Frederick would be emerges from the first half of this report and from his own character. But even were they still less favourable than in my opinion they are it would seem to be a European interest of the highest order that he should be prevailed upon to accept. If his candidature falls through I think there will be a republic in Spain either straight away or after a civil war, and it will not be a transient phenomenon but a permanent institution born of the conviction that a monarchic solution was impossible. What would be the consequences in Italy, or at a change of sovereign in France?

The Constitution has been under consideration by their Royal Highnesses the Crown Prince and the Prince of Hohenzollern. For your greater convenience in studying it I humbly append a copy of the passages relating to the marriage.

BUCHER

Annex: *Articles 74, 110, 111, 112 of the Spanish Constitution*

Annex [Spanish]
Article 74

The King must receive authorization by a special law:

6. To enter into matrimony and to allow to enter into matrimony those persons who are his subjects and have the right under the Constitution to succeed to the throne.

Article 110

The Cortes, either on their own initiative or on the proposal of the King, may sanction the reform of the Constitution, indicating for this purpose the article which they have to change.

Article 111

This declaration having been made, the King will dissolve the Senate and the Congress and will summon new Cortes which will meet within the next three months. Into the edict summoning them will be inserted the resolution of the Cortes mentioned in the preceding article.

Article 112

The co-legislating bodies will have the character of constituent assemblies but solely for the discussion of the reform, continuing thereafter as ordinary Cortes.

While the Cortes are constituent assemblies, neither of the co-legislating bodies may be dissolved.

107. *Bucher to Thile*

(Original) [German]   Berlin, 28 April, 1870

I humbly submit to Your Excellency a reprint[1] of the statistical report issued by the Madrid Central Statistical Office covering the period from 1 October, 1868 to 31 December, 1869. If the work can no longer serve the purpose for which it was given to me, its contents still retain a permanent value.   BUCHER[2]

108. *Salazar to Baron von Canitz, Prussian Minister at Madrid*

(Original) [French]   [Madrid, 29.4.70]

MY DEAR BARON,

I beg you to send off the enclosed telegram and shall be very grateful to you for so doing.

Your humble servant
E. DE SALAZAR Y MAZARREDO

*   *   *

Expressions attributed to the Emperor are inventions.[3]

M. Desein left yesterday delighted with his trip.   ALONSO

109. *Salazar to Bucher*

(Original) [French]   Madrid, 29 April, 1870
                                              pr. 6 May via Herr v. Versen

M. GAMA[4] to HERR BUCHER.

The news published by an Alphonsine journal that the Emperor opposed Prince Frederick Charles's candidature has made no impression on the public. Napoleon III would not hear of Don Fernando of Portugal

---

[1] Marginal note by Bucher: "Placed in the library."
[2] Marginal note by Bucher: "Entered in the files. Br. 6/5."
[3] See Doc. No. 112.
[4] Marginal note by Bucher: "(Salazar)."

because a strong nation on this side of the Pyrenees does not fit in with his political ideas. He is also against the Duke of Genoa because the aggrandisement of the House of Savoy in the Mediterranean would be adverse to France.

In so far as his personal influence may weigh with the princes of other countries, it may be harmful, but in regard to Prussia, as it is not in his power to alter her decisions, all he can say is utterly unavailing.

On the contrary the Spanish character is so sensitive about anything in the nature of a protectorate that M. Castelar, the leader of the Republicans, said to me yesterday: "I am going one day to say in public what everybody has already realized, namely that the Emperor, by his desire to keep our affairs unsettled, is the sole cause of the continuance of the provisional regime. He is the open enemy of our country's Constitution whether as a republic or in the form of a monarchy."

The day approaches and you will see the consequences.

The desire is that if the loan cannot be arranged the reply will not be final, for who knows what may happen in the near future? In that case the reply would of course be a written one, not a telegram, and might dwell on the delays due to the circumstances of the moment, in short on some cause or other which does not entirely slam the door for the *future*.

I am still not without hope, for I cannot think that such a brilliant offer can be declined, made as it is under the most favourable auspices that have occurred for a long time.

Not only is there perfect tranquillity, but what is more, it is based on the chronic and complete impotence of all that could threaten public order.

Just think that even the name of Prince Frederick Charles, who is a Protestant, has not alarmed the Catholics and his name of victor of Sadowa does not appal those who might see in this choice an open desire to challenge France. So great is the weariness of the interim regime and of the Emperor.

A Catholic prince would in a very short time be the darling of the whole nation.

Herr von V[ersen] is delighted with his trip.

110. *Baron von Canitz, Prussian Minister at Madrid,*
to Count von Bismarck

(Telegram. Decipher) [French]   Madrid, 30 April, 1870. 1.40 p.m.
arrived 8.42 p.m.

Expressions attributed to the Emperor are an invention.[1] M. Desein left yesterday delighted with his trip.   signed: ALONSO.

CANITZ

[1] See Doc. No. 112.

111. *The King of Prussia to Thile*

(Original) [German]   B[erlin] 30.4.1870. 8.45 [a.m.]

Having just spoken with D.B.,[1] I wish him to start off this evening for Düsseldorf and would send by him a letter to Prince H[ohenzollern]. In the same way as I am unable to change my mind I likewise anticipate that the Prince and his son will not do so either. All that remains to be decided is the form of the refusal, and there I think it must frankly be said that Prince F[rederick] does not feel he is capable of taking on such a position so that on that ground I can never either persuade or command him to dedicate himself to it.

Send me at once the letters . . . by you which D.B. brought with him and come here at 4 o'clock for a conference.

WILLIAM

112. *Thile to the King of Prussia*

(Original) [German]   Berlin, 1 May, 1870

In delivering to Your Majesty with my humble duty the enclosed telegram[2] from Madrid, I respectfully remark that I have no further knowledge of the "expressions attributed to the Emperor" mentioned in it than that according to a telegram in the Vienna "*Presse*", reproduced below, the Emperor Napoleon is said to have spoken of the acceptance of the Spanish throne by Prince Frederick as a *casus belli* against Prussia. Whether there is any connexion between this and the expressions used by Napoleon to the Spanish Ambassador in Paris, which M. Salazar mentioned to Bucher[3] but later avoided specifying more closely, must remain a matter for conjecture.

In the matter of whether Major von Versen shall be summoned to us immediately or not until after Bucher's return from Düsseldorf,[4] I may expect Your Majesty's command.

V. THILE

[1] Marginal note by Bucher: "I was announced under the name of Dr Braun."
[2] See Doc. No. 110.
[3] See Doc. No. 103.
[4] Marginal note by the King of Prussia: "Yes", referring to "after Bucher's return from Düsseldorf".

Telegram in "Die Presse"

Annex:

Paris, 28 April ("*Presse*" telegram).

It is definitely stated here that Prince Frederick of Hohenzollern's candidature is being seriously considered by Spanish statesmen but that the Emperor told the Spanish Minister Olozaga that this solution of the question of the Spanish throne would be for France a *casus belli* with Prussia.

113. *Bucher to Thile*

(Original) [German]   Berlin, 1 May, 1870

YOUR EXCELLENCY!

Will you in forwarding Versen's report[1] be so kind as to ask for His Majesty's command as to whether Major v. Versen is to return now or go on to Catalonia.

Salazar has asked me to let him know by a private telegram, the wording of which has been prearranged by us, whether the obstacle consists only in Prince Frederick's will or also in opposition on the part of France. I was not able to convince him that France would never attempt such opposition because Prussia would never brook it. To remove such foolish ideas I respectfully crave permission to send off the telegram.[2]

BUCHER

114. *Note of Prince Karl Anton of Hohenzollern*[3]

(Original) [German]   [1.5.1870]

For return to my archives:
Letter of General Prim to the Hereditary Prince. Madrid, 17 February.
Letter of Don Salazar to me of April.

*   *   *

[1] See Docs. Nos. 97,104.
[2] Marginal note by Bucher: "I did not receive permission. B[ucher] 28/5."
[3] Marginal note by Bucher: "Documents of 8th and 9th for the Prince of Hohenzollern."

Next kindly let me see Legation Counsellor Bucher's reports[1] from Madrid.

PRINCE OF HOHENZOLLERN

115. *Bucher to Count von Bismarck*

(Original) [German]   Berlin, 2 May, 1870

I respectfully inform Your Excellency that His Majesty the King commanded me to wait upon him on the 30th ult. His Majesty began by saying that he desired to hear something of my journey to Madrid but at once proceeded to lay down his own views, which may be resumed as follows:

The Hereditary Prince declined lest the danger should arise that the princely line should disappear entirely from Germany; His Majesty thought very highly of him for this. Prince Frederick felt no vocation, did not think he possessed the qualities, and consequently His Majesty could not command him to accept the crown.

His Majesty commanded me to travel that evening to Düsseldorf to report to the Prince, saying in an interrogative tone as he was dismissing me: "Did you come back with favourable impressions?" I answered that I had been instructed by Your Excellency to obtain information on three points; only on one, relations with Rome, had I been able to form an independent judgement and that was in fact a favourable one. As regards the two others I could only report what Prim had said to me.

His Majesty gave me no opening to enter more fully into these points or even into the first one, but dismissed me with the order to tell the Secretary of State to return to His Majesty Prim's letter to Your Excellency[2] and Major v. Versen's report,[3] both of which Herr v. Thile had received His Majesty's authorization to open, and with the announcement that in the course of the day I would receive a letter from His Majesty to take to the Prince of Hohenzollern.

On arriving at Düsseldorf on the morning of the 1st inst. I delivered His Majesty's letter at the Prince's residence with the message that I would return in an hour; I wanted to give H.R.H. time to read the rather voluminous letter at leisure. I found him still reading it when I was ushered in, and he began by reading it out to me but only as far as the sentence: "Versen and Bucher have let themselves be dazzled by the brilliant aspects"; from the remainder he only quoted the words: importance of the mission, failure, and passed over all the rest. (I venture to interpose the respectful remark that I do not know how the ideas displayed

[1] Marginal note by Bucher: "H.R.H. means those of 14 and 20 April."
[2] See Doc. No. 102.   [3] See Doc. No. 97.

148

in these partly complete, partly fragmentary phrases, can have originated in His Majesty's mind. My reports are impersonal statements giving no personal opinion; and although I was deeply impressed with the importance of the *matter at issue*, my own *mission* was purely to collect information. If the affair came to nothing it would do so here and the thought never crossed my mind that anyone here or in Madrid could hold me responsible for it.)

H.R.H. then invited me to tell him what Marshal Prim had said and interrupted several times with expressions of satisfaction especially over the gentle methods used in reducing the vast ecclesiastical benefices and the military effort in Cuba. He asked me whether I had set this all down in writing, to which I replied in the affirmative. To the further question whether my reports had been submitted to His Majesty I could give no information.

The Prince's whole attitude during this conversation of nearly two hours showed that he wished his son Frederick would accept. But, to repeat his own words: "I have promised my youngest born not to exercise compulsion but to place the decision in His Majesty's hands. If the King so much as expresses a wish, for my son it will be a command."

With special interest he enquired what in my opinion would happen in Spain if this candidature came to naught. I replied that I had come to the conviction from the press that none of the native candidates was strong enough to set aside the rest either in the Cortes or in a civil war. The Prince of Asturias, I said, unfortunately suffered from the detestation felt for his mother and from the widely believed rumour of his illegitimate birth. The Duc de Montpensier was equally ruled out, as devoid of any rights, by both the rival parties, by the Queen's adherents because as Captain General of the army he never stirred in September, 1868, by their opponents because he did not make common cause with them. In the one case, as they say, Isabella would still have been Queen, in the other he, himself, would have been King. Lastly, the Carlists were utterly disintegrating. I could therefore imagine no other development than towards a republic, either immediately or after some transitional phase. I ventured to add that in my view the republic would have prospects of permanency as resting on the conviction resulting from experience that all monarchic expedients had been exhausted and I thought that the example of Spain would have an infectious influence on Italy and, in the event of a change of sovereign, also on France, in France not permanently, but probably permanently in Italy.

The Prince asked me to return again in the evening and gave me a letter for His Majesty; I delivered it at the Royal Palace this morning immediately on my arrival.

BUCHER

116. *Thile to Baron von Canitz, Prussian Minister at Madrid*

(Telegram. Draft for cipher)[1] [French]   Berlin, 4 May, 1870. noon

Communicate as follows to Anastasio Alonso:

It is deeply regretted that "the loan" cannot be arranged.

After a conscientious examination of his own personality and capacities in relation to a task as noble as it is arduous the young man does not feel justified in taking on the responsibility that would be laid on him by such a generous manifestation of trust.

THILE[2]

117. *Abeken to the King of Prussia*[3]

(Original) [German]   Berlin, 4 May, 1870

YOUR MAJESTY,

I have the honour to submit to you with my humble duty the telegram[4] which in obedience to Your Royal command has been sent off avoiding the Prince's name and the reference to the Spanish nation. The

---

[1] A draft telegram in Bucher's hand has the following text: "Communicate all that follows to Anastasio Alonso.

It is deeply regretted that 'the loan' cannot be arranged.

After a conscientious examination of his own personality and capacities Prince Frederick definitely declares that he does not feel equal to the no less glorious than arduous task to which he might be called by the trust of the Spanish people."

Another draft telegram in Thile's hand runs as follows:

"To Herr von Canitz.

After mature reflection and a conscientious examination of his own personality and capacities, Prince Frederick has finally declared that he does not feel equal to the no less glorious than arduous task to the fulfilment of which he might be called by the trust of the Spanish $\left\{ \begin{matrix} \text{people} \\ \text{Cortes} \end{matrix} \right\}$?

Prince Leopold, as you know, had already pronounced in a similar sense. Kindly bring the above to the knowledge of M. Salazar with the expression of our sincerest regrets and our good wishes for the future of a great and generous nation.

Tell Herr von Versen to return to Berlin."

The draft for cipher is in Abeken's hand.

[2] Cf. Hesselbarth: "(15) 4 May from Bismarck to Salazar. It is deeply regretted that the loan cannot be arranged. After a conscientious examination of his own personality and capacities with reference to a task no less glorious than arduous, the young man does not feel justified in taking on the responsibility that would be laid upon him by such a generous manifestation of trust. THILE." (*Drei psychologische Fragen*, p. 30.)

[3] Marginal note by King of Prussia: "Agreed. W. 4.5.70."

[4] See Doc. No. 116.

Secretary of State, von Thile, who is still confined to his room, hopes that Your Majesty will find it in conformity with your intentions and will in pursuance of Your Majesty's command send a copy to His Royal Highness the Prince of Hohenzollern.

In deepest respect I am
Your Majesty's
Most humble and obedient
servant and subject

ABEKEN

118. *Abeken to Bucher*

(Original) [German]   B[erlin], 4.5.70

MOST HONOURED COLLEAGUE!

Herr Thile has sent me a verbal reply that he would be very grateful to you if you would undertake to give the news to Düsseldorf.

For this purpose I enclose the complete set of papers in order that they may be kept together. The King's "Agreed"[1] enables you to say to the Prince that the telegram went off at His Majesty's command; I leave it to your judgement whether you mention that from the Prince's letter brought here by you the King drew the conclusion that the matter was regarded as *settled* and that only the *form* of the refusal was to be discussed.

With cordial greeting
Yours

ABEKEN

119. *Bucher to Prince Karl Anton of Hohenzollern*

(Draft) [German]   Berlin, 4 May, 1870

YOUR SERENE HIGHNESS,

At the command of H.M. the King and on instructions from the Secretary of State, who is ill, I have the honour most obediently to send herewith to Your Royal Highness a copy of the telegram[2] which at His Majesty's command was today dispatched to Madrid. The delivery of the documents[3] desired by Y.R.H. will follow without delay as soon as Herr v. Thile has recovered.

I remain
Y.R.H. etc.

B[UCHE]R

[1] See Doc. No. 117, note 3.
[2] See Doc. No. 116.
[3] See Doc. No. 114.

120. *Bucher to Prince Karl Anton of Hohenzollern*

(Draft) [German]   Berlin, 8 May, 1870

YOUR SERENE HIGHNESS,

On instructions from the S[ecretary of] St[ate] I send you with my respects Marshal Prim's letter to His Serene Highness the Hereditary Prince of 17 February.[1] M. Salazar's letter to Y.R.H.[2] is not in the files and is probably in the keeping of the Chancellor.

In accordance with Y.R.H.'s command I have the honour to append my reports of 14 and 20 April[3] with the humble request that you will most graciously have them returned to me.[4]

I remain, with respects,
Y.R.H.'s
most obedient Servant
B[UCHE]R

121. *Bucher to Prince Karl Anton of Hohenzollern*

(Draft) [German]   BERLIN, 9 May, 1870

YOUR SERENE HIGHNESS,

I have the honour to send you with my respects M. Salazar's letter of 14 April of this year[5] discovered at a final tidying up of the papers.[6]

I remain etc.
B[UCHE]R

122. *Thile to the King of Prussia*

(Original)[7] [German]   Berlin, 11 May, 1870

Major von Versen has just informed me that Your Majesty is willing to sanction his going to Varzin in order to report to Count Bismarck on the Spanish matter. I said to him that this would no doubt be very useful but that I knew from repeated experience that when, as now, the Minister is ill and nervously excited he would find it very unpleasant without

---

[1] Marginal note by Bucher: "Copy is in the files."—See Doc. No. 3.
[2] See Doc. No. 83.
[3] See Docs. Nos. 82 and 99.
[4] Marginal note by Bucher: "Returned by H.R.H. by private letter on 12 May."
[5] See Doc. No. 83.
[6] Marginal note by Bucher: "Letter to be appended. Copy entered in the files."
[7] Marginal note by King of Prussia: "Agreed. W. 11.5.70."

preliminary arrangement to receive a visitor at his country house for the purpose of discussing business. I, therefore, believed I was acting in accordance with Your Majesty's wishes in writing at once to Count Bismarck giving a clear summary of events and asking him to telegraph whether his condition will allow of his receiving Major von Versen.

I can receive this telegram by tomorrow morning and humbly beg permission to report tomorrow to Your Majesty on this and other matters.

v. THILE

123. *Salazar to Baron von Canitz, Prussian Minister at Madrid*

(Original) [French]   Thursday, 12 [May, 1870]

MY DEAR BARON,

I beg you to send to Berlin the telegram you will find on the next page. Excuse me, and believe always in the feelings of gratitude of your humble servant

E. DE SALAZAR Y MAZARREDO

*   *   *

Telegram[1]

Marshal Prim received with great regret telegram of 4th.[2] He desires to know if Count Bismarck's state of health will allow him to reply to his last letter in 10 or 15 days. Reply might come securely by special messenger, Prussian Legation.

124. *Baron von Canitz, Prussian Minister at Madrid,* *to Count von Bismarck*

(Telegram. Decipher) [French]   Madrid, 12 May, 1870. 3.30 p.m. arr. 9.50 p.m.

Telegram from Alonso: Marshal Prim received with great regret telegraphic dispatch of 4th.[3] He desires to know if Count Bismarck's state of health will allow him to answer his last letter in ten or fifteen days. Reply might securely come by special messenger, Prussian Legation.

(signed) CANITZ[4]

[1] Here Canitz adds: "telegram from Alonso."
[2] See Doc. No. 116.
[3] See Doc. No. 116.
[4] Cf. Hesselbarth: "(16) 12 May to Bismarck. Chevalier Prim received telegram with regret. Desires to know whether Bismarck's state of health will allow of a reply to his last letter in 10 or 15 days. SALAZAR." (*Drei psychologische Fragen*, p. 30.)

125. *Thile to Count von Bismarck*

(Original)[1] [German]   B[erlin], 12 May, 1870

HONOURED CHIEF,

I am really distressed to have to bother Your Excellency with so many Spanish telegrams, and in driblets into the bargain.

It would give me great happiness if you would order me to telegraph to Madrid let them in God's name proclaim Don Leopoldo. Then the tooth would be out.

Most faithfully and obediently   THILE

126. *Salazar to Baron von Canitz, Prussian Minister at Madrid*

(Original) [French]   Sunday[2]

MY DEAR BARON,

If I did not have the honour of seeing you yesterday [it was] because there is nothing new. On the other hand I have been much occupied at the Cortes. Yesterday evening's vote did not have the importance people have wanted to ascribe to it. We voted against a bill of the Finance Ministry because we think its administration of the finances is disastrous; but we are ready to give a vote of confidence to Marshal Prim. Explanations will be given and all will come right in the end as so many other times. It is a minor matter.

I have the honour to greet you very affectionately,

E. DE SALAZAR Y MAZARREDO

127. *Salazar to Baron von Canitz, Prussian Minister at Madrid*

(Original) [French]   Sunday, 13[3]

MONSIEUR LE BARON,

I have been to see you twice to beg you to listen to me a moment on an urgent matter relating to important interests of the Province of Biscay and the City of Hamburg.

Tomorrow Monday, Tuesday and Wednesday I have to go early to the Cabinet meeting and after that I have, of course, to attend the Cortes.

---

[1] Marginal note by Roland: "Received by His Serene Highness in January 1877 for the files. Roland."

[2] An inventory made in 1877 by the Madrid Legation gives this and the following document as of 13 and 14 May, 1870.

[3] See the note to the previous document.

I should be very grateful if you would receive me between 9 and 10 in the evening, and in that case I would ask you to have me ushered through a room in which there are not other persons, for I have been suffering for several days from a very obstinate cold in the head and the doctor has ordered me not to wear evening dress.

I apologize, M. le Baron, for taking the liberty of intruding on your moments of leisure, and I beg you to believe the sincere sentiments with which I have the honour to be your very humble and devoted servant

E. DE SALAZAR Y MAZARREDO

128. Baron von Werthern, Prussian Minister at Munich, to Count von Bismarck

(Copy in Bucher's hand) [German]

Extract A 1528   Munich, 15 May, 1870

H.R.H. Prince Leopold has in these last days gone to Vienna. I surmise that it is a question of a marriage with Princess Amalie, the daughter of Duke Augustus of Saxe-Coburg.   (signed) V. WERTHERN[1]

129. Thile to the King of Prussia

(Original) [German]   Berlin, 16 May, 1870

Only now am I in a position to report to Your Majesty with my humble duty the Minister-President's reply in the matter of the Spanish throne. Count Bismarck does not see any practical purpose in Major von Versen's going to Varzin to report verbally on his latest impressions but on the other hand will make a point of examining in Berlin the report already drawn up by Major von Versen for this purpose.

In these circumstances I may be allowed to expect Your Majesty's command that I am to authorize Major von Versen, who is awaiting further instructions in Dresden, to return to Posen.[2]

The Minister further writes me that if his condition does not grow worse he will return to Berlin in the next few days in order to attend the Reichstag discussions, and he expresses the hope that Your Majesty will most graciously excuse his non-appearance during the visit of His Majesty the Tsar, since thereby exertions and activities would be imposed upon him to which he does not yet feel equal.[3]   THILE

[1] Marginal note by Bucher: "For the files. B[uche]r 22.5."
[2] Marginal note of the King of Prussia: "Yes, immediately. Let him return!"
[3] Marginal note of the King of Prussia: "Certainly. W. 16.6.70."

130. *Thile to Eichmann, Prussian Minister at Dresden*

(Telegram. Draft for cipher) [German]

No. 3   B[erlin], 16 May, 1870. 2.45 p.m.

Will Your Excellency inform Major von Versen that according to H.M.'s decision nothing more prevents his return to his garrison and it is left to him to see that the documents he wishes to submit should reach me by a trustworthy channel.

TH[ILE]

131. *Eichmann, Prussian Minister at Dresden, to Count von Bismarck*

(Telegram. Decipher) [German]

Dresden, 17 May, 1870, 12.45 p.m.
arr. 1.50 p.m.

No. 6
Answer to telegram No. 3.[1]

I made the relevant announcement to Major von Versen yesterday evening.

(signed) EICHMANN

132. *Salazar to Baron von Canitz, Prussian Minister at Madrid*

(Original) [French]   Tuesday, 17 [May, 1870]

MY DEAR BARON,

Would you have the goodness to tell me whether the last telegram[2] was received in due time at Berlin?

Marshal Prim is quite astonished to see that there is no reply after so many days and I would beg you to give a reminder [*un recuerdo*].

Does it mean that Count von Bismarck is still ill?

I have the honour to greet you very cordially.

E. DE SALAZAR Y MAZARREDO

[1] See Doc. No. 130.
[2] See Doc. No. 124.

133. *Baron von Canitz, Prussian Minister at Madrid, to Salazar*

(Draft) [French]   Tuesday, 17 [May, 1870]

DEAR SIR,

The telegram of the 12th[1] reached Berlin about 7 p.m. on the same day.

Count von Bismarck is convalescent but still at Varzin.

I attribute the delay in replying to the hope on the Count's part that he will be able to answer the General's letter within 10 or 15 days. Since the Count has certainly received the telegram if his state of health already allows him to attend to business, I cannot on my side remind him of my having sent off a telegram addressed to him on the 12th.

As soon as a reply arrives I will send it to you.

Yours

C[ANITZ]

134. *Thile to Count von Bismarck*[2]

(Original)[3] [German]   Berlin, 18 May, 1870

HONOURED CHIEF,

Benedetti was here today to say that he is intending to start on his long-planned journey to Paris on Saturday evening. He said he had absolutely nothing special to say to you; if you wanted to give him any messages for Paris[4] (say, in connexion with the change at the Foreign Ministry in Paris) he would be very willing to put off his departure until *Sunday* evening, having heard that Your Excellency is expected on Saturday.

I of course did not hold out any hope to Benedetti of your seeing him but *could not do otherwise* than inform you of the above at his wish.[5] Perhaps Your Excellency will be so good as to telegraph a word or two to me as to what answer to give Benedetti.

Ever with esteem

Your most obedient

THILE

---

[1] See Doc. No. 124.

[2] Marginal note by Bismarck: "2 months later there was war."

[3] Marginal note by Roland: "received from His Serene Highness in January 1877 for the files. Roland."

[4] Marginal note by Bismarck: "!".

[5] Marginal note by Bismarck: "!!".

135. *Count von Bismarck to Prince Karl Anton of Hohenzollern*

(Copy)[1, 2] [German]   Berlin, 28 May, 1870

MOST SERENE PRINCE,
> YOUR MOST GRACIOUS HIGHNESS,

On my return to affairs I learned of the latest negotiations about the candidature for the Spanish throne and cannot resist the impression that in them German interests have not received their due. The reports coming in in the interval show that the interim rulers have endeavoured, not without success, to create order in the finances, the army and the general administration, and that this nation of 17 millions, depending like ourselves on the preservation of peace in Europe, is already capable in the event of European complications of casting a weight in the scales which would not be without practical importance to us. Today no less than before I feel no doubt that Germany has a vital interest here, and that at critical moments the pointer on the scales might well register differently according as we know Madrid to be a friend or an enemy. I have once more begged H.M. the King to reconsider the question in this light and received the answer that as soon as any Prince of the House of Hohenzollern showed any inclination to accept the crown he would raise no opposition whatever to this inclination. This I regard as the fullest reply which can be expected from H.M. in the present state of things, since the King will certainly never make a decision to *command* a member of the Royal House to undertake a mission the success of which lies predominantly in the sense of *vocation* personally felt by him who undertakes it. I believe that public opinion and the judgement of posterity will agree with this when the facts become known in detail. In my opinion H.M. the King cannot be expected to undertake a personal responsibility in a matter which does not involve his own decision but is a command to other members of the Royal House to undertake a responsibility.

I do not doubt that this view is fully shared by H.R.H. the Crown Prince. If His Serene Highness the Hereditary Prince or one of Your Royal Highness's younger sons were inclined to render service to *both* countries and earn the gratitude of Spain and Germany I think that a still unanswered telegram addressed to me by Marshal Prim *after* the latest refusal would afford a possibility for me to reopen the question.

Graciously accept the expression of the deep respect with which I remain

Y.R.H.'s most humble servant

(signed) v. BISMARCK

[1] The text of this document has been published by Thimme, *Bismarck. Ges. Werke*, VIb, No. 1557.

[2] Marginal note: "Original taken by hand by L. R. Bucher, 31 May."

136. *Bucher to Prince Karl Anton of Hohenzollern*

Draft[1] [German]   Berlin, 29 May, 1870

SERENE HIGHNESS, MOST GRACIOUS PRINCE,
    On instructions from the Ch[ancellor] of the C[onfederation] I have
the honour to send Y.R.H. herewith
    (1) Extract of a report of Count Brandenburg of 23rd inst.[2]

[1] Marginal note by Bucher: "For the next report."
[2] Marginal note by Bucher: "Append the bracketed passage, A 1685, pp. 1-4."
    The following is the text of Count Brandenburg's report: "Lisbon, 23 May, 1870.
A 1685. received 29 May, 1870.
    Political report: No. 11.
    The lower Chamber met today again for a sitting at which the decree was submitted
for the prorogation of the Cortes session until 20 June. It was a very lively sitting. A
number of deputies, headed by the former Finance Minister Senhor Braankamp, who
had been prevented from attending the sitting on the 21st, declared their support for
the Da Cunha proposal passed by the Chamber at that sitting and on which I had the
honour to report to Your Excellency on the 22nd, basing their declaration on the sharpest
condemnation of the military revolt led by Marshal Saldanha. Next Senhor Bereiro Diaz
made an indignant speech about the present state of affairs. He said it was unheard of that
now, 5 days after the revolt, the ringleader of the rebels had set himself up as dictator,
had not yet showed his face, and had done nothing to create an ordered government.
That he was unable to do so was the best proof that nobody could be found to share responsibility with the man who by armed force was leading the unhappy country to its
ruin. He denounced the decree proroguing the Chamber as an act of mutinous dictatorship.
At the end of his speech he drew attention to the impression produced by these events in
the neighbouring countries according to Spanish press accounts, an impression unfortunately confirmed by Marshal Saldanha's utterances. This allusion to the Iberian tendencies
always attributed to the Marshal and to the threat to the country's independence, allusions
which no one so far had ventured to make, threw the whole house into an uproar.
Senhor Barros da Cunha said he did not think the Marshal capable of an outrage against
the independence of Portugal but hoped that, if he were, the whole country would rise
as one man to oppose the plans of a degenerate Portuguese. He was followed by the
deputy Santos Silva who, after condemning the Marshal's revolt in the strongest terms,
adjured the house to take a solemn vow to unite in the struggle against every attempt to
strike Portugal off the roll of nations. The house did not give him time to finish, all the
deputies left their seats and enthusiastically adopted the proposal by acclamation. The
galleries by now densely packed broke into applause and so the last sitting came to an end;
after this tempestuous scene the deputies left the house in order not to listen to the prorogation decree. It is remarkable that the Marshal allowed the two Chambers so much
time to meet and declare against him with such unanimity. I am told that he wanted to
avoid as much as possible behaving like a dictator and that he intended to prorogue the
house only after forming a Cabinet. It must be added that demonstrations in the Chambers
make much less impression on the public than one might think. The Marshal's biggest
difficulty was to form a Cabinet. He has no political party of his own and no connexions
with any but with Count Peniche and his radical following, with whom he joined up for
his revolutionary aims and who are now said to be a burden to him. His whole enterprise
was purely aimed at revenging himself against the Loulé Ministry by whom he had felt

2. Extract from a report made by me to the Federal Chancellor dated 27 April.[1]

I am instructed to inform you that Señor Rascón ascribes the latest happenings in Lisbon to the idea of proclaiming the Crown Prince of Portugal as King of Iberia under the regency of Espartero, or possibly of Saldanha, but that in the opinion of Baron von Canitz, who has no personal contacts with the present rulers of Spain and is inclined to think them capable of many things, the idea of a Saldanha regency "does not probably exist in any Spaniard's head except Rascón's".[2]

I remain etc.

B[UCHE]R

himself deeply offended and he had no plans thought out for what was to happen after the fall of the Government. He is now trying to win over the Bishop of Vizen and his party which is particularly numerous in Porto and the northern provinces; and although the Bishop has refused to come here and is behaving very coolly towards his pressing representations, the Marshal is said not yet to have given up hope of finding among his friends men willing to form a ministry. For this purpose his alliance with Count Peniche is of course an obstacle, while the Count on his side insists on entering the Cabinet. How these difficulties are to be solved it is not yet possible to see.

The present second Chamber will, of course, not meet again but will be dissolved during the recess. The Marshal intends then to promulgate a new electoral law at the same time abolishing the members' expenses allowance, this latter on financial as well as political grounds. He makes no secret of the fact that he is in no hurry to summon the Cortes and that some time will elapse before the new Chamber meets.

So far no sort of manifesto or proclamation has been issued by the Marshal.

BRANDENBURG"

[1] Marginal note by Bucher: "Append the passage in brackets, pp. 10-11." See Doc. No. 106. The passage indicated by Bucher begins: "If I am correctly informed it is chiefly on two counts. . . ." and ends: "in favour of a cadet line of the princely House."

[2] Text of telegram of Canitz: "Madrid, 26 May, 1870. A 1691. pr. 29 May 1870. Decipher.

To my telegram of yesterday that Saldanha's revolt in Portugal was a failure in so far as it planned to set up an Iberian kingdom, and could not be otherwise on account of Portuguese hostility to the idea of union with Spain, I add that, in spite of all the declarations of the Spanish Government, this does not rule out the possibility, though even the Portuguese Minister here does so, that the Spanish Government had cognizance of General Saldanha's plans and even financed them. [Marginal note by Bucher: "my information on Prim's attitude towards union with Portugal is entirely at variance with this assumption."] The Spanish Government's position is such that it grasps at everything offering a ray of hope of finding a way out of the present untenable situation. It is possible that Saldanha's energy has here raised hopes of success which was unattainable by other means, what has been left out of account being the aversion of the Portuguese for Iberian union.

The Empress of the French, according to my observations here, favours a restoration with the Prince of Asturias and I incline to think that the Emperor is not against the idea either. Apart from Rascón, no Spaniard has ever thought of a Saldanha regency in an Iberian kingdom.

(signed) CANITZ"

137. *Count von Bismarck to Baron von Canitz,*
Prussian Minister at Madrid

(Telegram. Draft for cipher) [German]

No. 3   Berlin, 30 May, 1870. 5.40 p.m.

In a few days a special messenger will leave here with my reply to
Marshal Prim. Meanwhile pardon the delay brought about by my illness.

v. B[ISMARCK]

138. *Baron von Canitz, Prussian Minister at Madrid,*
to Count von Bismarck

(Telegram. Decipher)[1] [German]   Madrid, 30 May, 1870. 2 p.m.
                                                                arrived 9.40 p.m.
                                                   A 1711. pr. 31 May, 1870

Bernhardi in Southern Spain whence he is soon expected back. Says
he will report as soon as he leaves for Portugal.

CANITZ

139. *Baron von Canitz, Prussian Minister at Madrid,*
to Count von Bismarck

(Telegram. Decipher)[2] [German]

No. 22   Madrid, 30 May, 1870. 2 p.m.
                                                        arrived 10.20 p.m.
                                               A 1712. pr. 31 May, 1870

According to present arrangements the election of the King by the
Cortes is to take place on 9 June. The Duc de Montpensier assures intimates
that Prim has now promised him his vote and influence. However it is
very doubtful whether in the election the Duke will receive the necessary
majority of half the Cortes members, as a part of the Ministers and of the
monarchist Democrats mean to make the election impossible by leaving
the Chamber when the vote is being taken.

CANITZ

---

[1] Marginal notes: "Duplicate. 1 copy submitted to H. Ex."
[2] Marginal note by Bismarck: "Copy to H. Majesty."

140. *Baron von Canitz, Prussian Minister at Madrid, to Salazar*

(Draft) [French]   Madrid, 31 May, 1870

DEAR SIR,

Count von Bismarck today informs me by telegraph[1] that a courier
will soon be leaving Berlin with the Count's correspondence for Count
de Reus.

In the meanwhile tender excuses to His Excellency for the delay caused
by the illness of the Federal Chancellor.

Your most devoted

signed CANITZ

141. *Prince Karl Anton of Hohenzollern to Count von Bismarck*

(Original)[2] [German]   Nauheim, 31 May, 1870
                                                    pr. 1 June [1870][3]

YOUR EXCELLENCY,

Your momentous letter of the 28th inst. was brought to me by Legation Counsellor Bucher. The eminently statesmanlike appreciation of the
question at issue is such that I cannot but qualify it unreservedly as out-
standing. After a sharp struggle between higher duties and family feeling
I have now come to the conviction that in existing circumstances a refusal
would be a failure to understand the situation, the historic mission and
the workings of Providence.

Although I have made and could make no communication to my son,
the Hereditary Prince, about the reopening of the question with us, I know
with absolute certainty that he will be willing for any sacrifice if, as in the
present case, interests of state are involved.—Great as is the weight of our
family interests which viewed from any aspect are not favourable to
acceptance of the crown, they can no longer *today* constitute the sole
decisive factor. In anticipation of His Majesty the King's assent and with
the express reservation of my son's right to make his decision I think I may
already leave it to Your Excellency's discretion to let Madrid know that
under conditions yet more exactly to be formulated a modification of the
previous decision in favour of a refusal might be admissible.

Before all else it is the *question of time*. If the Spanish rulers succeed in
maintaining the status quo until the autumn, this would constitute another

[1] See Doc. No. 137.
[2] Marginal note by Bucher: "Presented by L. R. Bucher."
[3] Marginal note: "Shorthand copy made."

moral obligation for us not to offer resistance, i.e. to accept the fait accompli of an election carried by a sufficient number of votes.

Family considerations of many kinds compel me to demand this delay —as well as the recasting of many clauses of the Hohenzollern Famil Law—all of them things needing time and thought before they can be submitted to His Majesty's sanction.

Legation Secretary Bucher can give Your Excellency information verbally on many points which I have not time to explain in writing— for I think the most important thing is to let Your Excellency know my views on the *main question* as soon as possible.

Reserving more detailed information for a later letter, I remain with gratitude and esteem

Your Excellency's devoted
PRINCE OF HOHENZOLLERN

142. *Count von Bismarck to Salazar*

(Telegram en clair)[1] [French]   Berlin, 1 June, 1870. 2 p.m.

The two machines will be delivered together, by Tuesday if can be.
BRAUN

143. *Count von Bismarck to Marshal Prim*

(Draft) [French]   Berlin, 1 June, 1870

MONSIEUR LE COMTE,

I am seizing the first moment of quietude to thank Your Excellency for the letter you were so kind as to write me on 24 April.[2] I only received it on my return from the country[3] not yet quite recovered from a very serious indisposition which made it entirely impossible for me to attend to any business. I trust that in spite of so long a delay Your Excellency will not doubt my eagerness to give account to you of the steps I have

[1] The telegram was not sent direct to Salazar. Bismarck requested the head of the telegraph office at Hanover to send the text signed Braun to: "Pedro Sierra, Concepcion Geronima 28, Madrid." Braun stood for Bucher.

[2] See Doc. No. 102.

[3] Can Bismarck's illness explain why the Hohenzollern candidature was not revived until the end of May? Bismarck had been suffering from jaundice in Varzin since the 14th of April. This letter suggests that Bismarck did not know of Prim's letter of the 24th of April until he came back to Berlin at the end of May. Admittedly this would seem at first sight highly improbable, but we have not found either in the documents or in the registers any indication that Prim's letter was actually communicated to Bismarck whilst he was in Varzin, though Canitz's telegram of the 12th of May, forwarded to Bismarck, mentioned the existence of Prim's letter.

taken with a view to the realization of plans so much in accord with the regard I have for you and for the welfare of your country.

Having come to the conviction that Prince Frederick must be entirely ruled out, I took up the thread of negotiations afresh and today I think that in spite of his previous refusal we have succeeded in proving both to the Prince and to his august father that the misgivings and anxieties with which they had at first regarded the plan and the state of affairs in Spain were ill-founded. But the general difficulties which I had the honour to mention to Y.E. in my letter of 11 April[1] still stand in the way of a definite resolve. I have just received from H.R.H. the father the assurance that his son, the Hereditary Prince, no longer maintains his refusal on personal grounds. To this statement the father adds the promise that his eldest son would accept the result of the voting provided that by then an understanding could be reached on the conditions and the future position of the King in matters not regulated by the Constitution. Whether or not the Spanish Government is in a position to agree to such an arrangement is a question outside my competence. Still hoping that the presence of M. de Salazar might hasten the final solution I have requested him by telegraph to come to Berlin.[2] Whatever turn the affair may take I beg Y.E. to be convinced that I have done and will do all in my power and that if I do not in time enough achieve the result desired by us both it is only because of the difficulty of bringing about an agreement between persons of that rank as quickly as would have been necessary.

I am deeply touched by your good wishes for my health and I beg you to believe that I shall be most happy to be of service to you personally and to your country.

Accept, *M. le Comte*, the expression of the high esteem with which I have the honour to be

Your Excellency's

144. *Bucher to Count von Bismarck*

(Original) [German]   1.6.[1870]

If by chance the letter to Prim *cannot* be delivered by Herr v. Canitz (as would probably be preferred by both of them) the courier should receive instructions[3] to enquire by a note when he is to present himself to effect delivery and make sure that he does not present himself in uniform[4]

---

[1] See Doc. No. 79.

[2] Bismarck is perhaps alluding to Doc. No. 149, i.e. a telegram he intended to dispatch.

[3] Marginal note by Bismarck: "yes."

[4] Marginal note by Bismarck: "he must not travel in uniform at all, and especially not in Madrid."

at the Marshal's residence. The Marshal had me ushered in by a back door into his private dwelling. Salazar may not be in Madrid when the courier arrives.

BUCHER

145. Count von Bismarck to Baron von Canitz, Prussian Minister at Madrid[1]

(Draft) [German]

No. 5   Berlin, 1 June, 1870

Your Excellency will remember the communication dated 28 October, 1868, which I addressed to your deputy, Baron von Saurma.[2] The idea expressed in it, that as regards the events accompanying the change of sovereign in Spain we should maintain an attitude of dispassionate observation of a historic fact and judge future developments by the test of our own interests, finds application to circumstances which could not then be foreseen now that responsible quarters in Spain have made known the wish that one of the princes of the princely line of the Royal House should accept the throne. The highest officials of various departments, whom H.M. the King has taken into his confidence in order to hear their

[1] Marginal notes: "Secret—by King's Messenger—Royal Chasseur, Lieutenant Rohrbeck on 2 June."

[2] Text of Bismarck's instructions to Saurma of 28 October, 1868: "Berlin, 28 October, 1868. A 3341. Your Excellency's recent reports, especially Nos. 33-5, written in the midst of events, reveal in many passages the mood which the downfall of a time-honoured monarchy is calculated to evoke. But the greater the sympathy felt by the observer for the vanquished and the more easily this develops into antipathy towards the institutions and personages who replace it, the more steadfastly we must at present take care that the mutual relations of the two Governments are guided solely by the interests of the respective states.

The fallen Government was hostile to us. Although in the political field there was no point of immediate contact between it and us we had, when anything happened, to count it on the side of our opponents. Moreover the principles it pursued in economic questions were not favourable to the German tariff union. Its fall is thus an event of value to our policy. We shall therefore have to regard dispassionately as facts of history the happenings which always necessarily accompany any such change and, without prejudice, judge future developments by the test of our own interests.

For this reason in my telegram of the 21st inst. I invited Y.E. to give a friendly form to your relations with the personalities and authorities in Madrid. I would also ask you to maintain a similar tone in your dispatches. These will then harmonize with the lines of our policy; and they cannot then by any chance, in the event of their falling into unauthorized hands, be used to raise doubts of our sincerity in the provisional Government. If in the course of a frank, objective account you are obliged to convey information or express judgements which might give rise to doubts of our friendliness towards the present Spanish Government, be so kind as always to use cipher in accordance with my telegram of the 22nd inst.

VON BISMARCK."

views, have unanimously expressed the opinion that acceptance is dictated by the interests of Germany. H.R.H. the Crown Prince has also expressed himself in favour of the plan. H.M. the King, though not insensible of the political considerations which speak in favour of acceptance, has declined to pronounce a decision between these and his solicitude for the fate of the two Princes, so long as they themselves do not more clearly manifest a vocation and a willingness to assume so burdensome and perilous a mission. For me in my official position what is of importance is the political consideration, and as the King's official adviser I uphold this pending His Majesty's decision. I request Y.E. in drawing up your reports to bear in mind the interests of the Prussian State and the international relations of the two countries. It goes without saying that every important *fact* must be taken into consideration in the final decision, and the more Y.E. enters into the facts, the more objective the light in which you place them, the more welcome to me will be your reports. I would be especially grateful to Y.E. if you could inform me more fully than hitherto as to the state of our commercial relations and the prospects of their development and as to legislation; and as an example and standard of what is wanted I take the liberty of mentioning a law, the text of which has reached me by another channel: the law of 23 April of the current year relating to the powers of the authorities and the methods of procedure when the suspension of basic rights has been proclaimed in a district. On the other hand I beg you to exclude from your dispatches everything that falls into the category of doubtful conjecture. For instance in the dispatch of the 24th inst.[1] Your Excellency expresses the surmise that Marshal Saldanha's action had the support of the Spanish Government. It is possible that you may be right but it is certain that a series of facts can be adduced which speak against it. Observation at close range has its advantages and also its disadvantages, and where it is a question of forming a judgement on a question like the Hohenzollern candidature which encroaches on the field of general policy the best foundations for a sound estimate are as a rule to be sought at the centre where responsibility lies.

H.E.'s signature on fair copy

v. B[ISMARCK]
B[UCHE]R 3/5

146. *Count von Bismarck to Crown Prince Frederick William*

(Draft) [German]   Berlin, 1 June, 1870

I have the honour to send to Y.R.H. with my respects a copy of my letter of the 28th[2] to the Prince of Hohenzollern together with the original

---

[1] See Doc. No. 136, note.   [2] See Doc. No. 135.

of his reply of the 31st[1] ult. in pursuance of my report of yesterday and with the humble request for its return.

B[UCHE]R

147. Salazar to Baron von Canitz, Prussian Minister at Madrid

(Original) [French]   2 June [1870]

MY DEAR BARON,

I beg you to send off the enclosed telegram as soon as possible.

Most gratefully yours

E. DE SALAZAR Y MAZARREDO

★   ★   ★

Engineer will be able to assemble the two machines at the same time on the appointed day if there is good hope of casting tubes of diameters Nos. 4 and 6 in Hanover.

SIERRA

148. Baron von Canitz, Prussian Minister at Madrid, to Count von Bismarck

(Telegram. Decipher) [French]   Madrid, 2 June, 1870. 9 p.m.
arrived 1.30 a.m.

For Herr Bucher. Engineer will be able to assemble the two machines at the same time on the appointed day if there is good hope of casting tubes of the diameters numbered four and six in Hanover.

Signed: SIERRA

CANITZ[2]

149. Count von Bismarck to Baron von Canitz, Prussian Minister at Madrid

(Telegram. Draft for cipher) [French]
Berlin, 3 June, 1870. 12.5 p.m.

For Sierra. Mould No. 6 no longer exists. Manufacture of tube number

---

[1] See Doc. No. 141.

[2] Cf. Hesselbarth: "(17) 2nd June to Bucher from Prim. Engineer will be able to assemble the two machines at the same time on the appointed day if there is good hope of casting tubes of the diameter in Hanover. SALAZAR." (*Drei psychologische Fragen*, p. 30.)

four begun but would be speeded up by personal supervision of fitter.
Signed BRAUN.

Fair copy signed by H.E.

B[UCHE]R. 3.6.[1870][1]

150. *Salazar to Baron von Canitz, Prussian Minister at Madrid*

(Original) [French]   Friday [3 June, 1870]

Urgent!

MY DEAR BARON,

I beg you once again, and forgive me all this bother, to send off as soon
as possible the telegram written on the next page.

I have the honour to greet you most cordially,

E. DE SALAZAR Y MAZARREDO

*   *   *

M. Bucher.

After mature reflection it is *indispensable* for success manufacture that
the Doctor should come here immediately to compare the state of our
machines with the dimensions of the tubes. This co-operation will enormously facilitate engineer's task. They would go back together.

SIERRA

151. *Baron von Canitz, Prussian Minister at Madrid,*
to Count von Bismarck

(Telegram. Decipher) [French]   Madrid, 4 June, 1870. 10.35 a.m.
arrived 7.28 p.m.

To the same.[2] After mature reflection it is indispensable for success
manufacture that the Doctor[3] should come here immediately to compare
state of our machines with dimensions of tubes. This co-operation would

---

[1] Cf. Hesselbarth: "(18) 3 June to Bismarck. "Mould number 6 no longer exists. The
manufacture of the tubes numbered 4 would be speeded up by the personal supervision
of the fitter, Braun. SALAZAR." (*Drei psychologische Fragen*, p. 30.) The reader will note
how much the text published by Hesselbarth differs in the present case from the
authentic text.

Marginal note by Bucher: "i.e. to Herr Bucher."
Marginal note by Bucher: "i.e. Dr Braun."

enormously facilitate engineer's task. They would go back together.
SIERRA.

CANITZ[1]

152. *Prince Leopold of Hohenzollern to Crown Prince Frederick William*

(Copy) [German]   Benrath, 4 June, 1870

MOST GRACIOUS COUSIN,

Having returned from Nauheim yesterday evening I hasten to reply
to your gracious letter of 31 May[2] which reached me at the moment of
my departure. The previously arranged visit to my father could not therefore have come at a more appropriate moment when for the 3rd time this
question faces us.—In anticipation of my assent Count Bismarck's letter[3]
had already been answered by Papa.[4] Letter and reply are doubtless known
to you, I therefore need only add that I cannot but associate myself with
their point of view since more prolonged resistance to those paramount
Prussian and German interests of state repeatedly stressed in Count
Bismarck's letter as likely to be injured by a refusal must necessarily
produce an impression of faint-hearted pusillanimity;—this way of looking
at the matter makes it easier for me to sacrifice my independent, happy
existence since I shall be able to serve my country from a distance and I
trust that in this consciousness I shall find strength and perseverance for a
task about which I have no illusions—and to which no ambition could
impel me. Forgive this anything but objective attitude which I freely
confess to you; but after all I am more a man of feeling than of reason.

Both my father's and my own view in the matter of reopening this
question is that after H.M.'s rejection the initiative cannot in any way
come from us but only from the Spanish Government; further, my father
has made the stipulation that in the event of resumption a certain interval
must elapse before publication to permit the settlement of questions
connected with both family law and the entail, as well as to give time for
him and all of us to have needed spa treatment; finally, in order that later
on, when, God willing, William has come of age, the possibility may be
granted on both sides for me to come home again in order to look after
the interests of our son Ferdinand as next heir to the entail.

The immediate future will no doubt shed light on the question; in the

---

[1] Cf. Hesselbarth: "(19) 4 June to Bismarck. After an examination it is indispensable
that the Doctor should come here immediately, to compare state of our machines with
dimensions of the tubes. This collaboration would enormously facilitate engineer's task.
They would go back together. SIERRA—SALAZAR." (*Drei psychologische Fragen*, pp. 30-31.)

[2] The letter in question has not been found [in the files of the German Foreign
Ministry, but in the Sigmaringen Archives. See Appendix.]

[3] See Doc. No. 135.

[4] See Doc. No. 141.

meantime I await events with an easy mind and pray to God that He will order all for the best and, in the event of acceptance, for the honour and happiness of our House and our two countries, as you so finely put it in your letter.—

We are just off for a holiday in the Bavarian highlands. Please be so gracious as to give my cordial greetings to the Crown Princess and continue to bestow your love and favour on me.

Your devoted and obedient servant and cousin
signed LEOPOLD HOHENZOLLERN

153. *Count von Bismarck to Baron von Canitz,*
Prussian Minister at Madrid

(Telegram. Draft for cipher) [French]

Berlin, 5 June, 1870 [8.15 a.m.]

For Sierra. Doctor coming.

Fair copy signed by H.E.[1]

154. *Count von Bismarck to Baron von Canitz,*
Prussian Minister at Madrid

(Telegram. Draft for cipher) [German]

Berlin, 6 June, 1870. 8.30 a.m.

Keep courier waiting till further orders.

fair copy signed by H.E.

v. B[ISMARCK]
B[UCHE]R 5.6.[1870][2]

155. *Baron von Canitz, Prussian Minister at Madrid,*
to Count von Bismarck

(Telegram. Decipher) [German]   Madrid, 6 June, 1870. 2.30 p.m.
arr. 8.12 p.m.

Your Excellency's despatches, including No. 5,[3] received by King's messenger today.

CANITZ

---

[1] Cf. Hesselbarth: "5 June to Salazar. Doctor coming. BISMARCK." (*Drei psychologische Fragen*, p. 31.)
[2] Marginal note by Bucher: "To be sent off on 6th."
[3] See Doc. No. 145.

156. *Salazar to Baron von Canitz, Prussian Minister at Madrid*

(Original) [French]   8 June [1870]

MY DEAR BARON,

Yet another telegram and it will not be the last. To save you work I leave it to your discretion whether the words underlined below [italicized here] can be sent en clair.

I have the honour to greet you cordially.

E. DE SALAZAR Y MAZARREDO

*   *   *

Telegram

Law for election of King passed yesterday; it requires absolute majority of the 350 admitted deputies; this clause ends all hopes of partisans of Espartero and Montpensier. The latter about to depart.

Letter received. Awaiting Doctor. Next week decisive for monarchic principle. Immediate election of King would not preclude time demanded for preliminary arrangements. Delay spells defeat. Almost all the deputies are present pending a decision; their fatigue is extreme and a great number will not return again.

ALONSO

157. *Baron von Canitz, Prussian Minister at Madrid, to Count von Bismarck*

(Telegram. Decipher)[1, 2] [French]

Madrid, 8 June, 1870. 2.15 p.m.,
arrived 9.24 p.m.
A 1795. pr. 9 June, 1870

Law for election of King passed yesterday; it requires absolute majority of three hundred fifty delegates. This clause removes all hope of partisans of Espartero and Montpensier. Montpensier about to depart.

Letter received. Awaiting Doctor. Next week decisive for monarchic principle. Immediate election of King would not rule out time demanded for arranging plan. Delay spells defeat. Almost all the deputies are present

---

[1] Marginal note: "laid before H.R.H. 7.7."

[2] Marginal note by Abeken: "Provisionally to be put in the files. B[erlin] 9.6.70 Ab[eken].—Thile."

in expectation of a decision. Their fatigue is extreme and a great number will not come back again.—ALONSO.—

(signed) CANITZ[1]

158. *Crown Prince Frederick William to Count von Bismarck*

(Original)[2] [German]   Potsdam, 8.6.1870

Enclosed is a letter received a few days ago from the Hereditary Prince[3] which I should be glad if you will return and which will demonstrate to you beyond doubt the Prince's readiness to accept.

Therewith I regard the matter as settled; should difficulties of a new kind arise they will not be attributable to members of the Hohenzollern House but to the Spaniards.

FREDERICK WILLIAM OF HOHENZOLLERN

159. *Versen to Count von Bismarck*

(Original)[4] [German]   Berlin, 8 June, 1870

NOBLE COUNT!

Esteemed Chancellor of the North German Confederation, Minister-President and Major-General!

I have the honour most obediently to report to Your Excellency that I have just been received by the Crown Prince. I executed Your Excellency's order. He again talked at length about the further course of the affair and gave me the enclosed letter for Your Excellency.[5] He will receive M. Salazar, but this had better happen under some fictitious name.

He asked that Your Excellency should return H.R. Highness's letter[6] enclosed in his own, either by post or by some sure channel. From it Your Excellency will gather that the Hereditary Prince has already expressed his readiness; he will await the renewed offer of the crown and then ask His Majesty's permission to accept. I said to the Crown Prince that it

---

[1] Cf. Hesselbarth: "(21) 8 June to Bismarck. Law for election of King approved yesterday. It requires absolute majority of 350 deputies. Immediate election of king would not preclude time demanded for preliminary engagement. Delay spells defeat. Almost all the deputies are present in expectation of a decision. Their fatigue is extreme; a great number will not return again. SALAZAR." (*Drei psychologische Fragen*, p. 31.)

[2] Marginal note by Bismarck: "Foreign Ministry. Secreta."

[3] See Doc. No. 152.

[4] Marginal note by Bismarck: "Foreign Ministry. Secreta."

[5] See Doc. No. 158.

[6] See Doc. No. 152.

might be desirable for the Prince to apply for this permission now in case the crown is offered him again and to fix now a definite date for his departure, so that if M. Salazar comes the matter could soon be brought to a conclusion.

The Crown Prince leaves it to Your Excellency's discretion to act as Your Excellency thinks wise.

I have taken sick leave and think of going to Reichenhall on my own responsibility. The Crown Prince has given me a verbal message for the Hereditary Prince thanking him for his last letter and saying he regards the matter now as settled.

I most respectfully offer Your Excellency, on this quite private journey of mine, to bear any confidential messages, asking you to tell me whether I should suggest to the Hereditary Prince that he should address his request to His Majesty now or only when M. Salazar arrives. I shall also have to give the Hereditary Prince news about Herr Bucher's mission and the impending arrival of M. Salazar, and I venture, respectfully and subject to correction, to suggest that it might be well if I could exercise still further influence on the Hereditary Prince in order to counteract the inevitable influence of the ladies. At the short meeting at Benrath I was able to smooth away and confute his main scruples, but it would do no harm if he were to ask more questions and receive more information. If, on the other hand, Your Excellency has no further messages to entrust to me I would give up the journey and therefore will await your kind reply to Berlin—Hotel Windsor.

With the highest esteem I have the honour to remain
Your Excellency's most obedient
VERSEN
Major, General Staff

160. *Theodor von Bernhardi to Count von Bismarck*

(Original)[1] [German]   Madrid, 8 June, 1870

On my return from the provinces of the Crown of Aragon I have the honour most respectfully to report that according to my instructions I am at once—this evening—leaving for Lisbon.

A more detailed account of conditions, especially in Catalonia, which may become only too important, must for lack of time wait over for the next opportunity. But I feel I must respectfully report without delay that according to all I have seen and heard in the Aragonese provinces Spain will hardly escape without another civil war.

The old opposition between Castile and Aragon is more bitter than

[1] Marginal note by Versen: "Has been submitted to H.E. at Varzin."

at any time in the last two centuries, intensified in Catalonia by the growing consciousness of a nationality which is Provençal and non-Spanish.

If the Duc de Montpensier were to be elected King there would be a rising against him of the greater part of Aragon and the whole of Catalonia.

One of the most disquieting features is probably *that a separation of Catalonia from Spain in order to join up with France is not at all beyond the realm of possibility*. The well-off classes in Catalonia are generally in favour of it. They regard it as a means of escaping the Spanish financial collapse and fending off the socialistic republic which they certainly have every reason to fear.

Here in Madrid everybody is, as ever, entirely taken up with petty personal interests. General Prim is again making every effort to render the election of a King impossible while ostensibly promoting it. This time again he wants to keep things *in statu quo* until he believes his own time has come.

TH. V. BERNHARDI

161. *Salazar to Baron von Canitz, Prussian Minister at Madrid*

(Original) [French]   9 June [1870]

MY DEAR BARON,
    Another telegram.
    I beg you to believe in my most sincere sentiments.

E. DE SALAZAR Y MAZARREDO

You may suppress the words underlined [italicized here] because they would make the telegram too long and that might arouse suspicions in France.

*　　*　　*

To Count von Bismarck, for himself alone.

Doctor *is* here. Moment *has* arrived to convert *the* confidential démarches into official negotiations. Spanish Government will officially approach the Prussian Government as soon as Herr von Bismarck through his representative here sends word to the Ministry for Foreign Affairs that he is ready to receive communications in the sense of the Prime Minister's semi-official démarches.

I confirm yesterday's telegram.[1] Reply is therefore urgent. After election three months at least will be allowed for the arrival. According to law, *the* Prince's private fortune will appertain always to his person, not to the crown. Civil List proposed for the King would be five million francs.

[1] See Doc. No. 157.

162. *Salazar to Baron von Canitz, Prussian Minister at Madrid*

(Original) [French]   9 June [1870]

MY DEAR BARON,

I forgot two words in the telegram I have just sent you. It must be said that Herr von Bismarck's instructions to Herr von Canitz, that you are to pass on verbally to our Minister for Foreign Affairs, will have to be sent *by telegraph.*

Cordially yours

E. SALAZAR Y MAZARREDO

163. *Baron von Canitz, Prussian Minister at Madrid,*
to Count von Bismarck

(Telegram. Decipher)[1] [French]

Madrid, 9 June, 1870. 4.30 p.m.
arrived 10.30 p.m.
A 1801. pr. 10 June, 1870

Personal. Doctor here. Moment arrived for conversion of confidential démarches into official negotiations. Spanish Government will officially approach Prussian Government[2] as soon as Herr von Bismarck through his representative here sends word to the Minister for Foreign Affairs that he is ready to receive communications in the sense of the Prime Minister's semi-official démarches. I confirm yesterday's telegram.[3] Reply is therefore urgent. After election three months at least will be allowed for the arrival. According to the law the Prince's private fortune will appertain always to his person not to the crown. Civil List proposed for the King will be five million francs.

signed: SALAZAR

CANITZ[4]

[1] Marginal note: "Laid before H.R.H. 7.7."
[2] Marginal note by Bismarck: "The Prussian Government is not concerned with all this!"
[3] See Doc. No. 157.
[4] Cf. Hesselbarth: "(22) 9 June to Bismarck. Doctor here. Moment arrived to convert confidential démarches into official negotiations. Government here will officially approach Government there as soon as Bismarck sends word to the Ministry of State through Canitz that he is ready to receive communications in the sense of President Prim's semi-official démarches. Reply is urgent. After election three months at least will be allowed for the arrival; according to the law the caballero's fortune will always appertain to his person and not to the Crown. Civil List proposed for the king; Five million francs. SALAZAR." (*Drei psychologische Fragen*, p. 31.)

164. *Salazar to Baron von Canitz, Prussian Minister at Madrid*

(Original) [French]   9 June [1870]

MY DEAR BARON,
  Here is what you ask me for.
                                                              Yours
                                          E. DE SALAZAR Y MAZARREDO

⋆   ⋆   ⋆

Count von Bismarck.
  Y.E. is requested to send by telegraph instructions asked for by Herr
von Canitz.
                                                              SALAZAR

165. *Baron von Canitz, Prussian Minister at Madrid,*
to Count von Bismarck

(Telegram. Decipher) [French]   Madrid, 9 June 1870. 6 p.m.
                                            arrived 10.6. 4.15 a.m.
                                            A 1800. pr. 10 June, 1870

  Your Excellency is requested to send by telegraph instructions asked
for by Baron von Canitz.[1] SALAZAR.
                                                  (signed) CANITZ

166. *Salazar to Baron von Canitz, Prussian Minister at Madrid*

(Original) [French]   9 June [1870]

MY DEAR BARON,
  Here is another telegram. If you received the instructions asked for
yesterday,[2] I would beg you to apprise me before communicating them
to M. Sagasta, but I think that this other telegram will arrive in time.
The minutes are precious and after so many delays a little indecision might
ruin everything.
                                                              Yours
                                          E. DE SALAZAR Y MAZARREDO

  The telegram is too long and all the underlined [italicized] words may
be omitted.
⋆   ⋆   ⋆

---

[1] See Doc. No. 163.   [2] See Doc. No. 163.

To Count von Bismarck. Personal.

Vexation Montpensier *partisans* makes *them* hasten election King 10 days from now. In these circumstances official communications would take too long *a* time, *and* to offer candidature it will suffice for Herr von Bismarck to send by *special* courier *a* letter addressed *to* Marshal Prim, accepting the votes on *the* agreed terms, if it could be here by Friday 17th. More prolonged indecision would ruin everything. Dispatch *of* this letter might officially be announced to the Minister for Foreign Affairs the same day by Herr *von* Canitz. *A* reply from the Prince would help our plans even if it were merely announced. Court expenditure is greatly reduced but Civil List *of the* King would be at least five million francs. Prince Asturias provision apart.

SALAZAR

167. Baron von Canitz, Prussian Minister at Madrid, to Count von Bismarck

(Telegram. Decipher)[1] [French]

Madrid, 10 June, 1870. 1.35 p.m.
arr. 9.10 p.m.
A 1017. pr. 11 June, 1870

Personal. Departure of Montpensier hastens election of King in ten days' time. In the circumstances official communications would take too long, it would suffice to present candidate that Count von Bismarck should send a letter by courier addressed to Marshal Prim accepting vote on agreed terms if it can be here by Friday 17th. More prolonged indecision would ruin everything. Dispatch of that letter may officially be announced by Baron von Canitz to Minister for Foreign Affairs same day. A reply from the Prince would also help our plans even if it were not announced. Court expenditure is greatly reduced but the King's Civil List would be at least five million francs. Prince Asturias provision apart. Signed SALAZAR.

(Signed) CANITZ[2]

[1] Marginal note: "submitted Varzin. 21.6.—Duplicate."

[2] Cf. Hesselbarth: "(23) 10 June to Bismarck. Personal. Vexation Montpensier partisans causes hastening election of King 10 days from now. In the circumstances official communications would take too long a time and in order to present candidature it will suffice for M. Bismarck to send by courier a letter addressed to Marshal Prim accepting voting on the agreed terms, it could arrive by Friday the 17th. More prolonged indecision would ruin everything. Dispatch of this letter might officially be announced by Canitz to Sagasta. A reply from the caballero would also help our plans, even if it were only announced. Court expenditure is greatly reduced, but the King's Civil List would be at least five million francs. Prince Asturias provision apart." (*Drei psychologische Fragen*, pp. 31-2.)

168. *Count von Bismarck to Thile*

(Telegram en clair) [German]   Varzin, 11.6.70. 11.45 a.m.
                                A 1826. pr. 11 June, 1870

Provisionally, pending written intimation by this evening's post, I request you to telegraph to the Doctor in reply to his friend's urgent representations that I am away and without cipher, and that success can only be expected from negotiations with the one person directly concerned who is now independent and animated by the greatest goodwill. The affair would probably have been settled if, as I suggested a week ago,[1] A.[2] had come to Berlin instead of asking for the Doctor.

BISMARCK[3]

169. *Thile to Baron von Canitz, Prussian Minister at Madrid*

(Telegram. Draft for cipher) [French]
                              Berlin, 11 June, 1870. 2.55 p.m.
                                     A 1826

After receiving the two telegrams of the 9th,[4] Count Bismarck asks me to telegraph to the Doctor in reply to his friend's urgent representations, that he is absent from Berlin, that he is without cipher and that a result can only be obtained by communicating with the person directly interested, who now is independent in his decisions and animated by the best dispositions. The Count adds that the affair would probably be settled by now if at the suggestion he made a week ago[5] Alonso had come to Berlin instead of asking for the Doctor. Telegram No. 10[6] cannot be in the hands of the Count earlier than tomorrow, the 12th.

Fair copy for signature by Secretary of State

AB[EKEN] 11.6.70

v. TH[ILE]

---

[1] See Doc. No. 149.

[2] A. is Alonso, i.e. Salazar.

[3] Draft telegram drawn up by Bismarck and not sent to Thile: "I request you to telegraph to the Doctor in reply to his friend's urgent representations that I am absent and without cipher and that successful negotiations can only be carried on with the one person alone directly concerned, since he is of age and free to make his own decisions." Marginal note by Roland: "Received from His Serene Highness in January 1877 for the files."

[4] See Docs. Nos. 163 and 165.

[5] See Doc. No. 149.

[6] See Doc. No. 167.

170. *Baron von Canitz, Prussian Minister at Madrid, to Count von Bismarck*

(Telegram. Decipher)[1] [French]   Madrid, 11 June, 1870. 9.30 p.m.
arrived ?? p.m.
A 1898. pr. 12 June, 1870

General impression after patriotic declaration made today's sitting by liberal union is that candidate presented by government will receive almost unanimous monarchist vote. SALAZAR.

CANITZ

171. *Thile to Count von Bismarck*

(Original)[2] [German]   11.6.70

As with the recent telegrams I will not without Your Excellency's instructions lay before His Majesty the enclosed telegram from Madrid[3] which has just arrived.

THILE

172. *Count von Bismarck to Versen*

(Copy) [German]   Varzin, 11 June, 1870

Many thanks to Your Excellency for your kind communication.[4] I am, however, for the moment undergoing a drastic cure and, in the absence of all departmental resources, not in a position to attend to state business and hence to add anything new to the last detailed discussion. The difficulty now is how to bring those concerned, i.e. the two parties involved in the affair, into immediate contact with each other. In this matter I cannot do more than I did before I left.

With kind regards, etc.

(signed) v. BISMARCK

---

[1] Marginal note: "Submitted Varzin 26.6.—Duplicate."
[2] Marginal note by Roland: "Received from His Serene Highness in January 1877 for the files. Roland."
[3] See Doc. No. 167.
[4] See Doc. No. 159.

173. *Count von Bismarck to Thile*

(Original) [German]   Varzin, 11 June, 1870

HONOURED FRIEND,

I beg you to make a secret copy of the contents of enclosed envelope addressed to H.R.H. the Crown Prince,[1] including the Hereditary Prince's letter,[2] sealing it then with an engraved crystal private seal bearing my coat of arms which lies on my desk and sending it off; next do the same with the letter to Versen,[3] and finally telegraph asking Bucher to tell Salazar: "I had pointed out a week ago and repeat today that the only way to carry the affair to a successful conclusion was for someone to make the journey to see the Hereditary Prince at Reichenhall and settle with him what is to be done; the Hereditary Prince is of age and ready to negotiate; the family objections which were a previous obstacle have been overcome; the Prussian Government has no say in the matter and, according to letters which I have read privately, there is no doubt about his willingness to accept." Bucher can put this as my personal conviction; if no progress results I can do nothing about it and I wash my hands of the matter. Versen's letter,[4] to which the enclosed is a reply, will you please place in the files. I am sleeping very badly here because I have too much writing to do. For most of the items it would do no harm if they were marked to be produced again[5] in 3 months.

Yours

V. BISMARCK

174. *Count von Bismarck to Crown Prince Frederick William*

(Copy)[6] [German]   Varzin, 11 June, 1870

MOST SERENE HIGHNESS,
        MOST GRACIOUS CROWN PRINCE.

With respectful thanks I return His Serene Highness the Hereditary Prince's letter to your Royal Highness.[7] Before I left I let Madrid know of my wish that a confidential envoy should come to Germany to negotiate directly with the Prince [Karl Anton] and his son.[8] The answer

---

[1] See Doc. No. 174.   [2] See Doc. No. 152.
[3] See Doc. No. 172.   [4] See Doc. No. 159.
[5] reproducatur.
[6] This document is published by Thimme, *Bismarck. Ges. Werke*, VIb, doc. No. 1562.
[7] See Doc. No. 152.   [8] See Doc. No. 149.

came back with the wish that an agent from here should go to Madrid[1] to clear up the situation, and as a result of this L.R. Bucher went off at once to Madrid, he being the one who knows most about the intentions of the Princely House since he had just had a talk with His Highness, the Prince [Karl Anton]. Since then M. Salazar has reported the intentions of Madrid in private telegrams the content of which Herr von Thile will be able to explain more fully to Y.R.H. I am enclosing the copies which have been sent to me with the respectful comment that I attach no *official* importance to their contents. I have sent word to Salazar that in my opinion direct negotiations with His Serene Highness the Hereditary Prince are the only practical way of advancing matters, since the Prince is in an independent position, and has recently expressed his willingness to negotiate, and since the Prussian Government has no power or wish to prescribe what he shall do. I unfortunately lack all ways and means of carrying matters beyond the point they had reached at my departure, having exercised my good offices to the limit of what I can do without a command from His Majesty.

With deepest respects I remain

Y.R.H.'s humble servant

signed BISMARCK

175. *Thile to Baron von Canitz, Prussian Minister at Madrid*

(Telegram. Draft for cipher) [French]

Berlin, 12 June, 1870. 10.10 p.m.

FOR THE DOCTOR.

The Chief instructs you to say the following to Alonso: the only way to bring the matter to fruition is for someone to go at once to see the Hereditary Prince at Reichenhall in order to do with him whatever can be done. The Prince is of age and ready to negotiate. The objections on the part of his family have been removed. The Prussian Government has no orders to give him, but our Chief has read private letters proving that the Prince is desirous of accepting. The Doctor is to say all this as a personal opinion on the part of the Chief. Versen leaves tomorrow for Reichenhall.

THILE[2]

[1] See Doc. No. 151.

[2] Cf. Hesselbarth: "(25) 12 June to Salazar for the Doctor. The Chief instructs you to say the following to Alonso Salazar: the only way to bring the matter to fruition is for someone to go at once to see the caballero at Reichenhall to do with him whatever can be done. The caballero is of age and ready to negotiate. The objections on the part of his family have been removed. The Prussian Government has no orders to give him, but Chief has read private letters proving that the chevalier is desirous of accepting. The doctor is therefore to say this as an opinion of the Chief's. Versen leaves tomorrow for Reichenhall. THILE." (*Drei psychologische Fragen*, p. 32.)

176. *Baron von Canitz, Prussian Minister at Madrid, to Count von Bismarck*

(Telegram. Decipher)[1] [French]

Madrid, 12 June, 1870. 12.13 p.m.
arr. 4.45 p.m.
A 1840. pr. 12 June, 1870

Defeat of Montpensier in plan of calling at yesterday's sitting for immediate election of king or a decisive vote, enables Alonso leave for Berlin this week. Impossible before. If Prince well disposed, Marshal thinks all may be arranged in short time. Doctor and courier leaving tomorrow. SALAZAR.

(signed) CANITZ[2]

177. *Versen to Count von Bismarck*

(Original)[3] [German]   Berlin, 12 June, 1870

HONOURED SIR,

Most Honourable Chancellor of the North German Confederation, Minister-President and Major-General.

I humbly venture to beg Your Excellency in reply to the registered letter of the 8th inst.[4] graciously to let me know whether I may go to Reichenhall, am to remain here in Berlin, or am to come to Varzin to receive instructions from Your Excellency.[5] Until your gracious instructions reach me I would not return to garrison in Posen but stay here, Hotel Windsor.

With highest esteem I have the honour to remain
Your Excellency's most obedient
v. VERSEN
Major, General Staff

[1] Marginal note: "submitted Varzin. 20.6.—Duplicate."
[2] Cf. Hesselbarth: "12 June to Bismarck. Defeat of Montpensier in plan of calling at yesterday's sitting for immediate election of King as a vote censure enables Alonso leave for Berlin this week. Impossible before. Doctor and courier leaving tomorrow. SALAZAR." (*Drei psychologische Fragen*, p. 32.)
[3] Marginal note by Bismarck: "Foreign Ministry, Secret."
[4] See Doc. No. 159.
[5] Marginal note by Bismarck: "Telegraph reply. First sentence: I think your journey desirable. H.E. von Thile has from me the information you need."

178. *Salazar to Baron von Canitz, Prussian Minister at Madrid*

(Original) [French]   13 June [1870]

MY DEAR BARON,
    I leave tomorrow and trust that this will be the last telegram *por ahora*.
Yours
E. DE SALAZAR Y MAZARREDO

★   ★   ★

Doctor and I leaving together tomorrow for Reichenhall.
SALAZAR

179. *Baron von Canitz, Prussian Minister at Madrid,*
to Count von Bismarck

(Telegram. Decipher)[1] [French]   Madrid, 13 June, 1870. 5.10 p.m.
arrived 9.5 p.m.
A 1856. pr. 14 June, 1870

Doctor and myself leaving together tomorrow for Reichenhall.
SALAZAR.
(signed) CANITZ[2]

180. *Thile to Count von Bismarck*

(Original)[3] [German]   Berlin, 13 June, 1870

HONOURED CHIEF,
    The instructions contained in Your Excellency's letter[4] received yesterday evening have all been carried out. Versen left yesterday evening for Reichenhall taking with him notes of the contents of all last week's telegrams from Madrid inclusive of the enclosed most recent one,[5] and hopes to persuade the Hereditary Prince to approach H.M. at once for

---

[1] Marginal note: "submitted Varzin 21.6.—Duplicate."
[2] Cf. Hesselbarth: "(26) 13 June to Bismarck. Doctor and I leaving tomorrow for Reichenhall. ALONSO SALAZAR." (*Drei psychologische Fragen*, p. 33.)
[3] Marginal note by Roland: "Received from His Highness in January 1877 for the files. Roland."
[4] See Doc. No. 173.
[5] Probably Doc. No. 176 is meant.

permission to accept. I have arranged a sort of code[1] with Versen for Reichenhall.

I deeply regret the bad after effects of the many business demands on your sleep. On my part I will practise the utmost possible abstinence, at the same time with your authorization sending you until further notice such dispatches as require no instructions but are, God willing, tolerably interesting reading.

Today I have to report on various small matters, and will take occasion at the wish of (Court Marshal) von Eulenburg to drop a hint to His Majesty that the Crown Prince would very much like to receive a command from the King to wait on the Tsar on His return from Breslau.

Benedetti is back and said to me (with a certain purposefulness): [French] "as regards foreign policy there is nothing at all, we are taken up entirely with our home affairs."

Most obediently and faithfully   THILE

Postscript. According to enclosed telegram from Werther[2] Meding *seems* to be going to nibble at the bait.

The telegram you ordered to be sent to Bucher[3] went off yesterday evening and will therefore catch him in Madrid.

181. *Baron von Canitz, Prussian Minister at Madrid, to Count von Bismarck*

(Original)[4] [German]   Madrid, 13 June, 1870

Private. No. 25.
By King's Messenger.

As already announced by telegraph, I had the honour to receive on

---

[1] The following is the code arranged between Thile and Versen: "Code arranged with Herr von Versen.—Max von Versen, Reichenhall.

Prince will at once approach H. Majesty=Parcel to Leipzig going off.
Should difficulties arise=I am taking the parcel to Leipzig.

Appanage	= 5000 cigars.	Hohenzollern—father	= Werner
Bismarck	= Lehmann	King	= Schröder
Crown Prince	= Schwarz	Salazar	= Bock
Bucher	= Braun	Prim	= Erdmann
Thile	= Schmidt	Sigmaringen	= Schwarzburg
Hereditary Prince	= Arnold	remittance on xy day	= election desired not before xy day."

The three last items were agreed on only several days later. See Doc. No. 186.

[2] This telegram from Paris on 12 June 1870 (A 1841. pr. 12 June, 1870), which is contained in file *IA Ag 29, Umtriebe des Hannöverschen Hofes,* Bd. 9, May 1869–August 1870, has no connexion with the Hohenzollern candidature.

[3] See Doc. No. 175.

[4] Marginal note by Thile: "Submitted to His Ex. at Varzin."

the 6th[1] inst. Your Excellency's esteemed secret letter No. 5[2] and took note thereof with the keenest interest.

It was with most lively regret that I learnt from it that Your Excellency is not in agreement either with my ideas or with what I have been reporting on conditions here and that you invite me to be mindful in my reports of Prussian state interests and the international relations of the two countries. As long as I have had the honour and good fortune to serve my King and country I believe myself never to have lost sight of this guiding principle, and never to have either reported or taken official action on any other principle; I believe myself never to have penned a line, especially on the question of the candidature for the Spanish throne, that was not purely and after mature reflection dictated by Prussian state interests.

None of His Majesty's ministers abroad can be more convinced than the humble signatory of this present letter how indubitably right is the dictum that in judging of a question encroaching on the field of general policy, such as the Hohenzollern candidature, only at the centre, occupied with such success by Your Excellency, is there a convergence of adequate data for a correct evaluation of the political situation as a whole and that only from this centre is it possible to decide what is to be done or not done for the good of Prussia. I therefore fully acquiesce if in antithesis to the whole tenor of my reports a venture is undertaken in Spain of whose adverse issue in the near or distant future I cannot be otherwise than convinced by all my observations here; I acquiesce because I am not in a position to command a view of Prussian policy as a whole and can imagine that a hazard taken here, the difficulties of which have not been overlooked, may in a far distant field bring Prussia benefits and advantages far outweighing the damage to relations with Spain.

I will make every effort to fulfil Your Excellency's instruction to report more amply on the state of our commercial relations with Spain and the prospects of their development, also on Spanish legislation, although it will be difficult to say more than has hitherto been the case, since all consideration of such questions makes it practically impossible to leave the political situation in the country altogether out of count, and since by Your Excellency's telegrams of 4 and 5 December, 1868 and Your Excellency's letter of the 10th of that same month I have the strictest instructions either not to report at all or to report only in cipher unless a Prussian or an English opportunity presents itself by which the dispatch can reach you.

I did not—mistakenly as I with regret perceive—let you have the law of 23 April of the current year on the powers conferred on authorities and the procedure when suspension of the basic rights has been proclaimed in a district, the text of which has reached Your Excellency through other channels and not through me, the reason being that because

---

[1] See Doc. No. 155. [2] See Doc. No. 145.

of its purely detail regulations for states of emergency I regarded it, like many others of its kind, as not being of sufficient interest to be brought to the knowledge of the Royal Government, the more so as all such laws here in Spain are for short terms and mostly observed by nobody even while they are in force.

CANITZ

182. *Baron von Canitz, Prussian Minister at Madrid, to Count von Bismarck*

(Original) [German]   Madrid, 13 June, 1870
pr. 17.6

The King's Messenger, Rohrbeck, leaves Madrid today for Berlin, acting, so he tells me, on instructions reaching him direct from the Spanish Ministry.

As this impending departure was telegraphed[1] yesterday to Berlin by Alonso, hence was known there, I assume that it has Your Excellency's approval and in consequence regard the telegram of the 6th inst.[2] instructing me to retain the King's Messenger here until further orders as discharged.

CANITZ

183. *Thile to Versen*

(Telegram en clair)[3] [German]   B[erlin], 15 June, 1870

To HERR MAX VON VERSEN,
    Reichenhall.
Our friends Bock[4] and Braun[4] will arrive these days at Reichenhall.
SCHMIDT[4]

184. *Versen to Thile*

(Telegram en clair) [German]   Reichenhall, 15.6.1870. 5 p.m.

He has been killing time elsewhere for two days, will do no business without Werner,[5] will go straight to Werner.

MAX

---

[1] See Doc. No. 176.   [2] See Doc. No. 154.
[3] Marginal note by Roland: "Dispatched by me, 15.6, at 12.40 a.m."
[4] See Doc. No. 180, note. Bock=Salazar, Braun=Bucher, Schmidt=Thile.
[5] See Doc. No. 180, note. Werner=Hohenzollern—father.

185. *Versen to Thile*

(Telegram en clair) [German]   Reichenhall, 15.6.1870. 10.10 p.m.

Telegram received,[1] please detain our friends until I have settled the business with Werner[2] and Company and can send the parcel to Leipzig.[3] Should like to have a word with the friends before their journey here. Can they await me Munich Four Seasons? We travel 16th six p.m. to Werner's.[2]

MAX

186. *Versen to Thile*

(Original)[4] [German]   Reichenhall, 15 June, 1870

YOUR EXCELLENCY,

I beg to report that I arrived at Reichenhall on the morning of the 14th. The gentleman whom I venture in future to call Arnold[5] had stayed on in Munich and only arrived here this afternoon. He is ready to accept in the autumn but has objections to doing so in the immediate future as he would thereby inevitably receive an official rank and would have to mind his ps and qs wherever he goes, especially here in Reichenhall where he has only just arrived, has many relatives in the neighbourhood, and must pass the coming three weeks on account of the cure; he says he wants not to accept until autumn and then go straight there. I represented to him the urgency of the situation in M[adrid] and showed him in the telegrams the new offer from Erdmann[6] on which he had insisted, explaining to him that the deputies would never again assemble in such large numbers whereas he was attaching importance to a large number of votes, etc., etc.

Of course I did not show him the telegram of the 12th June, noon,[7] since it again affords full latitude for procrastination, and in the intervening time other influences might again interfere with the whole business.

He slowly realized the change in the situation and the necessity for

---

[1] See Doc. No. 183.
[2] See Doc. No. 180, note. Werner=Hohenzollern—father.
[3] See Doc. No. 180, note. "Parcel to Leipzig going off"="Prince will at once approach His Majesty."
[4] Marginal note by Thile: "Has been submitted to H.E. at Varzin."
[5] Marginal note: "Hereditary Prince."
[6] Marginal note: "Prim."
[7] See Doc. No. 176.

making a fresh resolve, but has had to promise his father not to do anything without him. We are therefore leaving on the 16th for Sigmaringen
where the Father arrives on the 17th, and I hope then to get hold of
Arnold's[1] official letter to Schröder,[2] in which, on the basis of the latest
news reaching him, he now in advance asks permission to accept. If now
they definitely want not to do so for the time being, I will in any case
all the same insist on their fixing the date for acceptance as early as
possible.

By the time I have achieved that, Bock[3] and Braun[4] will doubtless
have arrived. I would of course like to acquaint them of the results of my
negotiations, as well as of other views of which they are unaware, before
they go to see Arnold[5] and before I take the letter to Schröder.[6] That is
why I at once telegraphed Y.E. asking that they should if still possible
receive word from Berlin asking them to await me in Munich at the
Hotel of the Four Seasons. If they can no longer be reached by telegraph
and are on the way to Reichenhall it will perhaps not matter. By their
latest news they will not manage to achieve an earlier date of acceptance.

I must add that Arnold[7] wanted not to receive anyone at Reichenhall.
I told him that Bock and Braun[8] were probably coming, which annoyed
him much. I received Schmidt's[9] telegram *after* the dispatch of my own
first telegram.[10]

I propose to call Sigmaringen Schwarzburg. Now that, as I have
already mentioned, what is at issue is no longer acceptance but only
postponement of the voting day which inconveniences Arnold[11] so much,
I respectfully venture to add to the code: remittance on . .th day=he
desires election not to take place before . .th day. Against the 5 thousand
cigars[12] he raised no further objection, though perhaps Werner[13]
will.

With highest esteem
Yours obediently

Max[14]

[1] Marginal note: "Hereditary Prince."
[2] Marginal note: "H.M. the King."
[3] Marginal note: " Salazar."
[4] Marginal note: "Bucher."
[5] Marginal note: "Hereditary Prince."
[6] Marginal note: "His Majesty, the King."
[7] Marginal note: "Hereditary Prince."
[8] Marginal note: "Salazar and Bucher."
[9] Marginal note: "Thile."
[10] See Docs. Nos. 183, 184.
[11] Marginal note: "Hereditary Prince."
[12] Marginal note: "appanage."
[13] Marginal note: "Prince of Hohenz[ollern]. Father."
[14] Marginal note: "Versen."

187. *Thile to Versen*

(Telegram en clair)[1] [German]   [16 June, 1870]

MAX VON VERSEN,
    Reichenhall.
    if gone away, Munich, Hotel 4 Seasons.
Friends[2] on the way, no longer possible to reach them with the news.
                               SCHMIDT[3]

188. *Versen to Thile*

(Telegram en clair) [German]
                    Sigmaringen, 17.6.1870. 5.13 p.m.
                    Delayed by breakdown. pr. 18.6.1870

Please wire here when our friends will probably be arriving at Reichenhall. Letter follows.[4]

                                    MAX

189. *Versen to Thile*

(Original) [German]   Sigmaringen, 17 June, 1870

Y.E.,
    I beg to report that Werner[5] has read a dispatch in the press here that the Cortes were prorogued the day before yesterday.
    Arnold[6] will now not send off the necessary letter to Schröder[7] until Bock and Braun[8] are here, I having held out the prospect of their coming.
    In order to produce a telegram of the latest date I have just telegraphed Schmidt[9] for news when the two will arrive at Reichenhall.[10] At Reichenhall they will find awaiting them a letter from me together with the request at Arnold's[11] house, to follow on here immediately.

[1] Marginal note by Roland: "Dispatched by me 16 June, 11.20. Roland."
[2] "Friends"=Bock and Braun, i.e. Salazar and Bucher, whose arrival at Reichenhall Thile announced by telegram on 15 June (see Doc. No. 183).
[3] Schmidt=Thile (see Doc. No. 180, note).
[4] See Doc. No. 189.
[5] Marginal note: "Hohenzollern—Father."
[6] Marginal note: "Hereditary Prince."
[7] Marginal note: "H.M. the King."
[8] Marginal note: "Salazar and Bucher."
[9] Marginal note: "H. v. Thile."
[10] See Doc. No. 188.
[11] Marginal note: "Hereditary Prince."

Werner[1] has raised no new difficulties and agrees to the terms but wants the election to be made public only in three months' time though the preliminary semi-official steps might be taken at once, for which reason Arnold[2] is to send the agreed letter to Schröder[3] as soon as everything has been settled with Bock.[4]

Had there not been the telegram about the proroguing of the Cortes then the parcel would have gone off at once to Leipzig.[5]

With highest esteem

Yours obediently

MAX V. VERSEN

190. *Thile to Versen*

(Telegram en clair) [German]   Berlin, 18 June, 1870[6]

The friends intended to leave on the 14th for Reichenhall.

SCHMIDT[7]

191. *Thile to Count von Bismarck*

(Original)[8] [German]   Berlin, 19 June, 1870

HONOURED CHIEF,

I have for some days refrained from troubling Y.E. with enclosures, but am obliged to trouble you today. Of the annexed items from Spain Canitz's apologia[9] came with the returning courier, who otherwise brought only a short note from Bucher to say that, after Salazar's meeting with the Hereditary Prince, which by now may very likely have taken place, he, Bucher, will at once come to Berlin, or alternatively to Varzin. Bernhardi's prophecies about Catalonia[10] seem to me rather fanciful.

The pseudonyms in Versen's letter[11] to me are based on a code[12] arranged between us.

Now I must report the following: a week ago the King said to me that

---

[1] Marginal note: "Hohenzollern—Father."
[2] Marginal note: "Hereditary Prince."
[3] Marginal note: "His Majesty."
[4] Marginal note: "Salazar."
[5] Marginal note: "then the Prince would at once have approached His Majesty."
[6] Marginal note by Roland: "Sent off by me 18.6. 12.35. Roland.'
[7] Schmidt=Thile (see Doc. No. 180, note).
[8] Marginal note by Roland: "received from His Highness in January 1877 for the files. Roland."
[9] See Doc. No. 181.
[10] See Doc. No. 160.
[11] See Doc. No. 189.
[12] See Doc. No. 180, note.

he was unpleasantly surprised by the revival of the question of the Spanish throne. Luckily H.M. asked me no questions about the details which would have put me in an awkward position.

Yesterday at the last submission before his departure, H.M. reverted more fully to the matter and expressed himself as follows: "the Crown Prince had told him, or rather '*let slip*', that Bucher had gone off to Spain again, and that Versen, whose return to Posen had long since been commanded by H.M., was travelling about again with orders from Your Excellency, that Salazar was coming again, etc.; that H.M. had known nothing of all this and that it was very extraordinary that this sort of thing was going on without his authorization.

H.M.'s standpoint in the whole affair was, need he say, unchanged. He would never command nor even desire that a Hohenzollern Prince should accept the Spanish crown, though if he felt a definite "vocation" for it, H.M. would not stand in his way. In any case nothing was to be done in the matter behind H.M.'s back and I am to write Your Excellency that the King desires to be informed of *everything that Salazar brings either by word of mouth or in writing*[1] before any action is taken."[2]

All this the King said not without a certain asperity, though at once adding that everything must be avoided that might put Your Excellency out of humour or "irritate your nerves".[3] I think that in the fulfilment of the above wishes His Majesty will rest content with fairly general indications, so that the course of negotiations need not thereby be interrupted. I await in due course Your Excellency's instructions in the matter.

For the sake of security I am sending the present letter by the Chancellery porter.

Your most obedient

THILE[4]

192. *Versen to Count von Bismarck*

(Original) [German]   Sigmaringen, 19 June, 1870

HONOURED SIR,
    Most Honourable Chancellor of the North German Confederation, Minister-President and Major-General.
    In spite of the course of treatment at the spa I venture to report the

---

[1] Marginal note by Bismarck: "that beats anything!"
[2] Marginal note by Bismarck: "so H.M. wants the affair treated *with official Royal interference*?!"
[3] Marginal note by Bismarck: "and that looks like Royal Prussian interference!"
[4] Marginal note by Bismarck: "The whole affair is only possible if it remains the limited concern of the Hohenzollern Princes, it must not turn into a Prussian concern, the King must be able to say without lying: I know nothing about it."

following to Your Excellency as it is, by way of exception, a piece of good news:

On receipt of the telegrams I travelled through to Reichenhall without stopping, getting there on the morning of the 14th. The Hereditary Prince did not arrive until noon on the 15th. He had, however, promised his father not to do anything without him and for many reasons definitely wanted the election postponed until the autumn, he remaining unmolested by it till then. I finally obtained his consent and on the 16th we made the journey to Sigmaringen where on the 17th the Prince arrived at the same time as ourselves. Unfortunately the Prince had seen in the newspapers a later telegram from Madrid saying that the Cortes had been prorogued and he thus thought that time had once more been gained. In the end I managed to obtain the letter from the Hereditary Prince in which he asked His Majesty's permission to accept "in conformity with the family law". It had just been drafted when Herr Bucher arrived with M. Salazar. They described the erroneous press telegram as a French intrigue and represented the situation in Madrid once more as so critical that this was positively the last moment, otherwise Archduke Salvador was being thought of, on whose behalf the French and Austrian Ministers in Madrid were intriguing. Thereupon father and son decided on acceptance.

Herr Bucher has just started off direct to His Majesty with the Hereditary Prince's letter and one from Prince Karl Anton, and, as no time was to be lost, also bearing verbal messages, and will from Ems telegraph to us here that, as may of course be presumed, His Majesty has "nothing against it".

M. Salazar is for the present remaining here, having sent the news to Madrid by telegraph in cipher, and will leave for Madrid with the Hereditary Prince's already drafted letter of acceptance to Marshal Prim as soon as His Majesty's telegram reaches here, as it must by Wednesday. According to M. Salazar's rough calculation the election will take place on 8 July and the appropriate delegation thereupon make the journey to Sigmaringen.

It was luck that the Princess is at the spa and is not allowed to be told anything during the treatment. Enclosed I am sending with my respects a letter from the Prince of Hohenzollern.[1] Now my mission is ended I return to Posen without delay and remain

With highest esteem

Your Excellency's most obedient

v. Versen

Major on General Staff of V Army Corps

P.S. M. Salazar has just sent along yet another note.[2]

[1] See Doc. No. 193.
[2] See Doc. No. 194.

193. *Prince Karl Anton of Hohenzollern to Count von Bismarck*

(Original) [German]   Sigmaringen, 19 June, 1870

YOUR EXCELLENCY,

I hasten to inform you with my respects that the Hereditary Prince, my son, has today sent the declaration to His Majesty the King that he will henceforward be resolved to accept the call to the Spanish throne.

According to the provisions and the express wording of our Family Law the approval of His Majesty, the Supreme Head of the whole family, is necessary for this step, and in view of the extreme urgency of the matter His Majesty has been humbly asked by us to have either "Agreed" or "Not agreed" telegraphed back in reply. In so doing His Majesty will only be carrying out the responsibilities laid down in the Family Law according to which the King has either to grant or to withhold His Royal approval of a decision *once it has been made.*

This great event will, accordingly, shortly be set in motion and, together with my son, I indulge in the hope that, in consideration of the heavy sacrifice we are making, Your Excellency will steer it into tranquil waters.

With my best wishes for the restoration of your health and the assurance of my highest esteem, I have the honour to be

Your Excellency's most devoted servant
PRINCE OF HOHENZOLLERN

194. *Salazar to Count von Bismarck*

(Original) [French]   Sigmaringen, 19 June, 1870

H.E. Count von Bismarck is asked to be so kind as to mention in his reply to the paragraph in Marshal Prim's letter referring to M. Gama[1] that the latter in his conduct of the long and difficult negotiations has not proved unworthy of the high trust placed in him by the Spanish Government in entrusting such a delicate mission to him.

Only after a *tête à tête* conversation will Count von Bismarck be able to form an idea of the immense difficulties which have had to be overcome in order to attain this so greatly desired result.

[1] See Doc. No. 2.

195. *Prince Leopold of Hohenzollern to Marshal Prim*

(Draft of a letter in Bucher's hand) [French]

Sigmaringen, — June, 1870

Monsieur le Maréchal,

Conscientious self-examination in view of a task as noble as it is onerous, and private obstacles, worthy to be taken into consideration, have prevented me till now from replying to the letter of 17 February[1] which Y.E. with the authorization of the Government of His Highness the Regent was so good as to address to me through the medium of M. de S[alazar] et M[azarredo].

Today I am in a position to tell you that I will accept the crown of Spain if the vote of the Constituent Cortes proves that the majority of the country, rejecting all other dynastic solution, wills by my election to put an end to a state of things the prolonging of which would be incompatible with the paramount interests of Spain and not without danger for the whole of Europe. I would accept it, proud of so generous a trust and in the hope that God would aid my sincere endeavours to restore to your country the conditions for steady and peaceful progress laid down by the Constitution of 1869. Be so good, *M. le Marquis*, as to make this letter known to the Government of His Highness, the Regent of the Kingdom of Spain.

I cannot end this letter without expressing my lively sympathy for the attitude of firmness and abnegation so long maintained by you in the face of an extremely difficult and delicate situation.

196. *Count von Bismarck to Marshal Prim*

(Draft of a letter in Bucher's hand)[2] [French]   Varzin, June, 1870

Monsieur le Maréchal,

Great as is the length of time which has gone by since the receipt of the letter dated 17 February[3] which Your Excellency kindly wrote me, no less great is the satisfaction I feel in informing you that it today only depends on the Cortes vote for the plan of which your letter informed me to be put into effect. His Highness Prince Leopold of Hohenzollern will

---

[1] See Doc. No. 3.

[2] Marginal note by Bucher: "to H.E. Marshal Prim, Marquis de los Castillejos, President of the Council of Ministers. He is better known under the name of Count de Reus, but to us as Marquis d[e] l[os] C[astillejos], a Grandee of Spain." The above draft of a letter was never sent; see Doc. No. 209, note (6), also Doc. No. 260.

[3] See Doc. No. 2.

no doubt have informed you already that he is ready to respond to the desire of the Spanish nation expressed by the votes of its representatives. It is not for me to appraise the reasons which the Prince has been obliged to weigh or the obstacles which have had to be removed before he arrived at the decision to accept the lustre and the burden of a crown. Suffice it to say that those reasons were entirely personal, those obstacles entirely of a private nature. Such mature reflection, such careful clearing of the ground are but an additional guarantee that under the reign of Prince Leopold Spain will enjoy a well-being to which so long a series of misfortunes has been unceasingly detrimental.

I seize

197. *Versen to Thile*

(Telegram en clair) [German] Ulm, 20.6.1870. 10.5. a.m.

Parcel just going off to Leipzig.

MAX[1]

198. *Thile to Count von Bismarck*

(Telegram. Draft for cipher) [German] 21.6.1870. 11.50 a.m.

Bucher is at Ems, Versen just arrived here. Shall the latter go to Varzin?

TH[ILE]

199. *Thile to Baron von Canitz, Prussian Minister at Madrid*

(Telegram. Draft for cipher in Salazar's hand) [French]
Berlin, 21 June, 1870. 1.15 p.m.

Telegrams which Herr von Canitz is requested to dispatch to their destinations dated: "Tuesday, 21st, Sigmaringen Castle."
1. Marshal Prim
      I confirm telegram re Prince's acceptance.
2. M. Ruiz Zorrilla, President of the Cortes
      I confirm telegram of the day before yesterday: "Carlists conspiring again, keep a watch on Deputy No. 3." Seeing you again about the 26th.

[1] Marginal note: "Means: The Prince is immediately approaching His Majesty. v. Versen."

3. Anastasio Alonso, 34 Hortaleza, Madrid.
Health perfect. Returning soon.
(signed) GAMA

THI[LE][1]

200 *Abeken to Thile*

(Telegram. Decipher) [German] Ems, 21 June, 1870. 2.1 p.m.
arrived 2.44 p.m.

No. 1

For *immediate* submission to Herr von Thile.

With His Majesty's assent I request you to telegraph registered to Baron von Canitz: [French] "Inform Marshal Prim on Bucher's part Salazar is now able to send him prearranged telegram."

[signed] ABEKEN[2]

---

[1] The following is the decipher of this telegram preserved by the Madrid Legation:
"Cipher telegram Berlin, 21 June, 1870. 1 o'clock.
Madrid, 21 ditto. 5 o'clock.
A 2880

To the North German Minister, Madrid.

Telegrams which Herr von Canitz is requested to dispatch to their destinations dated, Tuesday twenty-first, Sigmaringen Castle.

Firstly Tuesday Prim.
  I confirm telegram re Prince's acceptance.
Secondly
  M. Ruiz Zorrilla, President of the Cortes.
  I confirm telegram of day before yesterday: 'Carlists conspiring again, keep watch on deputies numbers three', seeing you again about the ninth. (2776) [This cipher group between brackets has later been struck out.]
Thirdly
  Anastasio Alonso, thirty four Hortaleza—Madrid.
  Health perfect. Returning soon.
    (Signed)—GAMA THILE."

The reader will not have failed to note that the expression *seeing you again about the 26th* has been deciphered at Madrid as *seeing you again about the 9th*. It will become clear later what influence this variant had on the course of events.

Hesselbarth publishes the following text on the subject of this incident: "Intermezzo. On 20 June at 10 p.m. there arrived a telegram in cipher from Salazar to Zorrilla in which there were groups which seemed to mean: 'the 9th'. At least they were thus deciphered and forwarded. Who was to blame? The telegraphists of the North? No, because a check was made which proved that the groups arrived in France correct! Was it the telegraphists here or the deciphering clerks? Anything is probable. The one certainty is that the vote did not take place. If things had not happened thus, the gentleman would have been accepted and would have taken up his position after the war." (*Drei psychologische Fragen*, p. 33.)

[2] In conformity to these instructions Thile sent Canitz a telegram dispatched that same day at 8.50 p.m.

201. *Count von Bismarck to Thile*

(Telegram. Decipher) [German]

Varzin, 21 June, 1870. 2.30 p.m.
arrived 3.5 [p.m.]

Better not.[1] I do not wish to have anything more to do with it and have notified the King thereof through Abeken. What is Bucher doing in Ems? Privy Counsellor Abeken must show Bucher my yesterday's letter[2] before making further use of its content.

BISMARCK

202. *Thile to Abeken*

(Telegram. Draft for cipher) [German]

B[erlin], 21 June, 1870. 8 p.m.

The Minister-President wishes you to show Bucher his yesterday's letter[3] before you make further use of its contents.

THILE

203. *The King of Prussia to Prince Leopold of Hohenzollern*

(Copy in the hand of Prince Karl Anton of Hohenzollern) [German]

[The text of this letter has been already published by Fester, *Briefe*, No. 231, following Zingeler, *Karl Anton*, p. 246. As the Fester-Zingeler text is somewhat corrupt, the King of Prussia's letter is here published *in extenso*, the words omitted in the earlier publications being italicized.]

Ems, 21 June, 1870

MY DEAR COUSIN,

I have read your letter of the 19th inst.[4] not without deep emotion.

You have taken a decision which you previously, and in my opinion rightly, with full consciousness refused to entertain. *Now you regard the political views put forward in the winter of this year by Minister Count Bismarck as justified and incontrovertible from the statesman's point of view. Had that been my own view originally I should not so decidedly have approved of your rejection at that time of the Spanish crown.*

---

[1] See Doc. No. 198.
[2] This letter is not in the files relating to the Hohenzollern candidature.
[3] Cf. Doc. No. 201.
[4] Not contained in the files of the *Auswärtiges Amt*.

I still today abide by my pronouncement of that time, namely that I cannot encourage or command any member of my Hohenzollern House to undertake so great a hazard unless I receive assurance of an inward persuasion, a vocation, a conviction imposed by fate! Your letter now shows me that after mature consideration you have recognized this vocation and feel no longer able to resist the urgent appeal to accept that crown. Consequently in accordance with that pronouncement I cannot but give my consent though with a very heavy heart!—

The future alone can tell us whether we have done the will of God! May that be so! Then some day, perhaps long after I am no more, those who take my place may bless the hour when this hazardous resolve came to fruition.

If the result in Madrid is favourable then go in God's name whither your fate seems to beckon you.

My feelings will go with you and yours.

Your faithful cousin
William R[EX]

204. *The King of Prussia to Prince Karl Anton of Hohenzollern*

(Copy in Bucher's hand)[1] [German]   Ems, 21 June, 1870

My fateful telegram of today will already be in your hands! After our talk in Giessen I was far from thinking that once again, as in the winter of this year, the knife would be held to our throats and that—not merely in a few days, which at that time proved to be an exaggeration—but now actually in a matter of hours the same procedure would be adopted after your having so firmly ruled that not until after a recasting of our Family Law, i.e. in three months at the earliest, could there be any more question of the affair. A few days ago Prim himself publicly announced this time-limit *before* which he would not be able to make any statement to the Cortes on the subject of a candidate for the throne. This seemed to me a proof that he had acquiesced in the statement made by you both in this sense. That Bucher has been on a new mission to Madrid I only learnt from my son a few days ago, the Minister having said nothing about it to me. The report made on this mission together with the actual arrival a second time of the Spanish negotiator has, I see, resulted with you and your son in a complete reversal of your previous views.

As I told you in Giessen, after I had officially declined acceptance of the crown in the name of your two sons—as far as in *secret* negotiations

---

[1] Marginal note: "Copia Copiae." Marginal note by Bismarck: "A[uswärtiges] A[mt]. secr[eta]." Only a few lines of this letter have been published by Fester, *Briefe*, No. 232, following Zingeler, p. 247.

there can be any question of *officially*—I did not, and could not without utterly compromising myself, take any initiative to reopen them. It is now apparent that my withdrawal has in fact been quickly exploited and that Count Bismarck's views (which last winter were weighed by us but not regarded either by you or your son Leopold as turning the scales in favour of acceptance of the throne or by me as a reason for persuasion or an actual command) have now according to your son's letter and your own statements to me so gained the upper hand that the fateful decision has already been taken by you both, only my assent still being needed! I have given it with a heavy heart—for my opinion has been from the beginning until today the same, namely that I would only with reluctance see a member of the House of Hohenzollern run a risk which cannot as far as can humanly be judged turn out to his advantage. My pronouncement that I could only *give my assent* if one of your sons feels an *inner vocation* compelling him to obey the *call of fate* still remains irrevocably firm on my part today. Now that the letters of both of you bring me proof that you have harkened to this call of fate I can, in conformity with my pronouncement, give my assent! May God's way and will be other than, as I said above, I anticipate as being humanly to be expected, and may neither of you regret a step which previously and, in my opinion, with good conscience and after repeated and ample consideration, you both rejected!

Your son writes me that he will only accept the crown on terms and with provisos. As he did not specify these, Bucher has added the information that what was to be understood thereby was the Civil List and the position as regards his fortune, which according to a further statement by him had been shown by Prim on the basis of documents to be very advantageous.[1] If under those terms, etc., other items are included I expect a further communication on the point.

It is very painful to me to be unable to give my assent joyfully in so important a matter. We will leave everything in God's hands, and some day, even if long hence when I am no longer here to see it, time will show whether we have done *His Will*.

With deep emotion

Your faithful friend and cousin

(signed) William.

[1] Marginal note by Bucher: "I said to H.M.:
  1. The King's own fortune remains by law his private fortune not in any way to be included under the Civil List.
  2. The Civil List will amount to at least 5 million francs, excluding special provision for the Prince of Asturias.
  3. To the Crown are assigned under the law the palace in Madrid, the Alcazar in Seville, Aranjuez, La Granja, the Pardo, the Buen Retiro, the latter of which because of the building plots attached to it promises to become a profitable possession.—Bucher."

205. *General von Schweinitz, Prussian Minister at Vienna, to Thile*

(Copy. Excerpt) [German]   Vienna, 21 June, 1870
A 1931. (No. 56. Ems)

I can tell Your Excellency in confidence that at the State Chancellery
a tender feeling for us begins to stir; it manifests itself in personal contacts,
in the press, in the shops, especially in cases of frontier trespass and the
Elbe tariff convention.

In order not to nip the opening bud before it blooms or even fruits I
venture respectfully to suggest to Your Excellency that you should be so
kind as to take measures in order that the anniversary of Sadowa on
3 July shall not be commemorated by too ostentatious festivities nor
by paeans of victory in the press.

Of course the regiments cannot be forbidden to celebrate the glorious
day, but it should be possible to keep well within bounds those features of
such commemoration festivities which cause pain in Austria.

206. *Thile to Count von Bismarck*

(Telegram. Draft for cipher) [German]
Berlin, 22 June, 1870 [8 a.m.]

Instruction in yesterday's telegram[1] immediately executed. Why
Bucher has gone to Ems I do not know.   Th[ILE][2]

207. *Bucher to Count von Bismarck*

(Telegram. Draft for cipher) [German]
Berlin, 22 June, 1870. dispatched 10.30 a.m.

Just back. Royal assent obtained yesterday at Ems. Communications
delivered. Report follows today.   BUCHER

208. *Thile to Count von Bismarck*

(Telegram en clair) [German]
Berlin, 22 June, 1870. dispatched 3.20 p.m.

Canitz asking for long leave. May I recommend this to His Majesty?[3]
THILE

[1] See Doc. No. 201.
[2] Marginal note by Thile: "to be sent to the telegraph office at 8 a.m. on *22* June."
[3] Marginal note by Bismarck: "not yet."

209. *Bucher to Count von Bismarck*

(Original)[1] [German]   Berlin, 22 June [1870.] a.m.

I hasten respectfully to inform Your Excellency that I returned here via Reichenhall, Sigmaringen and Ems. At Ems at an audience lasting an hour and a quarter I obtained, not without difficulty, His Majesty's assent to acceptance of the crown. The King promised to telegraph "Agreed" immediately to Sigmaringen where father and son are together and Salazar awaits the answer and has permitted me to telegraph to Marshal Prim via Herr von Canitz that everything is in order.[2] On my calculation election day will be fixed for about 3 July. By then Marshal Prim, being unable to shake off an in my opinion baseless anxiety about complications with France, hopes to receive a full-length reply from Your Excellency to his letter of 17 February,[3] taking the line that it is not a question of a Prussian interest, a performance of a Prussian duty, but a Spanish interest and a personal act on the part of the Hereditary Prince; that no harm to the balance of power in Europe will result. I will, if possible, enclose with this report Prim's letter[3] and a draft for a reply on those lines.[4] As Castilian pride has been wounded by the long delay and the absence of any answer from the Hereditary Prince, a very friendly tone would have a good effect. In agreement with Salazar I drafted the Hereditary Prince's letter of acceptance to Prim and left it at Sigmaringen[5] as there was no time to get in touch with Your Excellency. I append the, alas, very rough draft.[5] I have informed H.R.H. the Crown Prince of the gratifying result.

BUCHER[6]

210. *Abeken to Count von Bismarck*

(Original)[7] [German]   Ems, 22 June, 1870. noon

YOUR EXCELLENCY,

I have just received your kind and gracious letter of the 20th inst.,[8] and

---

[1] Marginal note by Bismarck: "A[uswärtiges] A[mt]. secr[eta]."

[2] See Doc. No. 200.   [3] See Doc. No. 2.

[4] See Doc. No. 196.   [5] See Doc. No. 195.

[6] Marginal note by Bismarck: "I do not regard it as opportune to allow 'Royal Government' participation in the negotiations to come into being, still less become publicly known. The whole affair must officially remain one transacted between Spain and the Hereditary Prince without my name ever being mentioned. I have already answered Prim confidentially and do not intend to write more, certainly not to produce any sort of official document of an international character."

[7] Marginal note by Roland: "Received from His Highness in January 1877 for the files. Roland." Cf. Fester, *Briefe*, No. 233.

[8] This letter is not in the files relating to the Hohenzollern candidature. (See Doc. No. 201.)

I would like to use the short time before the post leaves to express my heartfelt thanks for your kindness and confidence, and add the assurance that its contents, of which I shall be able to make appropriate use only at the submission of tomorrow, will, to judge by my experience up to the present, fall on good ground well prepared by Herr Bucher's report. The telegraphed instruction to show the letter first to Bucher[1] reached me unfortunately only after his departure; but all that he has reported to His Majesty was so entirely in harmony with it that I can hardly feel regret. After Bucher's departure and after his telegram: Agreed—had really gone off to the Prince of Hohenzollern, His Majesty once again thoroughly talked the matter over with me, without any real trace of resentment— at most a little against the Hohenzollern Highnesses because of their shilly-shallying and their present eagerness in the matter; all of which He will no doubt have expressed in the letter to the Prince going off today to Sigmaringen by express post messenger. On the question itself He reiterated that it ran counter to His own personal views but that He would not take the responsibility of vetoing it. He recognized also that the revival of the affair originated in Spain; this is so completely confirmed by Your Excellency's lucid account that I may already beg you to feel no further concern on the score of His Majesty's resentment, He having taken comfort in the thought, uttered twice yesterday, that the Hereditary Prince, as having fought in the victorious campaign of 1866, would be acceptable to the Spanish army as well.

I will not inflict more to read on Your Excellency especially as Bucher will no doubt be making a personal report to you. When I have made my report to His Majesty I trust I may be allowed to write again; now I only add that Herr von Arnim's agreement to your intentions is also not likely to be a difficult matter.

That I write my best and most heartfelt wishes *in ink* for the success of your draughts of medicinal water will, I trust, not poison them; apart from this I will endeavour here and in Berlin to let the ink dry up as much as possible.

Most respectfully I remain
Your Excellency's very obedient

ABEKEN

211. *Count von Bismarck to Thile*

(Telegram en clair) [German]   Varzin, 23.6.1870. 11.30 a.m.

Bucher wants me now to answer the letter of 17 February.[2] As far as I know I answered it long ago and the draft must now be preserved in the

---

[1] See Doc. No. 201.   [2] See Doc. No. 2.

files;[1] if Bucher could come here with them that would be the easiest way to clear the matter up.

BISMARCK

212. *Salazar to Thile*

(Telegram en clair) [French]   Stockach, 23.6.[1870.] 3.30 p.m.

Shall arrive at my destination Monday with letter.[2] Hope Doctor will be calm.

ERQUELINE

213. *Prince Karl Anton of Hohenzollern to Abeken*

(Original) [German]   Sigmaringen, 23 June, '70
pr. B[erlin] 24.6.70

DEAR SIR,

I shall be greatly obliged if you will see that the enclosed letter reaches Count Bismarck.[3]

I would also beg you to be so very kind as to let me have cognizance of any telegrams from Madrid which in 8-10 days from now may be brought to the knowledge of H.M. the King in order that we may make our arrangements accordingly in connexion with a variety of matters.

With highest respect and devotion
PRINCE OF HOHENZOLLERN

214. *Prince Karl Anton of Hohenzollern to Count von Bismarck*

(Original)[4] [German]   Sigmaringen, 23 June, 1870

YOUR EXCELLENCY,

I should like briefly to let you know that the die has been cast in the great affair. Today the Hereditary Prince's letter of acceptance went off to Marshal Prim by Don Salazar.

I have given it a most careful revision and sent a copy to His Majesty the King at Ems.

His Majesty will no doubt have it put in the files.

---

[1] See Doc. No. 143.
[2] Marginal note by Bucher: "from Prince Leopold to Marshal Prim."
[3] See Doc. No. 214.
[4] Marginal note by Bismarck: "A[uswärtiges] A[mt]. secr[eta]."

There only remains for me to make a most urgent plea for your powerful support both at home and abroad—for we need encouraging not dispiriting . . .[1] in this great venture.

May the Carlsbad cure have all the good effects at Varzin that I wish from the bottom of my heart!

With highest esteem

Your Excellency's faithfully devoted

HOHENZOLLERN

215. *Baron von Canitz, Prussian Minister at Madrid, to Count von Bismarck*

(Telegram.[2] Decipher) [German]   Madrid, 24 June, 1870. 3.30 p.m.

arr. 25 June. 1.15 a.m.

A 1939. pr. 25 June, 1870

The Cortes have been prorogued until 1 November. Only 130 deputies were still present.

[signed] CANITZ[3]

216. *Abeken to Count von Bismarck*

(Original)[4] [German]   Ems, 24 June, 1870

YOUR EXCELLENCY,

I trust you will not regard it as an unfairness to the excellent curative waters if I make one more brief report on the submission made to H.M. as a result of your letter,[5] hoping that nothing further from your side at least will render it nugatory.

I did, of course, make literal use of Your Excellency's words and, as I expected, His Majesty gave his first attention to them. He remarked that He would write to Your Excellency Himself; as, however, He did not know how soon He would get round to it, I was for the time being to tell you the following:

In the matter itself He remained of the opinion He had always expressed to Your Excellency and the Prince of Hohenzollern; had He shared

---

[1] Word illegible.

[2] Marginal note by Bismarck: "A[uswärtiges] A[mt]."

[3] Marginal note by Bismarck: "For the next 2 or 3 weeks I cannot recommend a grant of leave to the Minister at Madrid. If after then he renews his request, steps are to be taken at the same time to find a suitable deputy. V[arzin] 27 June, 1870. v. B[ismarck]."

[4] Marginal note by Roland: "received in January, 1877 from His Highness for the files. Roland."

[5] Refers to the letter of 20 June which is not in the files. See Doc. No. 210, note.

your opinion, He would Himself have had to advise acceptance, nay even command it, which He was unable to do. However, as things have turned out, He could not on the other hand refuse His assent. *He entirely acquitted Your Excellency* of having acted behind His back; your letter to Prim which you showed Him after its dispatch was exactly what it should be, and He has never doubted that Bucher had no verbal instructions of a different kind. He also appreciated your reasons for sending such a personal mission. Had Your Excellency consulted Him beforehand He would have pronounced against the choice of Bucher as being so personally in favour of the venture—though He found no fault with him for that—that this could not fail to have its influence on Madrid and was eagerly seized upon for a renewal of contact; on the other hand He did not fail to understand that it would have been difficult to bring yet another person into this delicate matter.

His Majesty gave this message without a trace of displeasure either towards Your Excellency or towards Bucher, only jokingly remarking that both Bucher and Versen had come back from Madrid with their heads turned [*benebelt*].

When I ventured to remark that, as His Majesty had wished, Your Excellency had successfully cleared His Majesty entirely of all responsibility for influencing the Hereditary Prince's decision, leaving Him only to decide the question whether He would *veto* the matter, He observed: "Yes, so long as it is known how it all came about and what My attitude at the beginning was! But the whole blame will be laid on Me and My schemes!"

Slight annoyance was in evidence only against their Hohenzollern Highnesses because of their shilly-shallying and their behaviour, which He still does not understand. His Majesty talked freely to me about His discussions with Your Excellency in Ems and then with the Prince of Hohenzollern, repeatedly remarking that "there was a *point on which He was still in the dark*, namely how Your Excellency already knew at Ems that the Prince and the Hereditary Prince felt willing again, seeing that you did not then know of their letters to the Crown Prince,[1] as the latter had told him." I could only remark that the Prince must have told Your Excellency directly, adding that to my knowledge Herr von Thile, too, had the definite impression that the Prince at bottom felt willing and only wished to be given the command.

As I write there comes the post office official back from taking His Majesty's letters to Sigmaringen bringing the letters of reply for His Majesty, and for me a line from the Prince asking me to forward the unaddressed enclosure to Your Excellency, as I herewith do.[2]

[1] See Doc. No. 152, the Hereditary Prince's letter to the Crown Prince. See also Appendix on the Sigmaringen Archives.
[2] See Doc. No. 214.

In the matter of the Rome affair I also made a submission yesterday, reading out Y.E.'s comments. His Majesty fully agreed with them and commanded that Herr von Arnim should be instructed accordingly— only desiring that he be expressly told not to attend the ceremony in an official capacity and otherwise to abstain from all demonstration.

Craving your indulgence and the continuance of your favour and with the best, most heartfelt wishes for your cure I respectfully remain

Your Excellency's most obedient

ABEKEN

217. *Queen Isabella of Bourbon to the Tsar of Russia*

(Telegram. Copy)[1] [French]

[Dispatched from Paris. Reached Weimar via St Petersburg]
26.6.1870. 8.10 a.m.

With lively gratitude for the kindnesses and regard ever shown me by your imperial majesty I hasten to inform you of the act whereby I yesterday abdicated the crown of Spain in favour of my well-beloved son, the Prince of Asturias. I offer my prayers for the happiness of your majesty and all the imperial family.

ISABELLA

218. *Abeken to Count von Bismarck*

(Copy)[2] [German]   Ems, 26 June, 1870. ad A 1931

His Majesty the King graciously remarked when I was making my report yesterday:

He certainly wishes to avoid everything that might wound Austrian feelings. This He showed last year in not holding any celebrations on 3 July. This year again no anniversary will be kept by the Sovereign or the Army leaders or by the Government. This seems a token of consideration which will receive recognition by Vienna. But in the individual service branches the ceremony cannot be forbidden or circumscribed; it would be impossible to treat the army like that. Let the press, as far as it is dependent on the Government, be warned against wounding utterances.

H.M. desires that H.E. the Secretary of State shall write confidentially in this sense to the Prussian Minister, Herr von Schweinitz, requesting him

[1] Marginal note by Bucher: "Ad acta secreta [For the secret files]. B[ucher]."
[2] Marginal note by Abeken: "Copy of report sent to Berlin. For the files at [two words illegible] Ems. A[beke]n Ems, 27.6.70." Marginal note by Bucher: "For the files. B[uche]r. 16.7.—Th[ile]."

if he comes across any signs of sensitiveness to point out the consideration shown by *His Majesty himself* and His Government and the impossibility of forbidding the individual celebrations. (signed) ABEKEN

219. *Crown Prince Frederick William to Count von Bismarck*

(Original) [German]   Potsdam, 27.6.70

The Prince of Hohenzollern has just informed me of the latest happenings, and since Major von Versen had already prepared me for the probability of acceptance there exists no more doubt that the Hereditary Prince will go to Spain.

Thus that affair may be regarded as settled and done with, and the parties concerned have managed to come to terms with all the difficulties of the situation. Only a letter in His Majesty's own hand has had a depressing effect on the Prince, who, although it arrived after the acceptance had gone off to Madrid, yet feels that H.M. does not contemplate the venture with a joyous heart. For this reason the Prince asks me to let you see this letter of H.M.'s, a copy of which I enclose,[1] in the hope that you will feel all the more obliged to side with his family as it may become a question of defending their Hohenzollern Highnesses against unmerited reproaches.

I would ask you to return the copy. For my youngest daughter's impending christening, which is to take place at the end of July, I wish to have Italian godparents, to which idea H.M. is quite agreeable. Whom would you advise? Shall I ask Victor Emanuel or the Crown Prince and Princess? All three are too many, the Crown Princess alone perhaps rather strange?

On 1 July I am, at His Majesty's wish, to welcome the Tsar of Russia at breakfast in Breslau.

Your
devoted
FREDERICK WILLIAM OF HOHENZOLLERN

220. *Salazar to Baron von Canitz, Prussian Minister at Madrid*

(Original) [French]   Tuesday, 28 [June, 1870]

MY DEAR BARON,

Here I am back again. There was a misunderstanding in the telegram addressed from Berlin to M. Zorrilla, President of the Cortes, and I shall be much obliged if you would send me a copy of it.[2]

---

[1] See Doc. No. 204.   [2] See Doc. No. 199.

It is the one that speaks at the beginning of the Carlists.

There only remain still a few matters on the periphery of the great
. . . thing.

Yours ever
E. DE SALAZAR Y MAZARREDO

---

221. *Salazar to Baron von Canitz, Prussian Minister at Madrid*

(Original) [French]   Tuesday, 28 [June, 1870]

MY DEAR BARON,

I have just received your letter and the President of the Cortes is right.
But how comes it that Berlin can have made the mistake? In my written
dispatch entrusted to Herr von Versen I had put "Seeing you again about
the *26th*".[1] When M. Zorrilla saw that I could only come on the 9th he
hastened to prorogue the Cortes, whereas if, as had been agreed, I put a
date earlier than 1 July the Cortes would have gone on somehow or other.
It is a most unfortunate mishap which we are trying to put right, but I
will ask you to verify by telegraph to Berlin whether I put the 26th or
whether I was so far mistaken as to put 9 instead of 26.

With my apologies, yours ever
E. DE SALAZAR Y MAZARREDO[2]

---

222. *Baron von Canitz, Prussian Minister at Madrid,*
to Count von Bismarck

(Telegram. Decipher)[3] [French]

Madrid, 28 June, 1870. 2.15 a.m. arr. 9 a.m.

Salazar who is back again here desires to know for his own satisfaction
whether in the telegram entrusted to Herr Versen and meant for M. Ruiz
Zorrilla[4] he had put "seeing you again about the 26th" or "Seeing you

---

[1] See Doc. No. 199.

[2] Cf. Hesselbarth: "(27) 28 June to Canitz. I have just received your letter. The
President of the Cortes is right. But how comes it that they can have made the mistake
at the other end? In my written dispatch delivered by Versen I had written 'Seeing you
again about the 26th'. When M. Zorrilla saw that I could only come on the 9th he
hastened the prorogation of the Cortes, whereas if, as had been agreed, I put a date earlier
than 1 July, the Cortes would have gone on somehow or other. It is a most unfortunate
mishap which we are trying to put right; all the same I will ask you to verify by telegraph
at the other end whether I had put the twenty sixth or whether I was so far mistaken as
to put 9 instead of 26. SALAZAR." (*Drei psychologische Fragen*, p. 33.)

[3] Marginal note by Thile "1 copy to Varzin. 29.6.—Dup[licate]."

[4] See Doc. No. 199.

again about the 9th" as was telegraphed from Berlin to Madrid. The error of date caused the prorogation of the Cortes[1] were adjourned before Salazar's return, whereas otherwise they would have gone on "somehow or other" as M. Salazar writes.

(signed) CANITZ

223. *Salazar to Baron von Canitz, Prussian Minister at Madrid*

(Original) [French]   Wednesday [29 June, 1870]

MY DEAR BARON,

Herewith another telegram beginning the new series.

Yours ever   E. DE SALAZAR

*   *   *

To HERR VON THILE.

Cabinet meeting will take place Granja after return Marshal who has gone for a rest Toledo mountains thinking I would arrive the 9th. I really had put *about the 26th* in my dispatch for President of Cortes given to Herr von Versen.[2] This regrettable mistake has caused prorogation. It was impossible to keep Cortes sitting any longer without revealing everything.

We will try to summon an *ad hoc* sitting, for in a few days it will be difficult to keep the secret. Please communicate Princes and Herr von Bismarck.

signed GAMA[3]

224. *Baron von Canitz, Prussian Minister at Madrid,*
to Count von Bismarck

(Telegram. Decipher)[4] [French]

Madrid, 29 June, 1870. 6.50 p.m.
arrived 30 June. 2.30 a.m.

To HERR VON THILE.

Cabinet meeting will take place Granja after return Marshal who has gone for a rest to Toledo mountains thinking I would arrive the 9th. I

---

[1] Marginal note: "which."   [2] See Doc. No. 199.

[3] Cf. Hesselbarth: "(28) 28 June to Bismarck. Cabinet meeting will take place at la Granja after return of Prim who has gone for a rest Toledo mountains thinking I would arrive 9 July. I really had put 'about the 26th' in my dispatch to Zorrilla via Versen. This mistake is regrettable and has caused prorogation. It was impossible to keep the Cortes sitting any longer without revealing everything. We will try to summon an *ad hoc* sitting, for in a few days it will be difficult to keep the secret. Please communicate to the caballero. SALAZAR MAZARREDO; EUSEBIO." (*Drei psychologische Fragen*, p. 34.)

[4] Marginal notes: "No. 8 Varzin. pr. 1 July—submitted Varzin, 2.7."

really had put the 26th in my dispatch for President of Cortes given to Herr von Versen.[1] This regrettable mistake has caused prorogation. It was impossible to keep them in session any longer without revealing everything. We will try to summon an *ad hoc* sitting for it will be difficult to keep the secret longer without revealing everything. Please communicate *Prince* and Count von Bismarck: signed GAMA

(signed) CANITZ[2]

225. *Bucher to Thile*

(Original) [German]   Varzin, 30 June, 1870

No. 1. Varzin

His Excellency the Chancellor desires:

1. that by an examination of the original telegram of 21 June[3] it should be ascertained whether the words "about the 26th" have been correctly enciphered in Berlin;
2. according to the result of this investigation Salazar's question[4] is to be answered and he is to be asked whether in his arrangements with Ruiz Zorrilla the formula "about the 9th" occurs as well;
3. the King's Messenger who took the cipher to Madrid, Lieutenant Rohrbeck, is to be asked how he carried the cipher, whether in his luggage or on his person;
4. that if the suspicion arises that the cipher is compromised a new one is to be sent to Madrid observing the precautions shown by experience to be necessary;
5. the enclosed document[5] to be laid before H.M. with information as to the enquiry that has been opened;
6. H.R.H. the Prince of Hohenzollern is to be confidentially notified by H.E. the Secretary of State of the error that has occurred and of its consequences.

H.E. later reverted once again to the occurrence and said that in any case a courier must be sent to deliver a new cipher. The man could at the same time take with him the information for Salazar or alternatively the enquiry

---

[1] See Doc. No. 199.

[2] Marginal note by Thile: "I await Your Excellency's orders in this matter. Thile." The document is accompanied by a note from Bucher which arrived in Berlin on 12 July: "No. 8 Varzin has been submitted to H.E. who gave no instructions about it. Its contents should no doubt be incorporated in the communication intended for the Prince of Hohenzollern (Father). Bucher. 1.7."

[3] See Doc. No. 199.

[4] See Doc. No. 222.

[5] See Doc. No. 226.

to be addressed to him. Further, although a result is hardly to be expected, a check should be made at Herr von Canitz's end to see whether the group in question arrived correct at Madrid and whether by chance a mistake was made in deciphering it there.

B[UCHE]R

226. *Count von Bismarck to Crown Prince Frederick William*

(Copy in Bucher's hand)[1] [German]   Varzin, 30 June, 1870

THE CROWN PRINCE.

G[racious] S[ir],

I received Y.R.H.'s gracious letter of 27 inst.[2] yesterday evening with respectful thanks and return the enclosure[3] with humble regards.

The courageous decision of their Highnesses of Hohenzollern to undertake a hazardous mission in the international and national interest is the more a proof of the strength of an inward vocation the less it is the result of encouragement from without. I, too, had hoped, and would find my own position in the matter considerably easier were my hope to be fulfilled, that H.M. the King would gain a more joyful confidence in the future of the enterprise. In the meanwhile there will still be time for opinions to gain in clarity now that the Spanish Cortes have been prorogued in consequence of an error or a falsification in a ciphered telegram from M. Salazar to the Spanish Government. I am still in the middle of an investigation into the question whether Salazar's decisive telegram was wrongly enciphered here in Berlin or whether in transmission via France or in Madrid a falsification took place. It is difficult to believe that so fateful an error can have been fortuitous; in order to clear the matter up as far as that is possible a courier is leaving one of these days for Madrid. I wish the best of luck to Y.R.H.'s plan of associating the Italian Royal family with the forthcoming christening of the youngest Princess[4] and on a first impression would humbly advise in favour of the Crown Prince and Princess, who represent, more than anyone else, the coming age and social prestige; but I respectfully leave it to Y.R. Highness's judgement whether to have a cipher telegram sent by Thile to Count Bressier to find out whether King Victor Emanuel would feel hurt by being thus passed over, in which case preference would certainly have to be given to His Majesty.

(signed) V. BISMARCK

[1] This document is published by Thimme, *Bismarck. Ges Werke*, VIb, doc. No. 1564.
[2] See Doc. No. 219.   [3] See Doc. No. 204.
[4] See Doc. No. 219.

227. *Note by de la Croix*

(Original) [German]

P.M.[1]   30.6.70

The error in the telegram for Madrid dispatched from here on the 21st inst.[2] lies apparently entirely, or in the most favourable hypothesis *mainly*, at the door of the Madrid Legation; in the Cipher Office the telegram was actually deciphered before being sent off to the Telegraph Office and found perfectly correct.

The position is namely the following:

In the French cipher code, which had to be employed because the tel. was in French, although it is older than new German one, the arrangement of the groups in question is as follows:

$$5710 \text{ twenty two}$$

1	—	three
2	—	four
3	—	five
4	—	six
5	—	seven
6	—	eight
7	—	nine

The telegram received by the Legation either had 5717 (twenty nine) instead of 5714 (twenty six) or else the cipher clerk mistook the last figure 4 for a 7. Then, in any case, he would have had to decipher it as twenty nine, not nine as he has done, having entirely left out the word twenty, marked by a stroke.

DE LA CROIX II

228. *Baron von Werther, Prussian Ambassador in Paris, to Count von Bismarck*

(Original)[3] [Geneva]   Paris, 30 June, 1870

No. 110   A 2038. pr. 3 July, 1870

When I attended the diplomatic reception day at the Duc de Gramont's today, he remarked to me that he must have a talk with me about a lit . . . but disagreeable matter and in this connexion read out to me a telegram

---

[1] P.M.=Pro Memoria.   [2] See Doc. No. 199.

[3] The document is torn; missing words are indicated by dots.

Marginal note: "from Ems.—for the files, B[erlin] 20.7.70. A[beken]."

which . . . . Higher Command in Nancy has addressed to the War . . . Marshal Le Boeuf. According to it . . . that Herr von Weyher, the Captain of the Royal . . . Staff, had from Strasbourg . . . visited Lunéville, Sarrebourg, Bramont, Virey . . . Lützelburg. He had been directed . . . by a . . . Gendarmerie officer to Nancy. . . . There he had expressed the intention of travelling via Obereschw . . ., Donon, Saverne to Sarrebourg. This . . . journey was, said the Duke, unquestionably a military reconnaiss . . . (*reconnaissance militaire*), and the question had been asked what was to be done. Marshal Le Boeuf had replied that Captain von Weyher was to be required to return direct to Germany via Strasbourg. . . .

In making this communication to me the Duc de Gramont remarked that he did not wish the slightest animosity to be attributed to this procedure and that it must be assumed that this officer had made the journey incognito on his own initiative. Had he carried any letter of recommendation for it, added the Duke, he himself would have raised no objection to the officer's being allowed to move about unmolested.

WERTHER[1]

229. *Note by Bülow*

(Original)[2] [German]   Berlin, 2 July, 1870

The King's Messenger, Lieutenant Rohrbeck, who appeared personally at the Auswärtiges Amt, declared in reply to interrogation:

"At my departure from here for Madrid via Paris as courier on 2 June of the present year the Chief Clerk of the cipher room entrusted me with a single official packet of letters for the Madrid Legation. I kept this packet, which as I learn today contained among other things a new cipher code for the Madrid Legation, during the whole journey in the diplomatic bag which I all the time carried on my person, and on my arrival in

[1] An undated note by Abeken accompanies this document: "The expulsion of Captain von Weyher, which the Duc de Gramont in really the most shameless way communicated as an accomplished fact carried out simply on General Le Boeuf's orders, making no excuses for it and without alleging any lack of propriety on the officer's part, is almost more than one can stand and in my opinion cannot be passed over in silence. Is a Prussian officer, if his papers are in order, not to be able to travel in France with a map without being arrested or expelled?

Count von Treskow casually expressed the idea that the officers designated to attend the Chalons camp should have their acceptances sent in and then a statement should be sent that after such experiences they could not be allowed to attend.

What do you think of this?"

Thile adds to Abeken's note: "in my opinion Werther should receive instructions to say something *rude* to Gramont. Th[ile]."

[2] Marginal note by Bülow: "Copy of appended protocol to be sent to Varzin by tomorrow's post." B[erlin]. 2.7.—Th[ile].

Madrid personally delivered to the Minister, Baron von Canitz. The possibility that this packet may have been opened during the journey is therefore entirely ruled out.

I make the above statement on my oath as an officer."

v.g.u.[1]

ROHRBECK

Lieutenant, mounted Feldjäger Corps

a.u.s.[2] BÜLOW Wirkl[icher] Leg[ations] Rath

Actual Legation Counsellor

230. *Thile to Bucher*

(Telegram. Draft for cipher) [German]

Berlin, 2 July, 1870. [1.25 p.m.]

I regard it as proved beyond doubt by de la Croix's memorandum[3] which is before you at Varzin that the slip occurred at Madrid. Unless otherwise instructed I shall report in this sense to His Majesty and the Prince of Hohenzollern and countermand the further investigations[4] here ordered on 30th, especially as the cipher[5] used is not identical with the one conveyed to Madrid by the King's Messenger.

Fair copy signed by H.E.[6]

TH[ILE]

231. *Bucher to Thile*

Original [German]   Varzin, 3 July, 1870

I submitted to the Chief Your Excellency's telegram of the 2nd inst.[7] relating to the telegraphic error. He wishes to see the matter more thoroughly cleared up than by the de la Croix memorandum which contains only a hypothesis, however probable it may be. He asks in the first place for the request to be made in his name to the Head Telegraph Office to return the original telegram[8] for inspection together with the

[1] v.g.u.=vorgelesen (read out), genehmigt (approved), unterschrieben (signed).
[2] a.u.s.=actum ut supra.
[3] See Doc. No. 227.
[4] See Doc. No. 225.
[5] The decipher of this telegram bears the marginal note by Bismarck: "Then it is possible after all that it is known in France."
[6] Marginal note: "Bü[low] 2."
[7] See Doc. No. 230.
[8] See Doc. No. 199.

information whether the telegram went direct to Madrid or was relayed en route and, if so, where. Then the telegram is to be sent together with the cipher code used and a statement from the Cipher office how long this cipher code has been in use for Madrid.

The King's Messenger in Madrid can in my opinion be recalled, as the Chancellor intends to send out another. In the question of what is to happen about Herr von Canitz's leave I would prefer to wait a few days until it can be seen whether the *ad hoc* recall will take place soon or later.

As to what is to be laid before H.M. the Chief says that duplicates of everything telegraphed by Canitz *qua* Canitz are to be sent to Ems. Telegrams from Alonso he regards as private telegrams.

BUCHER

232. *Thile to Baron von Canitz, Prussian Minister at Madrid*

(Draft) [German]

No. 7   Berlin, 4 July, 1870

I have orders from the Chief to communicate the following to you with my respects.

On 21 June at the request of M. Salazar the following cipher telegram was dispatched to you:

[here follows the telegram of 21 June][1]

Of the three telegrams contained on this sheet of cipher the second, directed to M. Ruiz Zorrilla, reached him with its text in so far corrupt as instead of the final words:

"Seeing you again about the 26th"

it had:

"Seeing you again about the 9th".

What disastrous consequences this error has had, or in existing conditions still may have, I need not dwell on at length, in view of the cipher telegrams sent here by Y.E. on 28 and 29 June at the request of Salazar.[2]

The Chief has therefore ordered appropriate investigations to be made in order to discover on whom the blame falls in the affair.

In this connexion there exist three possible alternatives:

    1. The telegram was incorrectly enciphered at this end,

    2. or it was garbled in transit intentionally or accidentally,

    3. or, finally, it was incorrectly deciphered at Madrid.

(re 1) Of these three alternatives it seems, according to investigations set on foot here, that the first may be completely ruled out. According to

---

[1] See Doc. No. 199.
[2] See Docs. Nos. 222, 224.

the official statement[1] of the Chief Cipher Clerk, before the enciphered telegram was taken to Telegraph Office it was *re-deciphered* and found to be perfectly correct. I moreover had the copy of the cipher message yesterday called in from the Berlin Central Telegraph Office[2] and on being deciphered it was found to tally exactly with the original here.

(re 2) The second possibility, too, has scant plausibility in its favour. The French cipher code used for the telegram is not identical with the German one brought to Y.E. at the beginning of June of this year by the King's Messenger, Lieutenant Rohrbeck, and even were it so, the possibility of the latter code falling into the wrong hands in transit is ruled out by the statement made on oath by the above-mentioned courier, a copy of which is enclosed.[3] Even on the scarcely credible assumption that the cipher used was already compromised it is singular that precisely the passage in question, the meaning and implications of which could not well be known to a third person, should intentionally be garbled; still more incredible in this connexion would seem the play of sheer chance.

(re 3) Consequently the third of the above-mentioned possibilities is the most likely one and is further strengthened by the information mentioned above furnished by Secret Court Counsellor de la Croix and included in the annexes.

I am therefore under the necessity of asking Y.E. kindly to send me by the returning courier a copy of my telegram of the 21st ult.[4] *exactly as it reached you in cipher* and personally attested by you, at the same time stating by whom it was deciphered on arrival. Will Y.E. further, using the enclosed data, yourself undertake investigations of a nature to throw light on this fateful error and send me a full account of the results.

Finally I venture to request Y.E. kindly to hand M. Salazar (Gama) the enclosed memorandum[5] drawn up at his request to serve for his personal vindication, giving him at the same time from what is here written such explanations as may seem desirable, and finally asking him whether the formula "about the 9th" occurred in his arrangements with M. Ruiz Zorrilla. Will Y.E. be so good as to let me know M. Salazar's answer by the channel mentioned above.[6]

Secretary of State
THILE

Annex

(Draft) [French]

For Monsieur Gama

The error in the telegram for M. Ruiz Zorrilla of 21 June, which we cannot sufficiently regret, does not in any way fall to the responsibility

---

[1] See Doc. No. 227.   [2] Marginal note: "done, without a covering letter."
[3] See Doc. No. 229.   [4] See Doc. No. 199.
[5] Marginal note: "copy of enclosed memorandum: 'For M. Gama.'" See Annex.
[6] Marginal note: "Bü[low] 4th."

of M. Gama. The latter had put at the end of the telegram "Seeing you again about the 26th" and not "Seeing you again about the 9th" as stands in the decipher delivered to the person to whom it was addressed. We are still enquiring into the origin of this regrettable error.

Berlin, 4 July[1]

233. *Salazar to Baron von Canitz, Prussian Minister at Madrid*

(Original) [French]   Tuesday, 5 July [1870]

MY DEAR BARON,

I thought that Prince Leopold's grandmother, Princess Marie Antoinette Murat (born in 1793, died in 1847), was not the daughter of the former King of Naples but his sister or niece.

As the newspapers have begun to speak about this relationship I would beg you to tell me what you know about it. Otherwise I would be grateful if you would send a telegram at once to clear up this point which is important and a subject of controversy.

Your servant and friend

E. SALAZAR Y MAZARREDO

234. *Baron von Canitz, Prussian Minister at Madrid,*
to Count von Bismarck

(Telegram. Decipher) [German]   Madrid, 5 July, 1870. 2.25 p.m.
                                          arrived 6.20 p.m.
                                      A 2076. pr. 5 July, 1870

Salazar wants to know on authority whether Prince Leopold's grandmother was the daughter, niece or sister of the former King Murat of Naples as the newspapers are already taking an interest in this relationship.

(signed) CANITZ[2]

235. *Thile to Prince Karl Anton of Hohenzollern and to Abeken*[3]

(Draft) [German]   Berlin, 5 July, 1870

YOUR MOST SERENE HIGHNESS,

MOST GRACIOUS PRINCE,

The prorogation of the Spanish Cortes for several months which took place on the 23rd ult. and which at that stage of the throne question seemed

---

[1] Marginal note: "Bü[low] 4th."

[2] Marginal notes: "See cipher telegram of 6 July to Madrid (No. 6)—from H.R.H. 7.7." See Doc. No. 237.

[3] The same text except for a few changes which will be given in footnotes was sent to Abeken. The original of the letter to Abeken bears the marginal note: "pr. Ems, 6 July, 1870. Laid before His Majesty the same evening. Returned by H.M. ?/7."

most singular and almost incomprehensible has now found its explanation in news meanwhile received from Madrid. Unfortunately the cause of this important measure is to be sought in the garbling, whether fortuitous or intentional, of a telegram sent from here to Madrid. I am instructed by Count von Bismarck respectfully to inform Your Royal Highness of the following:[1]

On 21 June Major von Versen on his arrival from Sigmaringen brought me a telegram drafted there by M. Salazar and addressed to Ruiz Zorrilla, the President of the Spanish Cortes, adding in Salazar's name the request that the telegram dated "Tuesday, 21st, Sigmaringen Castle" should be sent in cipher to Baron von Canitz at Madrid for the purpose of delivering it to the addressee. This request was immediately fulfilled by me. The text of the telegram ran as follows:

"M. Ruiz Zorrilla, President of the Cortes,
   I confirm telegram of the day before yesterday: Carlists conspiring again, keep a watch on Deputy No. 3. Seeing you again about the 26th.   GAMA"

This telegram reached M. Zorrilla corrupt in so far as instead of the final words :

"Seeing you again about the 26th"
it ran:
"Seeing you again about the 9th".

The further details are given in the Minister, Baron von Canitz's telegrams of the 28th and 29th ult.,[2] forwarded here in cipher at M. Salazar's request, copies of which I enclose with my humble duty,[3] and which also dwell on the disastrous consequences of this error. To clear it up and settle the question whether blame attaches to anybody, and if so, to whom, the necessary investigations are being undertaken.

There exist three possible alternatives in this connexion:
   1. either the telegram was incorrectly enciphered at this end,
   2. or it was garbled in transit, intentionally or accidentally,
   3. or, finally, it was incorrectly deciphered at Madrid.

Of these three eventualities, as a result of the investigations made here, the first seems entirely ruled out; according to the official statement[4] of de la Croix, the head cipher clerk, a copy of which is enclosed with my respects,[5] the enciphered telegram before being sent to the telegraph office was redeciphered and found perfectly correct. The day before yesterday,

---

[1] This phrase is replaced in the letter to Abeken by the following: "I am instructed by His Excellency, the Chief, to inform you of the following in order that you may make it the subject of a report to His Majesty the King."
[2] See Docs. Nos. 222, 224.   [3] Letter to Abeken: "with my regards".
[4] See Doc. No. 227.   [5] Letter to Abeken: "with my regards".

moreover, I asked the Central Telegraph Office here to send me the rough draft of the cipher sheet, and upon its being deciphered it proved to tally exactly with the original we have here.

The second alternative, too, has little probability in its favour. Even assuming the French cipher used for the telegram to be compromised it would still be singular that precisely the passage in question—the meaning and implications of which could not well be known to a third person—and *only this* passage should intentionally be garbled; still more incredible in this connexion would seem the play of sheer chance.

Consequently the third of the above-mentioned possibilities is the most likely one and is further strengthened by the information[1] furnished by Herr de la Croix. I have therefore instructed Baron Canitz, in a letter delivered yesterday by King's Messenger, to send me by the returning courier a copy of the telegram of the 21st ult.[2] *exactly as it reached him in cipher*, personally authenticated by him, and at the same time stating by whom it was deciphered on arrival. The Minister is also instructed, using the enclosed data, to undertake any other suitable investigations of a nature to throw light on this fateful error and send me a full account of the results and finally to hand M. Salazar (Gama) the memorandum,[3] a copy of which is enclosed, and ask him, whether the formula "about the 9th" occurred at all in his arrangements with M. Zorrilla.

In due time I would propose[4] to send Your Royal Highness with my respects a report of Baron von Canitz's reply together with the final results of the various investigations. I only add that[5] in view of the possibility that the cipher in question is compromised I have sent a new French cipher to the Minister in Madrid by yesterday's courier.[6]

Will Your Royal Highness pray accept the expression of the deep veneration with which I remain

Y.R.H.'s humble servant
fair copy signed by H.E.[7]

---

[1] See Doc. No. 227.   [2] See Doc. No. 199.   [3] See Doc. No. 232, Annex.

[4] The text of the letter to Abeken goes on: "in due time to give you further information with my regards. For today I merely add that I have reported the circumstances to His Royal Highness the Prince of Hohenzollern, and".

[5] From this point the letter to Abeken follows the text of the letter to Prince Karl Anton.

[6] The following passage has been struck out: "In connexion with the above information I venture in conclusion to add that according to a telegraphed report from the Ambassador in Paris the news of His Highness the Hereditary Prince's candidature has caused great and unpleasant surprise in Paris Government circles. The French Chargé d'Affaires here questioned me yesterday about our position in the matter and I curtly replied that for the Prussian Cabinet *as such* the matter did not exist and that the Spanish nation and the Princely House of Hohenzollern were masters of their own will and pleasure. If the matter is raised at Paris Baron von Werther has instructions to make this reply approved by H.M. the King and Count Bismarck."

[7] The letter to Abeken has: "The State Secretary. Th[ile]—Bü[low] 5th."

236. *Thile to Abeken*

(Telegram. Draft for cipher) [German]   B[erlin], 6 July, 1870[1]
No. 11   A 2077

On orders from the Minister-President I am informing Prince Reuss by telegraph of our position in the Spanish question on the same lines as the reply given to France.

The last sentence of my yesterday telegram re Her Majesty the Queen[2] must of course serve only for your own information.

TH[ILE]

237. *Thile to Baron von Canitz, Prussian Minister at Madrid*

(Telegram. Draft for cipher) [German]   Berlin, 6 July, 1870[3]

Prince Leopold's grandmother was a niece of King Murat.
fair copy signed by H.E.[4]

TH[ILE][5]

238. *Abeken to Prince Karl Anton of Hohenzollern*

(Telegram en clair) [German]   Ems, 6 July, 1870[6]

H.M. the King commands me to enquire whether Y.R.H. would be reached in Sigmaringen by an express messenger leaving here tomorrow?

Actual Privy Legation Counsellor

ABEKEN

[1] Marginal note: "To Telegraph Office 6.7.—11 a.m."
[2] See Lord, *Origins*, doc. No. 14.
[3] Marginal note: "To Telegraph Office. 6.7.—3 p.m."
[4] Marginal note: "Bü[low] 6th."
[5] The Madrid decipher bears the marginal note: "Communicated to M. Salazar on 7th July."
[6] Marginal note: "same day. 7.15 p.m. to the Telegraph Office, Ems."

239. *Baron von Canitz, Prussian Minister at Madrid, to Count von Bismarck*

(Telegram. Decipher) [German] Madrid, 6 July, 1870. 9.10 p.m.
              arr. 7 July. 11.45 a.m.
              A 2087. pr. 7 July, 1870

Telegraphic dispatch 4[1] and 5[2] duly received.

              signed VON CANITZ[3]

240. *Abeken to the King of Prussia*

(Original) [German]   Ems, 6 July, 1870

YOUR ROYAL MAJESTY,

I have the honour humbly to submit the draft of the letter to His Royal Highness the Prince of Hohenzollern commanded by Your Majesty.[4]

At the same time I beg respectfully to announce that Legation Counsellor Bucher has announced by telegraph that a letter[5] from the Chancellor on the lines of yesterday's telegrams[6] is on the way. Since this will *probably*, although not certainly, arrive here in the course of tomorrow and is unlikely to contain anything *fundamentally different* from the telegrams—I await Your Majesty's command as to whether you think it important enough to delay the dispatch of the letter to His Royal Highness on that account.[7]

I have as yet no reply to my telegraphic enquiry at Sigmaringen.[8]

    In profound homage I remain
      Your Royal Majesty's
        most humble and loyal
          Servant and subject
             ABEKEN

[1] Published by Lord, *Origins*, doc. No. 9.

[2] Published by Lord, *Origins*, doc. No. 20.

[3] Marginal note: "For the files, B[erlin]. 7.7 Bü[low], Th[ile]."

[4] See Doc. No. 241. Marginal note by King of Prussia: "Quite agreed. W."

[5] See doc. published by Lord, *Origins*, No. 16.

[6] See docs. published by Lord, *Origins*, Nos. 7, 14.

[7] Marginal note by King of Prussia: "I think it better that without awaiting B[isma]rck's letter, what you have written should go off as soon as possible with the following enclosure from me. W. 6.7.70." The enclosure to which the King of Prussia alludes is no doubt his letter of 6 July, 1870, to Karl Anton, mentioned by Fester, *Briefe*, No. 294. The files of the *Auswärtiges Amt* do not contain a copy of this letter.

[8] See Doc. No. 238.

241. *Abeken to Prince Karl Anton of Hohenzollern*

(Draft) [German]   Ems, 6 July, 1870

> [The text of this letter has been published by Fester, *Briefe*,
> No. 295, following Zingeler, *Karl Anton*, pp. 249-50. The
> Fester-Zingeler text shows omissions which are italicized
> in the text reproduced here.]

YOUR SERENE HIGHNESS,
>   GRACIOUS PRINCE,

His Majesty desires to inform Your Royal Highness as quickly and
fully as possible of the news which has reached His Majesty of the first
impressions produced in Paris by the disclosure coming from Madrid of
the offer and acceptance of the candidature for the Spanish throne, and
has to that end commanded me to send Your Royal Highness a copy of
the account of it given by the Prussian Ambassador, Baron von Werther,
dated the 5th inst.,[1] and herewith enclosed with my respects.

This account has been brought here personally by Baron von Werther,
who some little time ago asked permission to wait upon His Majesty at
Ems, and his verbal report, as His Majesty does not wish to conceal from
Your Royal Highness, gives a still more forceful picture of the excitement now reigning in Paris under the first impact of surprise. The French
Ministers—says the Ambassador—have said that France could not let a
Hohenzoller rule over Spain and would set all means in motion to cause
his downfall if he were to be elected; which might involve personal danger
for the Prince; the Emperor himself has, it is true, preserved his wonted
calmness while expressing himself with great decision in the same sense
as his Ministers.—Baron von Werther had not embarked upon any discussion and had taken refuge in his genuine, complete ignorance. The
news itself, as Herr v. Werther mentioned, reached the French Government on the 3rd or 4th inst. in a report from the French Ambassador at
Madrid giving information of a special announcement made to him by
Marshal Prim.

Marshal Prim is REPORTED *as having said that the Hohenzollern candidature
was offered to him, not requested by him. Admiral Topete* IS SAID *to have declared
to the French Ambassador that negotiations with Count Bismarck had been going
on for months.*

*His Majesty the King regards it as an open question how much truth there is
in these latest French allegations about utterances of Marshal Prim and Admiral
Topete and how they are to be judged.*

As early as the 4th inst. M. Lesourd, the French Chargé d'Affaires at
Berlin, had said to the Secretary of State, von Thile, that his Government
had received this news and instructed him to ask whether the Prussian

---

[1] See doc. published by Lord, *Origins*, No. 11.

Government was involved in the matter. Herr von Thile had replied that the affair had no existence for the Prussian Government and that he was unable to give any information as to negotiations between Marshal Prim and Your Royal Highness or H. Highness, the Hereditary Prince.[1]

His Majesty the King has deigned to approve this reply and, after a telegraphic declaration from Count Bismarck in the same sense had reached him, has deigned to command that in accordance with Count Bismarck's proposal, the Prussian Embassy in Paris be instructed:

to express surprise at the enquiry and to declare that His Highness the Hereditary Prince and the Spanish Government are masters of their own will and pleasure.[2] If France raised with us questions which only concern Spain, the Embassy must refuse to discuss them and must refer the enquirers to Madrid. Respecting the independence of Spain and in the absence of a call to interfere in Spanish constitutional questions, we left these to the Spaniards and those to whom they addressed themselves. If France wanted to exercise influence in such quarters that was her affair, not ours. *What must above all be* AVOIDED *was that the behaviour of the Embassy should give the impression that it or His Majesty could be* INTIMIDATED.

The Minister-President, Count Bismarck, further remarked in his telegram[3] that acceptance of discussion would worsen our OTHERWISE IMPREGNABLE *position; and the Embassy must avoid undertaking in Paris any advocacy of His Highness, the Hereditary Prince's candidature thereby making it an official Prussian concern, this being precisely the point which has caused the agitation in France. On the other hand Count Bismarck requested His Majesty the King that His Highness the Hereditary Prince should be informed of the feeling of the French Cabinet and advises that His Highness should endeavour to gain the confidence of Paris in order to prevent French money and influence being at once employed by Paris for conspiracies in the Spanish army.*

His Majesty the King commands me to say that He Himself fully approves this advice, but that He must leave it to Your Royal Highness and to His Highness, your son, to judge in what way and by what channels Your Highnesses can best bring influence to bear on the mood of Paris and especially on the Emperor himself, *and that in His Majesty's opinion any personal visit of His Highness the Hereditary Prince to H.M. the Emperor Napoleon would seem possible only after the election had taken place.*

From Madrid His Majesty has so far received ABSOLUTELY no news— *and only today, from a report to Berlin, has learnt of the garbling of M. Salazar's telegram, about which the Secretary of State, von Thile, states that he has sent information directly to Your Royal Highness.*

[1] See doc. published by Lord, *Origins*, No. 1.
[2] This sentence, as published by Fester, runs: "The Ambassador in Paris expressed his surprise to the French Government at the enquiry and declared that H.H. the Hereditary Prince and the Spanish Government were masters of their own will and pleasure."
[3] See doc. published by Lord, *Origins*, No. 13.

In conclusion I beg Your Royal Highness to permit me humbly to add that His Majesty has graciously taken cognizance of this letter and pronounced it in accordance with his intentions.

With deep respect I remain
Your Royal Highness's

A[BEKEN] 6.7.70[1]

242. Abeken to Thile

(Original) [German]   Ems, 6 July [1870]

HONOURED PATRON,

Only a couple of words to thank you for what you have sent today and to tell you that I had already given myself the instructions contained in your today's telegram[2] for the final sentence of yours of yesterday.[3] What Werther is bringing here along with him you will see from his report, of which I enclose a copy in case of need.[4] By word of mouth he tells me of still *more extreme utterances*: Gramont is saying: "if the affair goes through and the Prince is elected—we shall *destroy* him! [*nous le briserons*]"—"He would not remain King for six months." "We shall use all our resources and we have some!"

However, personally Herr von Werther is not depressed, though he would be *against* the business if it were a case of beginning afresh. But he realizes that we cannot back down, least of all on account of French reactions, and has promised me not to alarm the King.

And now for your explanation of the prorogation of the Cortes! How right you are to call it *disastrous*![5] Perhaps the whole thing actually would never have transpired until it was a *fait accompli*. But I do not understand Prim either—Werther says on Ollivier's authority: 'Prim came to Mercier: I have a disagreeable thing to tell you—disagreeable for France and for the Emperor personally; for France I do not mind much, but for the Emperor I feel really sorry about it.' And then he told Werther the whole story. (The Chancellor is said to be highly annoyed about this parleying between him and France.) Prim went on to say that the Prince's candidature was proposed to him—but did not say by whom. But Topete told Mercier that negotiations had gone on for a long time between Prim and *Count Bismarck*.

For the time being Herr von Werther had taken shelter behind ignorance, merely remarking that very likely the whole business had gone on without the Prussian Government's knowledge and consent as in the case of the Prince of Rumania, where in fact the Emperor Napoleon seems to

[1] Marginal note by Abeken: "fair copy made 7.7.70."
[2] See Doc. No. 236.   [3] See Lord, *Origins*, Doc. No. 14.
[4] See Lord, *Origins*, Doc. No. 11.   [5] See Doc. No. 235.

have known more and earlier of the Prince's intentions than the King of Prussia—which Ollivier did not deny, merely remarking that *this* was an entirely different matter!

I have not seen the King today yet; he had a good night but stayed rather longer in bed in the morning and then, to avoid the intense heat that has suddenly set in, did not come along to the medicinal spring. Yesterday at the banquet he was well, only a *little bit* tired—*less*, one had the impression, than he said he was; he is always unhappy about his strength not coming back more quickly.

The Grandduchess of Baden had a terrific fight to get him to Gastein, he has *not* said a word of anything to her either.

Here comes a long telegram from Varzin which it will not be possible to have deciphered *before* the post goes out.

In haste your faithful   ABEKEN

243. *General von Schweinitz, Prussian Minister at Vienna, to Count von Bismarck*

(Copy) [German]   Vienna, 6 July, 1870
A 2119[1]

The Imperial Chancellor spoke to me today of the Hereditary Prince of Hohenzollern's candidature for the Spanish throne. His information from Paris was that the French Government took a very serious view of the matter, as can also be seen in the *Constitutionnel* articles. Count Beust went on to say that he understood the views of the French Cabinet, but they would not affect the attitude of the Austro-Hungarian Government, which was remaining completely detached in the matter. For the rest he confidently hoped that this cloud on the political horizon would soon pass, and when the Spanish Government realized the strong opposition in France encountered by the present candidate for the throne, it might perhaps turn to the Prince of Asturias, whose chances, according to his information, were not so unfavourable as was generally assumed.

With others of my colleagues Count Beust also emphasized the neutral attitude of the Austro-Hungarian Government in this question but did not conceal from them his displeasure at the most recent turn in the question of the Spanish throne.

It is characteristic of the Austro-Hungarian Government's attitude that, as I hear from a reliable source, the inspired press has received directions to treat the Hereditary Prince of Hohenzollern's candidature with diminishing goodwill in proportion as the opposition in France increases in strength.

signed v. SCHWEINITZ

[1] Marginal note by Bucher: "No. 76 Varzin pr[aesentatum] 9 July."

244. *Prince Karl Anton of Hohenzollern to Abeken*

(Telegram en clair) [German]   Sigmaringen, 7 July, 1870. 9.44 a.m.

I shall in any case be to be found here.

PRINCE ZU HOHENZOLLERN[1]

245. *The Prince of Reuss, Prussian Minister at St Petersburg,*
to Count von Bismarck

(Telegram. Decipher) [French]

[This document has been already published by Lord, *Origins*,
doc. No. 35, but is reproduced here because Lord did not
know of Bismarck's marginal note on the Varzin copy.]

St Petersburg, 7 July, 1870. 6 p.m. arrived 9.50 p.m.

No. 14   A 2102. pr. 8 July, 1870[2]

General Fleury has told Prince Gorchakov that if the Prince of
Hohenzollern accepted the Spanish crown, there would be war with
Prussia.

He further endeavoured to rouse him against us by proving that the
increase of the power of Prussia would be a danger for Russia as well. The
Chancellor answered (before seeing me) that the Prussian Cabinet would
say, if questioned, that the affair did not concern it, hence there was no
reason to hold it responsible in the matter. As for the danger, he did not
anticipate an increase of power but rather a weakening in view of the
complications. Moreover the relations existing between Russia and
Prussia were not of a nature to inspire fears.

Ambassador dissatisfied with this reply.

Prince Gorchakov foresees no danger, nevertheless he advises the
prudence and calmness of strength. The French Government, humiliated
by previous reverses, is, he thinks, indulging in these theatrical gestures to
please the country. Ollivier's words roused strong disapproval and of this
he made no secret.

The Chancellor still plans to leave on the 10th. He is pleased with the
statement I made to him. He tells me that the Archduke has asked the
Tsar's good offices towards a rapprochement between Austria and
Prussia.

REUSS[3]

---

[1] The following telegram from Sigmaringen had also been sent to Abeken at 9.2 a.m.:
"His Royal Highness the Prince of Hohenzollern is here. Telegraph Office. Büttner."

[2] Marginal note by Bucher: "No. 60. Varzin, pr. 9."

[3] Marginal note by Bismarck: "Let the reply be that we have long desired this
rapprochement as far as it can be achieved without harm to our relations with *Russia*."

246. *Count von Bismarck to Count von Bernstorff,*
Prussian Ambassador in London

(Telegram. Draft for cipher in Bismarck's hand) [German]

No. 36   [7 July, 1870][1]

We have in fact no interest in interfering in Spanish affairs, and there is no question of our support when Prussia has no concern in the matter. If France wants to interfere that is her business, if she wants to make war on us because the Spaniards elect a German as King, it would be quite unjustifiable quarrelsomeness. *We* shall never wage a war of the Spanish succession and the whole ado is premature as long as the Cortes have not voted. Should the French attack us, however, we shall of course resist.

247. *Thile to the Central Telegraph Office at Berlin*

(Draft) [German]   Berlin, 7 July, 1870

In order to clear up the question of a garbling occurring in a cipher telegram dispatched on 21 June of this year[2] from here to the Minister at Madrid, I request the (Director) on official orders from His Excellency, the Chancellor, to be so good as to let me have the *original* of the telegram for inspection. At the same time I would ask for kind information whether the telegram was sent direct to Madrid or relayed in transit, and if so where it was relayed.

Secretary of State of the Auswärtige Amt[3]

Th[ile]

248. *Prince Karl Anton of Hohenzollern to Thile*

(Original) [German]   Sigmaringen, 7 July, 1870
                                                      A 2135. pr. 9 July, 1870

Your Excellency,

I am all the more grateful for your kind message of the 5th[4] since the obviously premature disclosure of the Spanish affair has not only caused an uproar in the European press but also provided ways and means for uncalculable intrigues and political complications of the most disquieting sort.

[1] Marginal note by Bucher: "enciphered and taken to the Telegraph Office. 7.7.—7.15 p.m."   [2] See Doc. No. 199.

[3] Marginal notes: "Bü[low] 7th.—forwarded the same day [eod[em] ins[inuatum]]."

[4] See Doc. No. 235.

I await with intense interest the result of the investigations into the garbling of the telegram to which we unfortunately owe the present upset of the prevailing political calm. What a disturbing effect this news has necessarily had in Ems is shown by enclosed copy[1] of a telegram that has just arrived.

I could not understand what caused the prorogation of the Cortes, still less how Marshal Prim could deal with the candidature for the throne *now* when a constitutional settlement would lack all legal basis.

The doors were thus flung wide open to the French outcry, to which a *swift* fait accompli is no good as a remedy. In this extremely difficult situation I can only beg you to keep me amply informed.

To escape public attention and all indiscreet questions I shall stay here for the time being, and further kind communications will always find me here. If I have to absent myself I will at once telegraph Your Excellency.

For several days I have been without news of my son, who has gone on a mountain tour for relaxation and to restore his spirits.

It is with sentiments of the highest esteem that I remain

Your Excellency's most devoted

PRINCE OF HOHENZOLLERN

249. *Bleichröder to Count von Bismarck*

(Telegram en clair) [German]   Berlin, 8 July, 1870. 11.59 a.m.[2]

Telegram in *Börsenzeitung* about Benedetti's resignation not confirmed. According to Havas the *Constitutionnel* reports:

Paris Cabinet will recall Minister Madrid if Spain disregards representations and will request Prussia to refuse Royal assent as was done by other Cabinets with Nemours, Murat, Alfred. Several Great Powers take this view and intend to intervene Madrid–Berlin.   BLEICHRÖDER

250. *Salazar to Baron von Canitz, Prussian Minister at Madrid*

(Original) [French]   Friday, 8 [July, 1870]

MY DEAR BARON,

Will you send off the telegram you will read below?[3]

Yours ever

E. DE SALAZAR Y MAZARREDO

*   *   *

[1] i.e. Doc. No. 238.

[3] Marginal note by Bucher: "No. 46 Varzin. pr. 8 July. For the files. B[ucher] 8.7."

[3] This telegram was dispatched by Canitz on 8 June, 1870, at 1.57 p.m., arriving on 9 July at 11.55 a.m. at Berlin, whence it was forwarded the same day in German translation to Ems and Varzin at 3.55 p.m.

I am ill and Rear-admiral Polo is leaving today for Sigmaringen.

To vindicate Prussia I am publishing a pamphlet to say that she is ignorant of the negotiations and that the Prince notified the King of his definite acceptance out of courtesy.   GAMA

251. *Salazar to Baron von Canitz, Prussian Minister at Madrid*

(Original) [French]   Friday, 8 [July, 1870]

MY DEAR BARON,
    Will you dispatch this further telegram?[1]
                              Yours ever
                                          E. DE SALAZAR

                    ★   ★   ★

Telegram

    The rumour of a European conference which would meet at Brussels to demonstrate the true character of the Hispano-Hohenzollern question has been very well received here. It is thought that this would be a way to smooth away many difficulties, England[2] might take the initiative.
                                                    GAMA

252. *Prince Karl Anton of Hohenzollern to Abeken*

(Original) [German]   Sigmaringen, 8 July, 1870[3]

    [The text of this letter was published by Fester, *Briefe*, No. 346, following Zingeler, *Karl Anton*, pp. 250-1. The Fester-Zingeler text, however, shows omissions which are italicized in the text published here.]

DEAR PRIVY COUNSELLOR,
    For your obliging and detailed news[4] I offer you my most sincere thanks.

[1] This telegram was sent off by Canitz on 8 July at 10 p.m., arriving the next day at 11.45 a.m. at Berlin, whence it was forwarded in German translation the same day at 3.55 p.m. to Ems and Varzin.

[2] In the text reaching Berlin this word has been deciphered as "Prince". The Berlin decipher bears the marginal note by Thile: "In the adjacent telegram the contents of which have been today telegraphed to Berlin in cipher A 2141 it is respectfully noted that the underlined word 'Prince' has been supplied on the basis of a similarity in the groups, because the cipher group in question was unintelligible. Another but most implausible conjecture for an emendation would make the word out to be: Empereur des Français. Berlin, 9 July, 1870 evening. Th[ile]."

[3] Marginal note by Bucher: "pr. Ems, 10 July, 1870 5.45. a.m. Delivered by postal messenger [1 word illegible]."

[4] See Doc. No. 241.

It came at a moment when amid the babel of sensational newspaper articles I had great need of genuine information.

To the vehemence with which the French Government has reacted on learning of the candidature attention will have to be given at a later and more suitable time—but I agree that for the moment it will have to be reckoned with. *I almost feel inclined to think that in Spain French anger will result on election day in a still more decisive majority in the Cortes and that thereby our spark of unuttered hope for a majority that would prove just too slender for acceptance has finally been extinguished.*

The view that the question, now dragged into the light of day, is not a Prussian concern but a domestic concern of my own family is one that I fully share, and no utterance or allusion has ever been made by me in speech or writing whereby anyone could accuse me or my son of being in any way at variance with this view. *I not only dimly sensed but clearly foresaw that the whole business would touch France to the quick—but such a degree of intense and passionate embitterment exceeds my worst forebodings.*

To me it seems that a feeling of weakness and insecurity must lurk behind this seething outburst.

I wholeheartedly agree that after the election is over my son should endeavour to achieve a personal rapprochement and understanding with Paris, provided on the other hand it does not wound Spanish national pride for the King of their choice to seek as it were absolution from the Emperor Napoleon.

If His Majesty the King were to approve of the Hereditary Prince's sending an explanatory letter to the Emperor, will you at once acquaint me of the expression of His Majesty's will.

Such a letter might simply notify him of the decision in favour of acceptance saying that with my agreement and after close consideration the Hereditary Prince thought he ought not to resist so generous an offer, and that in accepting the crown he was conscious that he would thenceforward think and act purely as a Spaniard. —But now that French suspicion has been roused it remains to be considered whether such a letter of apology to the French Emperor is compatible with our personal dignity and whether it does not seem more advisable to let the boiling point of French indignation pass—for the fury is too intense to be lasting.

I am most eager to learn what Marshal Prim's explanations will be like when they come. To judge by the antecedent causes the French information sounds highly improbable.

The attitude of the Austrian press in the question is singular. It has not definitely taken sides but is if anything more hostile to France than to us!

Requesting you kindly to keep me further informed in order that I may con-

tinue to act in harmony with the views and wishes of H.M. the King and His Foreign Ministry.

I remain ever with highest regard
Yours respectfully
PRINCE OF HOHENZOLLERN

P.S. In order to avoid all idle gossip and inquisitiveness I am for the present remaining quietly at Sigmaringen, as will my son when he returns from the Alps.

253. *Prince Karl Anton of Hohenzollern to the King of Prussia*

(Original) [German]   Sigmaringen, 8 July, 1870[1]

> [The text of this letter was published by Fester, *Briefe*, No. 345, following Zingeler, *Karl Anton*, pp. 251-2. The Fester-Zingeler text shows omissions which are italicized in the present text.]

YOUR ROYAL MAJESTY,

My most humble thanks for Your so gracious and confiding letter.[2]

With deep emotion I am compelled to recognize that this question of the candidature for the throne seems to be assuming dimensions which had not been included in the political calculations. France or rather the Imperial dignity in person is making capital of an affair to which it is entirely extraneous the better to cover over internal weaknesses and deficiencies.

The misunderstood cipher telegram to Madrid[3] is the source of all the complications which have arisen, and now at last I am clear about the prorogation of the Cortes.

When I read the news of the prorogation a weight was lifted from my heart, my only thought being that the whole election question would be postponed until the reassembly of the Legislative body, and that was why I was able humbly to report to Your Majesty on the 28th ult. that we had gained three months' respite.

What can have induced Marshal Prim thus immediately to publish the names of the persons involved to the whole of Europe is still wrapt in mystery.

---

[1] Marginal note by Abeken: "pr. H.M. the King, Ems, *10 July* 7.30 a.m. (brought by postal messenger [1 word illegible])." The copy in Abeken's hand bears the following marginal notes: "Letter of H.R.H. the Prince of Hohenzollern, of 8 July, brought by postal messenger and pr. Ems in the night of 9-10 July.—Copy to Varzin. 11.7."

[2] See Doc. No. 241.

[3] See Doc. No. 199. The telegram of 21 June, 1870.

231

Pray let Your Majesty graciously remain convinced that both my son and I will conscientiously maintain the standpoint adopted by Your Majesty, namely to pass the whole candidature off as an internal family matter, a question in which the Prussian Government and State have no say—even about Your Majesty's consent as required by Family Law the strictest silence shall be observed, since for the initiate it is no secret while there is no necessity for outsiders to know about it.

Accordingly we will remain silent and let things take their course. Only it must be confessed that this is not an auspicious but a thorny inauguration for the new dignity.

As regards our personal attitude towards France I have written my impressions to Privy Counsellor Abeken, who will lay them before Your Majesty.[1]

Since the recent events as reported to Your Majesty by me on the 19th and 28th of last month,[2] *nothing at all of any note has happened that it would have been my duty to mention. The untruthfulness of the telegram about deputations etc. is evident from the fact that the interviews are represented as having taken place all the time at Düsseldorf where we were thought to be staying, whereas we have been here now for nearly four weeks.*

Finally in reply to His Majesty's enquiry about Legation Counsellor Bucher I respectfully remark that I took his words about the prorogation of the Cortes to mean that they are to remain prorogued for several months and not to be recalled again for an ad hoc sitting, the members from the colonies being no longer within reach.

By their blundering rage the French have positively played into the hands of the nationalistic Spaniards; the more France takes sides against a candidate the higher will probably be the esteem in which he is held in Spain.—I can assure you on my honour that until a few days ago I indulged in the silent hope that perhaps at the eleventh hour non-acceptance might be based on the grounds of an insufficient majority in the voting—since the disgraceful scene in the Chamber in Paris I have lost even this anchor-hold—for it now seems a point of honour for both Spain and ourselves not to yield to intimidation.

If, however, the course of events and the good of the state make it advisable to yield, a hint from Your Majesty will be sufficient. In the same submissive spirit as the offer was finally accepted it will now joyfully be declined, though, for reasons of honour, no longer declined of our own free will.

My son is away on a tour in the Alps, that is why I was unable to procure the copy of Your Majesty's letter.

I expect him back at any hour now and will duly procure the copy.

I trust Your Majesty will not hold us personally responsible for the many unpleasant impressions intruding on Your Majesty's cure at the spa

[1] See Doc. No. 252.

[2] These letters are not in the files of the Auswärtige Amt. Fester, *Briefe*, No. 223, publishes a version of the letter of 19 June, 1870.

as a result of the Spanish question. This question is merely the signal for the flare-up of long smouldering hate for the new role of Prussia in world affairs resulting from the victories of 1866.

I remain with the most profound respect
Your humble servant and cousin

F. v. HOHENZOLLERN

I beg Your Majesty to excuse the hurried conclusion. I made a mistake in taking a copy of my letter. No time for a new one because the post is going out.

254. *Baron von Canitz, Prussian Minister at Madrid,*
to Count von Bismarck

(Original) [German]   Madrid, 8 July, 1870
A 2263. pr. 13 July, 1870

I have had the honour to receive Your Excellency's communication, No. 7,[1] of 4 July relating to the unfortunate garbling of M. Salazar's telegram of 21 June[2] to M. Ruiz Zorrilla and at once took steps to ascertain whether the fateful error of deciphering "about the twenty sixth," which M. Salazar had written, as "about the ninth" was a mistake made in the Chancery of our Legation here.

The telegram in question arrived at the Legation at 7 p.m. on 21 June and was immediately deciphered by the chancery clerk Kleefeld, part of it in my presence. The not very legible writing of the telegram caused difficulties in deciphering certain of the groups. The group representing "nine", however, caused no difficulty as I clearly remember. I am not in a position to furnish a copy of the telegram of the 21st[2] *as it reached me in cipher*, authenticated by my signature, since under Point 2 of the Instructions for the use of cipher codes, which the Prussian Legation had the honour to receive by Your Excellency's communication of 21 July, 1867, "the rough sheets of the decipher are to be destroyed immediately after the fair copy has been made when the decipher for purposes of checking has been entered either below or above the relevant groups" (as is always the practice here), and consequently I am no longer in possession of the original of the telegram.

In order to make up for this loss I have requested and received a copy of the telegram in question from the Telegraph Office here, attested by the Director, which I have the honour respectfully to enclose. In it at the relevant place there stands, it is true, the cipher group 5714, expressing the number twenty six, and to explain the error that has been made it can only be assumed that either by a mistake on the part of the Telegraph Office clerk here who dealt with the matter this cipher group 5714 of the original was not written as such, which is not very probable, or that

<hr>

[1] See Doc. No. 232.   [2] See Doc. No. 199.

it was written very illegibly, which is likewise improbable, since the deciphering of it presented no difficulty, a fact which, as I wrote you above, I clearly remember, or else, lastly, the chancery clerk, Kleefeld, who carried out the deciphering, in looking up the groups in the code book had the misfortune to make a slip, which might happen all the more easily since "about the ninth" made as good sense as "about the twenty sixth".

The note on the error[1] for M. Salazar, intended to serve for his personal justification, sent to me for delivery to him, has by my orders been given to him today by Herr Kleefeld. In receiving the document M. Salazar expressed his thanks for this kind attention and his regret for the trouble he has given. To the enquiry whether in his arrangements with M. Ruiz Zorrilla the formula "about the 9th" also had a meaning he replied in the negative.

CANITZ[2]

Annex

Berlin 21 June 1 h.
Madrid 21 June 5 h.

To the Minister of North Germany. Madrid.

4090	7912	122	1171	3686	6064	2116	
4438	205	1471	4759	310	1669	661	
1009	1479	1659	3505	5709	20	1046	
1487	5084	2476	3424	4778	3726	2504	
3747	6075	4420	79	3906	4457	3423	70
2111	1243	196	7912	7901	343	1829	
4462	3971	5023	72	3686	4924	2755	
5874	5877	4619	4878	3249	3251	20	
4437	1640	1340	5327	4939	27	79	
3111	1243	203	7912	658	2692	4461	
6068	1283	200	1471	3770	16	5279	274
1629	3897	5486	5164	7120	4655	5748	
5652	3286	5714	(2776)[3]	5353	73	491	575
5297	5084	3903	442	4016	5117	20	
5455	64	4569	2701	4923	442	2246	
311	63	6520	33	4151	4977	38	2111
4852	236	765	20	74	86	5093	9164
2478	3424	31	1460	2754= Thile			

Copy
Madrid 8 July 1870
Head of Department
L. BONET

[1] See Doc. No. 232, Annex.
[2] Marginal notes: "laid before H.M. 15.7.—submitted Ems 16.7. For the files. B[uche]r 17.7., Th[ile]."
[3] Marginal note by Canitz: "intervening stop lacking."

255. *Count von Bismarck to the Prince of Reuss,*
Prussian Minister at St Petersburg

(Telegram. Draft for cipher in Bucher's hand) [German]

Varzin, 9 July, 1870.[1] No. 60

No. 1   A 2102

We have long desired the rapprochement with Austria as far as can
be done without harm to our relations with Russia.

Fair copy signed by H.E.

256. *Abeken to the Ministry for Foreign Affairs*

(Telegram. Draft for cipher) [German]   Ems, 9 July, 1870[2]

No. 15   A 2149

Immediate.

If the Minister's letter to Prim, taken by Bucher on his second journey,
is in the files I am commanded by His Majesty to ask for a copy to be sent
here this evening.

A[BEKEN] 9.7.70

257. *Thile to Bucher*

(Telegram. Decipher) [German]

[Although already published by Lord, *Origins*, No. 64,
this telegram is reproduced here for Bismarck's marginal
notes on the decipher, to which Lord did not have access.]

Berlin, 9 July, 1870. 9.1 p.m.
arrived 10.15 p.m.
No. 71. Varzin, pr. 9 July, 1870

No. 13

Solms telegraphs from Paris today noon: "The situation grows every
moment more serious. French already arming. My colleagues and others
best able to know have the certainty[3] that unless within the next few days
Prussia does not definitely prevent the Hohenzollern candidature, a

---

[1] Marginal notes: "Enciphered and taken to Telegraph Office 9.7. 11.40 a.m.
B[uche]r. Copy per courier to Auswärtiges Amt, same day."

[2] Marginal note: "That same day, 4.15 p.m., taken to Telegraph Office, Ems."

[3] Marginal note by Bismarck: "Who can have that? Not even Napoleon himself."

French declaration of war is immediately imminent. France thinks this occasion for war particularly advantageous because the issue is not a German one[1] and this war is popular here. Duplicate to Ems."

THILE

258. Count von Bismarck to Thile

(Telegram. Decipher) [German]   Varzin, 9 July, 1870, 9.10 p.m.
                                                              arrived 10.10 p.m.
No. 16   A 2159. pr. 10 July, 1870

Answer to Salazar:

Question of congress or conference depends entirely on Spanish attitude. It all depends on whether Spain is willing to agree to a discussion of her affairs with other Powers. *We* have no occasion to pronounce an opinion on this matter as long as there is not a declaration from the Spanish Government.[2]

BISMARCK

259. Salazar to Baron von Canitz, Prussian Minister at Madrid

(Original) [French]   Saturday, 9 [July, 1870]

MY DEAR BARON,

I send you several copies of my pamphlet, which I beg you to send to Berlin, and to the Prince at Sigmaringen, near Bâle. Your coat of arms will ensure their being passed by the postal authorities.

It was read yesterday evening in all the [three words illegible] and the effect was superb.

Yet another telegram which you will find on the next page.

Ever yours

E. DE SALAZAR Y MAZARREDO

I am sending you the Imparcial.

★   ★   ★

(Telegram)[3]

Admiral bearing letter thanks started off yesterday. Pamphlet explaining everything and defending Prince producing very good effect. Opinion strengthening at moments.[4] Number of votes stipulated, amply covered.[5]

---

[1] Marginal note by Bismarck: "Nonsense. Attack on Germany is always entirely a German issue."

[2] This telegram was dispatched to Madrid on 10 July at 9.30 a.m.

[3] This telegram was dispatched to Berlin on 9 July at 3.30 p.m.

[4] "moments" was deciphered at Berlin as "monarchists".

[5] This sentence was deciphered at Berlin as: "number of senators' signed votes ample".

It is hoped Prince will stand firm and reply Tuileries that he is no longer his own master. Please communicate Prince. Usefulness of exploiting ill will Paris advanced press[1] towards Empress who openly favours Bourbons. Conference announced might let us gain time until election.

260. *Thile to Abeken*

(Original in Bülow's hand) [German]

Berlin, 9 July, 1870. evening
in A 2149

Reply to today's telegram No. 15[2]

According to the records Bucher on his second journey to Madrid last month did *not* take with him a letter from our Chief to Prim.

However the King's Messenger sent to Madrid on 2 June did bear such a letter.[3] The draft of it is here enclosed.[4] It is true it has not been initialled by the Minister nor does it bear a dispatch stamp, but entries in the day book of the cipher room leave *no* doubt that the dispatch actually took place.

Under the date 21 June Bucher on his return reports among other things to the Chief that Prim wanted from him (Count Bismarck) a reply[5] that he could show to others; he at the same time included a draft for a letter in this sense.[6] However the Chief did *not* agree to this proposal. The relevant documents are also among the enclosures; all enclosures are to be returned *as soon as possible.*   THILE

To HERR ABEKEN. Personal.[7]

How many of the enclosed are to be submitted to H.M. is left to your discretion.   TH[ILE]

261. *Bleichröder to Count von Bismarck*

(Original)[8] [German]

Berlin, 9 July, 1870
A 2157a. pr. 9 July, 1870

YOUR EXCELLENCY

permitted me this morning to telegraph that Havas yesterday evening reported "that in Toulon the equipment of 6 warships was being carried forward with all speed and that they were certainly not bound for China."

[1] These words were deciphered at Berlin as: "useful exploit ill will pressant avoncer Paris . . ."

[2] See Doc. No. 256.   [3] See Doc. No. 144.   [4] See Doc. No. 143.

[5] This is in reality Doc. No. 209, to which we assign the date 22 June, not 21 June.

[6] See Doc. No. 196.   [7] This postscript is in Thile's hand.

[8] Marginal note by Roland: "Received from His Highness in January, 1877 for the files. Roland."

The Paris newspapers without exception are loudly blowing the war trumpet! As regards the arming of the 6 vessels they are said to be bound for Algiers to fetch troops. After the Wimpffen affair I cannot quite believe that, and after all 6 vessels do not represent more than 6 battalions.

According to the latest reports from Paris the excitement there is intense and my faithful informant, who is very intimate with Gramont's First Secretary, says: "do not for Heaven's sake let the Spanish business be taken lightly," for French interests are too deeply engaged in the nomination to the Spanish throne. On my part I do not believe in the extreme seriousness of the political situation[1] and have therefore not yet done any selling on Your Excellency's account. Should I, however, be mistaken and should Your Excellency think that many more unpleasant incidents are to be expected, I respectfully beg you to warn me thereof by a single syllable.

With best regards I remain
Your Excellency's most devoted
GERSON BLEICHRÖDER

262. *Thile to Bucher*

(Original) [German]   B[erlin], 9 July, 1870
A 2135. Cf. A 2206

In obedience to instructions I had sent Prince Anton an account of the circumstances of the fatal cipher error (9th instead of 26th) by office messenger to Sigmaringen.[2] The office messenger has just brought me back the enclosed.[3] I await directions as to whether and how much I am to inform the Prince of the present situation by express messenger to S[igmaringen] or whether I am to leave this entirely to the correspondence which has been begun between Ems and Sigm[aringen].   THILE

263. *Thile to Bucher*

(Telegram. Decipher) [German]   Berlin, 10 July, 1870. 7.19 a.m.
arrived 8.15 a.m.
No. 78. Varzin, pr. 10 July
No. 15

Answer to No. 15.[4] Count Waldersee is back in Paris. On the other matters a discussion will take place with Chauvin and Weishaupt. General v. M[oltke] is in Silesia. For the moment I will have a talk with Colonel v[on] Stieble who is taking his place. Reports from Solms warlike in tone follow by post.   THILE

[1] Marginal note by Bismarck: "!".
[2] See Doc. No. 235.   [3] See Doc. No. 248.
[4] See doc. published by Lord, *Origins*, No. 68.

264. *Count von Bismarck to Count von Solms,*
Prussian Chargé d'Affaires at Paris

(Telegram. Draft for cipher in Bismarck's hand) [German]

[10 July, 1870]

[The text of this draft for cipher differs slightly from that published by Lord, *Origins*, No. 76.]

When people talk to you[1] of war, I request you to answer coldly and curtly that if it were declared on us we would fight. We are prepared and are in a position to defend ourselves and you should leave no one in doubt about this who addresses you on the matter.[2]

265. *Count von Bismarck to Thile*

(Telegram. Draft for cipher) [German]   Varzin, 10 July, 1870
                                                            No. 72

No. 18

[The text of the draft for cipher reproduced here contains three words omitted from the text published by Lord, *Origins*, No. 79.]

Conversation between Olozaga and Gramont in Telegram No. 14[3] to be printed somewhere or other as Paris Correspondence.

Time now for semi-official press to sound note of moral indignation[4] over Gramont's presumptuous demand and threat.

Fair copy signed by H.E.[5]

266. *Count von Bismarck to Count von Bernstorff,*
Prussian Ambassador in London

(Telegram. Draft for cipher) [German]   Varzin, 10.7.70
                                                            No. 79

No. 2

Provided Y.E. can for the time being do without Krause, please be so

---

[1] Lord's text has "offen" (openly) instead of "Ihnen" (to you).

[2] Lord's text has "anredete" (addressed) instead of "anredet" (addresses). Marginal note by Bucher: "2. Excellency von Thile. Duplicate. No. 17. Berlin. Enciphered and taken to Telegraph Office, 10.7., 9 a.m."

[3] See doc. published by Lord, *Origins*, No. 65.

[4] The words "of moral indignation" are lacking in Lord's text.

[5] Marginal note: "enciphered and taken to Telegraph Office, 10.7. 10.15 a.m."

kind as to let him have leave for a few weeks and send him here without delay. I intend to give him a temporary secret mission.

(Signed) v. B[ISMARCK][1]

267. *Count von Bismarck to General von Schweinitz,*
Prussian Minister at Vienna

(Telegram.[2] Draft for cipher) [German]   Varzin, 10 July, 1870
Nos. 60, 75

No. 1

According to a telegram from Reuss Archduke Albrecht has appealed to the Tsar for his good offices to bring about a rapprochement between Austria and Prussia. I have replied that we have long desired this so far as it can be done without harm to our relations with Russia.

Fair copy signed by H.E.[3]

268. *Abeken to Prince Karl Anton of Hohenzollern*

(Telegram en clair) [German]   Ems, 10 July, 1870

Hereditary Prince's letter of the tenor indicated in Your Royal Highness's letter to me as a plain exposition of the situation leaves the decision entirely to H.M. the King.   ABEKEN[4]

269. *Count von Bismarck to the Prince of Reuss,*
Prussian Minister at St Petersburg

(Telegram. Draft for cipher) [German]   [10.7.70]

No. 2

I do not think that in the present state of things you can leave St Petersburg as long as the Tsar is there, for business reasons.[5]

fair copy signed by H.E.[6]

---

[1] Thile was at the same time informed by special telegram of the communication to Bernstorff. Marginal note: "Enciphered and taken to the Telegraph Office 10.7.—10.15 a.m. K[eudell]."

[2] The text of this document has been published by Thimme, *Bismarck. Ges. Werke*, VIb, No. 1589.

[3] Marginal note by Bucher: "enciphered and taken to the Telegraph Office 10.7. 11 a.m. B[uche]r."

[4] Marginal notes: "Same day, 12.10 p.m. taken to the Telegraph Office, Ems. The statement expected from the Hereditary Prince is awaited here after his return from Alpine tour."

[5] See doc. published by Lord, *Origins*, No. 69.

[6] Marginal note: "Enciphered and taken to the Telegraph Office 10.7. 6.15 p.m. B[uche]r."

270. *Abeken to Count von Solms, Prussian Chargé d'Affaires at Paris*

(Telegram. Draft for cipher) [German]   Ems, 10 July, 1870

No. 2

If you receive intended list of officers for Chalons, you will now of course keep it back until further orders.

A[BEKEN] 10.7.70

271. *Baron von Canitz, Prussian Minister at Madrid, to Salazar*

(Draft) [French]   Ma[drid], 10 July, 1870
                                            Sunday evening

DEAR MONSIEUR DE SALAZAR,

I am instructed by Count von Bismarck[1] to reply to your telegram of the day before yesterday[2] that the question of a congress or conference depends entirely on the attitude that will be taken by Spain. All depends on whether Spain is willing to enter into negotiations with other Powers about her own affairs. We have no reason to pronounce an opinion in the matter so long as a declaration has not been made in this connexion by the Spanish Government.

Ever yours

C[ANITZ][3]

272. *Abeken to the Ministry for Foreign Affairs*

(Original) [German]   Ems, 10 July, 1870
                                           A 2196. pr. 11 July, 1870

H.M. the King desires that the enclosed letters[4] from the Prince of Hohenzollern, delivered here this morning by express messenger, shall be brought to the knowledge of the Chancellor as soon as possible. I have been obliged to prepare the copies in the greatest haste and therefore ask you, as there will be time enough to do so, to have legible copies made by your department for the Chancellor.

ABEKEN[5]

[1] See Doc. No. 258.
[2] See Doc. No. 251.
[3] Marginal note: "dispatched same day, 10 p.m. C[anitz]."
[4] See Docs. Nos. 252, 253.
[5] Marginal notes: "from Varzin, 13.7.—Now for the files. B[erlin] 13.7. Bü[low]. Thile."

273. *Abeken to Prince Karl Anton of Hohenzollern*

(Telegram en clair) [German]   Ems, 11 July, 1870

On account of difficulties of written and telegraphic communication His Majesty has sent a trusted army officer to Your Royal Highness for discussions by word of mouth. This officer left here yesterday evening.

ABEKEN[1]

274. *Strantz to Abeken*

(Telegram en clair)   Bruchsal, 11 July [1870]. 10.35 a.m.
                                        arr. at Ems 6.5 p.m.

Train has missed connexion, not arriving at destination therefore before evening.   (signed) STRANTZ

275. *Salazar to Baron von Canitz, Prussian Minister at Madrid*

(Original) [French]   11 July [1870]

MY DEAR BARON,
    I beg you to dispatch this telegram.
                            Kind regards
                                E. DE SALAZAR Y MAZARREDO

*   *   *

Telegram
    Telegram of 9th explains object Conference. Spain is mistress in her own house. Rear-admiral Polo is sole official envoy with Cabinet powers. Since his departure Cabinet opinion has not changed. France's attitude makes official candidate very popular. Please communicate Prince.

GAMA[2]

276. *Salazar to Baron von Canitz, Prussian Minister at Madrid*

(Original) [French]   11 July [1870]

MY DEAR BARON,
    Here is another telegram for Herr Thile, since the Count is still at Varzin.
                            Ever yours
                                E. DE SALAZAR

*   *   *

---

[1] Marginal note: "5.11 a.m. sent to the Ems Post Office."
[2] This telegram was dispatched by Canitz that same day at 2.20 p.m.

Natural anxiety makes us desire to know as soon as possible whether present state of negotiations between Prussia and France will render conflict inevitable.

GAMA[1]

277. *Thile to Bucher*

(Telegram. Decipher) [German]   Berlin, 11 July, 1870. 3.32 p.m.
arrived 4.35 p.m.
No. 109. Varzin, pr. 11 July

No. 22

Prince Gorchakov arrives here tomorrow morning intending to go on to Frankfort-on-Main on the morning of the day after tomorrow.

THILE

278. *Count von Eulenburg to Count von Bismarck*

(Telegram en clair) [German]   Berlin, 11.7.1870. 4.7 p.m.

Have you any objection to my coming tomorrow to Varzin for a few hours?

EULENBURG[2]

279. *Prince Karl Anton of Hohenzollern to Abeken*

(Telegram en clair) [German]   Sigmaringen, 11.7.1870. 5.25 p.m.

Officer not arrived, letter[3] still kept back by way of precaution, a copy of it will be in your hands by tomorrow.

PRINCE OF HOHENZOLLERN

280. *Count von Bismarck to Thile*

(Telegram. Draft for cipher) [German]   Varzin, 11 July, 1870

No. 27

For Monsieur Oubril.

Arriving Tuesday evening in Berlin, should be very pleased to see the Imperial Chancellor, having missed him twice.[4]

[1] This text was sent off by telegram the same day at 2.20 p.m.
[2] Marginal note by Bismarck. "Tomorrow evening I shall be in Berlin, summoned by the King to Ems, and shall hope to see you with Roon at my house for dinner. v. B[ismarck]."
[3] See Doc. No. 289.
[4] Marginal note by Bucher: "On directions from H.E. translated and enciphered.— Enciphered and taken to Telegraph Office. 11.7. 6.30 p.m. B[uche]r."
The text in Bismarck's hand runs: "Oubril. J'arrive à Berlin mardi soir et serais enchanté revoir Chancelier, l'ayant manqué à deux reprises."

281. *Count von Bismarck to Abeken*

(Telegram.[1] Draft for cipher) [German]   Varzin, 11 July, 1870
No. 115

No. 19
    If Herr von Werther is still there I should be glad if H.M. were to allow him to stay on until I arrive.
Fair copy signed by H.E.[2]

282. *Abeken to Prince Karl Anton of Hohenzollern*

(Telegram en clair)[3] [German]   11.7.70

    Colonel Strantz missed connexion because train late, must arrive tonight.
[signed] ABEKEN[4]

283. *Abeken to the King of Prussia*

(Original) [German]   8.20 p.m.

    I at once telegraphed:
        To his Royal Highness the Prince of Hohenzollern, Sigmaringen. Colonel Strantz missed connexion because train late, must arrive tonight.
(signed) ABEKEN[5]

284. *Count von Bismarck to the Prince of Reuss,*
Prussian Minister at St Petersburg

(Telegram. Draft for cipher) [German]   [11.7.70]

No. 3
    The passage in square brackets[6] to be inserted with what is written above, then continue:

[1] Lord noted the absence of this telegram from the files to which he was allowed access (*Origins*, p. vii, note 4).
    [2] Marginal note by Bucher: "enciphered and taken to Telegraph Office 11.7. 8 p.m."
    [3] Published by Fester, *Briefe*, No. 419.
    [4] Marginal note: "On 11.7 at 8.10 p.m. to Telegraph Office, Ems."
    [5] Marginal note by King of Prussia: "Do you know what letter the Prince means of which he promises you a copy? W. 11.7.70." See Doc. No. 289.
    [6] The passage in square brackets is Schweinitz's telegram of 11 July, 1870, published by Lord, *Origins*, No. 106.

As Solms reports[1] that Paris is making preparations and by all accounts intends a coup de main without mobilization, we too shall have to be mindful of our security. I am off to Ems tomorrow. If possible tell the Tsar this in confidence.[2]

285. Count von Bismarck to Thile

(Telegram. Draft for cipher) [German]   V[arzin] 11.7.70
                                                      No. 107
No. 23

Please ask Monsieur Oubril when Prince Gorchakov is arriving and how long he is staying, letting me know the result. I probably have to go to Berlin tomorrow and would be happy to see the Prince.

Fair copy signed by H.E.

286. Count von Bismarck to Thile

(Telegram. Draft for cipher) [German]   Varzin, 11.7.70
                                                      No. 111
No. 26

I wish to see Minister von Roon and Count Eulenburg tomorrow evening, preferably at dinner at my house, 6.30 p.m.

Will Your Excellency kindly arrange this, also requesting Minister of Commerce to have if possible a saloon coach ready on Wednesday morning for journey to Ems.[3]

287. Director General of Telegraph Service to Thile

(Original) [German]   Berlin, 11 July, 1870
                                            A 2204. pr. 11 July, 1870
                                            2 annexes[4]

Herewith enclosed the undersigned Director General has the honour respectfully to forward to Your Excellency the originals of the two cipher telegrams dispatched to Madrid from here on 21 June of the current year for which by your esteemed letter of 7 July[5] you asked the Berlin Central Telegraph Office; the obliging return of the same after use is requested.

[1] See doc. published by Lord, *Origins*, No. 112.
[2] Marginal note: "enciphered and taken to Telegraph Office 10.10 p.m. B[uche]r."
[3] Marginal note by Keudell: "enciphered and dispatched. K[eudell]."
[4] Marginal note by Thile: "To the Director General of the Telegraph Service in Berlin. 28 July."   [5] See Doc. No. 247.

The enquiries which have been made have shown that the telegrams in question were dispatched as follows:

1. No. 5241, to Madrid from Berlin, handed in on 21 June of the current year at 1.56 p.m., was received *correct* at Frankfort-on-the-Main and at 3.15 p.m. the same day telegraphed from Frankfort-on-the-Main to Paris from whence on being collated all the groups were returned *correct*.

2. No. 6251, to Madrid from Berlin, handed in on 21 June of the current year, 9.40 p.m., arrived correct at 10.15 p.m. at Frankfort o.M. and at 11.25 p.m. of the same day was telegraphed from Frankfort o.M. to Paris from whence likewise on being collated all the groups were returned correct.

Director General of Telegraph Service

Acting Director   MEYDEM

Annex
(Copy)
authenticated copy[1]

To the Minister of North Germany. Madrid.

4090	7912	122	4571	3686	6064	2116
4458	305	1487	4759	310	1669	661
1009	1479	16	59	3505	5709	20
1046	1487	5084	2476	3424	4878	3746
					(cancelled	
2504	3747	60	75	4420	by stamp)	79
3506	4457	3423	70	3111	1243	196
7912	7901	343	1825	4462	39	71
5023	72	3686	4924	2755	5874	5887
4615	4878	3249	3251	20	4437	1640
1340	5327	4935	27	79	3111	1243
203	7912	658	2692	44	61	6068
1283	200	1487	3870	16	5275	274
1629	3897	5486	61	64	7120	4655
5748	5652	3286	5714	27	76	5353
73	491	575	5297	5084	3903	442
4016	5117	23	5455	64	4569	2701
4923	442	2246	311	63	6520	33
4151	4977	37	3111	4852	236	765
30	74	86	5093	91	64	2478
3424	31	1460	2754			

(L.S.)[2] v. THILE

in place of original
Berlin, 2 July, 1870
Central Telegraph Station   v. . . . .

[1] Marginal note by Bülow: "keep here. Bülow."
[2] (L.S.) means: locus sigilli=seal.

288. *Crown Prince Frederick William to Count von Bismarck*

(Original) [German]   Potsdam, 11 July, 1870[1]
                                       A 2278. pr. 13 July, 1870

In accordance with your wish I wrote the Prince of Hohenzollern on the lines of your letter to me.[2]

Meanwhile according to reports from Paris the situation has assumed so serious and threatening an aspect that one can no longer close one's eyes to the possibility in certain eventualities of a general European war and an immediate conflict between France and Germany.

I have been in favour of the candidature of the Hereditary Prince of Hohenzollern ever since it came under discussion this spring as I assumed it would meet with no serious difficulties and could in no way lead to the danger of a conflict between France and . . .[3]

On this assumption it seemed to me that the accession of a Hohenzoller to the Spanish throne would *not* be without advantage to German interests and to the position of the dynasty and therefore deserved acceptance rather than rejection.

But as things now are this hypothetical advantage can no longer be thrown into the scales against the possibility, nay probability, of a terrible general war which this question threatens to conjure up over Prussia and Germany. In view of the provocative attitude assumed by the French Government our own Government will feel scruples about taking any steps which might have even the appearance of a withdrawal in the face of French threats.

However, in order to avert the danger of war it would seem an acceptable solution if the Hereditary Prince were to issue a declaration that in view of the changed situation and in consideration of the duty not to involve his fatherland in a war on his account he voluntarily withdrew his candidature! Should it not seem feasible for a suggestion on these lines to be made to the Hereditary Prince by the King or yourself, I declare my willingness at H.M. the King's command to take the necessary steps with the Hereditary Prince in the above-mentioned direction and have written in this sense to H.M.

Your most devoted

FREDERICK WILLIAM[4]

---

[1] Marginal note by Bismarck: "pr. 12."

[2] This correspondence is not to be found in the files of the German Foreign Ministry. The Sigmaringen Archives, however, contain the Crown Prince's letter of 8 July 1870, forwarding the letter addressed by Bismarck which has already been published by Thimme (Bismarck's *Gesamelte Werke*. Vol. VIb, Doc. No. 1569.).

[3] Word probably missing here.

[4] Marginal note by Bülow: "Executed by telegram to H.R.H. of 12 midnight. For the files. B. 13/7. Bülow—Th[ile]." Cf. telegram of 12 July, No. 294.

289. *Prince Karl Anton of Hohenzollern to Abeken*

(Original) [German]   Sigmaringen, 11 July, 1870
                                                       pr. Ems 12.7—2 p.m.

DEAR SIR,

Your telegram of yesterday,[1] sent to me at the command of H.M. the King, led me at once to write a letter to the Emperor Napoleon. It went[2] off today and I enclose a copy[3] for His Majesty's information. I deemed it necessary to adhere to the point of view taken today by the semi-official press and am enclosing a copy of my son's letter to Marshal Prim because it most clearly shows that the acceptance of the candidature was voluntary and not the result of pressure. As this letter will in any case be published it can do no harm if the Emperor receives the first intimation of its content.

I have also had a copy sent to Count Bismarck.

With my deepest respects and regards

PRINCE OF HOHENZOLLERN

290. *Strantz to Abeken*

(Telegram en clair) [German]   Sigmaringen, 12 July, 1870
                                                       handed in at 3.15

Found everybody already favourably prepared. My arrival turned the scales, induced betrothed to renounce alliance, returning noon tomorrow.

STRANSS [*sic*]

291. *Prince Karl Anton of Hohenzollern to the King of Prussia*

(Telegram en clair) [German]

Sigmaringen, 12 [July, 1870.] 2.25 p.m.
arrived 4.30 p.m.

Telegram to Prim announcing withdrawal sent off, likewise copy of same to Olozaga in Paris.[4] Letter with all details[5] will be brought tomorrow at 10 by officer on his return.

PRINCE OF HOHENZOLLERN

[1] See Doc. No. 268.

[2] Marginal note by Abeken: "kept back once more after yesterday's telegram from H.R. Highness the Prince." Cf. Doc. No. 279.

[3] Published by Fester, *Briefe*, No. 420.

[4] See Doc. No. 297.   [5] See Doc. No. 295.

292. *Salazar to Baron von Canitz, Prussian Minister at Madrid*

(Original) [French]   Tuesday, 12 [July, 1870]

MY DEAR BARON,

I beg you to send off the following telegram as a matter of extreme urgency.

Yours ever

E. DE SALAZAR Y MAZARREDO

   ★ ★ ★

FOR HERR THILE

Veuillez prier Prince tenir réservée [*sic*] comme mon opinion particulière, conseils sur réponse aux Tuileries.

[Please request Prince keep entirely to himself as my personal opinion advice on reply to Tuileries.]

GAMA[1]

293. *Crown Prince Frederick William to Count von Bismarck*

(Telegram en clair) [German]

Potsdam, Neues Palais, 12.7.70. 9.20 p.m.
A 2281. pr. 13 July, 1870

Can I write on the lines of the final passage of my letter to you?[2] The King, as he telegraphs me, is in favour.

CROWN PRINCE

294. *Count von Bismarck to Crown Prince Frederick William*

(Telegram en clair) [German]

Official news of Hereditary Prince's withdrawal has arrived here from Werther via Madrid and Paris.

signed BISMARCK[3]

---

[1] This telegram was dispatched by Canitz the same day at 4 p.m., arriving the following day at 10.55 a.m. in Berlin, where its decipher was found unintelligible: "A. Aquila. Vice-consul Prince se tenir réservé; comme mon opinion phare, conseil sur réponse aux Tuileries."

[2] See Doc. No. 288.

[3] Marginal note: "Taken to Telegraph Office 12.7.—10.50 p.m."

295. Prince Karl Anton of Hohenzollern to the King of Prussia

(Original)[1] [German]

> [Fester has published (*Briefe*, No. 455) an incomplete text
> of this letter which he reproduces from Zingeler, pp. 256-7.
> The omitted passages are italicized in the text below.]

Sigmaringen, 12 July, 1870

YOUR MAJESTY,

*With a beating heart I received Your letter[2] this morning from the hand of
Colonel von Strantz.*

*Before opening it I opened my heart to the Colonel, telling him that I only
awaited his arrival to send off the telegram, held ready in advance,[3] about the
decision to renounce the throne.*

The thought of an imminent casus belli because of a purely family
matter had become so unbearable that I had to hold myself in leash not to
publish the decision already yesterday. *But I thought it my duty first of all
to await Colonel von Strantz's arrival.*

Of Napoleon's PERSONAL desire to keep the peace I have today striking
proof. Namely he has expressed it as his wish to King Leopold of the
Belgians and requested him to press us for a withdrawal.

I was fortunate enough to be able *today* to inform the King by my
daughter Marie, who has been staying here, that the decision had already
been made.

All this concourse of events has made this day an important and
decisive one.

It now rests with the French Government to prove itself in earnest
about the preservation of peace now that the PRETEXT for war has been
removed. If not, then it is clear that Napoleon is the submissive tool of the
war party, which he is obliged blindly to obey for dynastic reasons.

If France wants war à tout prix, that will make the position incompar-
ably more favourable for us— the cause of war will no longer be a minor
family concern—England will morally and perhaps also materially take
her stand against the wanton disturber of the peace and public opinion
will everywhere be in our favour—the war will retain a national character and the German question will be brought nearer to its needed
solution.

*If we keep the peace until next spring the most favourable solution of the
army question can be expected during the winter session.*

In this way the tables will be turned against France; and whereas in

---

[1] Marginal note: "By Colonel Strantz."

[2] A version of this letter is published by Fester, *Briefe*, No. 399.

[3] Cf. Doc. No. 297.

the Spanish war question her position was compact and advantageous, now her position at home and abroad will become precarious if she shows herself to be seeking merely for PRETEXTS, not for genuine causes. My son is not yet back from his Alpine tour—*I do not know where to find him*—*tomorrow my daughter-in-law returns from Reichenhall—she does not say where her husband is roaming.*

I am therefore acting on my son's behalf in all this and take full responsibility upon myself for all I do and omit to do. It need not be known publicly that he is absent for the moment. Probably he will read in the *Augsburger Zeitung* tomorrow about his assuredly welcome fate!

If the French were better versed in geography and if they did not always look in Düsseldorf for him it would not be surprising if the press were to launch a rumour that he had slipped off incognito to Spain!!!

May Your Majesty ever favour us with Your Royal grace and not reproach us too much for the unrest and excitement we have caused Your Majesty in such abundant measure as a result of all these events.

With the greatest devotion, loyalty and veneration I remain
Your Majesty's most humble and obedient
servant and cousin
KARL ANTON, PRINCE OF HOHENZOLLERN

296. *Prince Karl Anton of Hohenzollern to the King of Prussia*

(Original) [German]   S[igmaringen] 12.7.70

P.S. with my humble duty.[1]

I have just received from Reichenhall the original of Your Majesty's letter of 21 June[2] to my son.
I enclose a copy thereof with my humble duty.
PRINCE OF HOHENZOLLERN

297. *Prince Karl Anton of Hohenzollern to the King of Prussia*

(Original)   Sigmaringen, 12 July, 1870

[German] Enclosed with my humble duty are drafts of the telegrams dispatched today to the press in Madrid and Paris.
PRINCE OF HOHENZOLLERN

★   ★   ★

[1] Cf. Doc. No. 295.   [2] See Doc. No. 203.

Sigm[aringen], 12 July, 1870

Telegram (French)

To the Spanish Ambassador, Paris.

I think it my duty to inform you, the representative of Spain in Paris, that I have just dispatched the following telegram to Marshal Prim at Madrid:

In view of the complications which my son Leopold's candidature for the throne of Spain seems to meet with and the difficult situation created for the Spanish nation by recent events placing it in a dilemma in which it cannot be guided otherwise than by its own feeling of independence, and being convinced that in such circumstances its vote could not have the sincerity and spontaneity on which my son had counted in accepting the candidature, I withdraw it in his name.

PRINCE OF HOHENZOLLERN[1]

*   *   *

[German] The telegram to Olozaga went off first, the one to Prim *later*, that being the best way for me to bring its content to the knowledge of the French Government.

*   *   *

The following paragraph has been sent to the *Schwäbische Merkur* in Stuttgart and the *Augsburger Allgemeine Zeitung*:

"In order to restore to the Spanish Government its freedom of initiative the Hereditary Prince withdraws his candidature for the throne —firmly resolved not to allow a minor family concern to develop into a pretext for war."

298. *Salazar to Baron von Canitz, Prussian Minister at Madrid*

(Original) [French]   13 July [1870]

MY DEAR BARON,

Here is another telegram which I beg you to dispatch.

Ever yours

E DE SALAZAR Y MAZARREDO

*   *   *

Secret. Council of Ministers and opinion consider Prince's withdrawal a new title to Spanish esteem. Last passage father's statement leaves future open: we shall ask for Congress to state our case and then act as we choose. Reassembly Cortes deferred to avoid discussion. Telegram date error

[1] The text of this telegram to Prim is well known. See Fester, *Briefe*, No. 452.

ruined everything. But for deferment Prince would have been elected the seventh. Opinion much roused against Napoleon and Montpensier.

GAMA[1]

299. *Prince Karl Anton of Hohenzollern to Abeken*

(Original) [German]   Sigmaringen, 13 July, 1870

DEAR SIR,
   Will you obligingly receive from the hands of my Court Librarian, Court Counsellor Dr Lehner, the letter in question[2] to His Majesty the King, and kindly arrange that His Majesty should grant him a few minutes' audience as a highly *reliable* and trusted man.
   You would do me a great service if by Dr Lehner you would inform me of any reversion of public opinion at home and abroad.

Your humble and obedient servant
P[RINCE] O[F] HOHENZOLLERN

300. *Prince Karl Anton of Hohenzollern to the King of Prussia*

(Original) [German]   Sigmar[ingen], 13 July, 1870

YOUR MAJESTY,
   I hereby submit to you with deepest respect the copy of a telegram[3] received this morning from the Spanish Embassy in Paris showing that Olozaga did not lose a minute in notifying the French Government of the withdrawal from the candidature for the throne.
   Further I submit with my humble duty a copy of the reply of the King of the Belgians.[4] This reveals that the Emperor Napoleon seeks a peaceful line of escape. Although now the letter is overtaken by events I think it too important after all not to be placed in Your Majesty's hands at once by courier.

With humble homage
P[RINCE] O[F] HOHENZOLLERN

[1] This telegram was dispatched by Canitz the same day at 9.30 p.m., arriving at Berlin 14 July at 6.40 a.m. The decipher bears the marginal note by Bismarck: "Did this go via Falmouth or via France?" Roland's reply to this enquiry runs: "Received via Paris; the instruction to telegraph via Falmouth went off on 13 July a.m."
[2] See Doc. No. 300.
[3] See doc. published by Fester, *Briefe*, No. 469, following Zingeler, pp. 258-9.
[4] See doc. published by Fester, *Briefe*, No. 367, following Zingeler, p. 254.

301. *The King of Prussia to Abeken*

(Original) [German]   [14.7.70]

Make a copy of the enclosed[1] or get one made, if you can, in order that I may have the full collection of copies which I already have put in the files.

W[ILLIAM] 14.7.70

302. *The Landgrave of Heyden to the King of Prussia*

(Original)[2] [German]   Villa Giulia, near Bellagio, Lake Como.
15.5.70
A 2857. pr. 21 July, 1870

MOST GRACIOUS KING,

An official letter from the Spanish and Portuguese Consul General at Copenhagen, Baron Gedelia, reached me a few days ago, and I take the liberty of sending it to Your Majesty herewith in a German translation.— I should not have thought it of enough importance to trouble Your Majesty with it if recent events had not urged me to greater caution. Perhaps in this case similar capital could be made of the fact that I am married to a Prussian Princess as has recently been made of the Hereditary Prince's relationship to the Royal House. Even the most remote possibility of involving Your Majesty in complications is important enough for me to bring the matter to Your Majesty's knowledge.

As far as my own attitude to the matter is concerned Your Majesty will certainly approve of my decision to decline the proposal.

I have the honour to sign myself Your Majesty's most humble and devoted nephew

FREDERICK
Landgrave of Heyden [3, 4]

[1] See Doc. No. 253.

[2] Marginal note by the King of Prussia: "Put with the previous Spanish documents." —Marginal note by Bismarck: "A[uswärtiges] A[mt] *secr*[eta]."

[3] Marginal note by the King of Prussia: "I think one experience is enough for us. W[illiam] 20.7.70."

[4] Marginal note by the King of Prussia: "Your letter of 15th of this month received by me yesterday. After the experiences I have just had in a similar case, you can well imagine that I have no intention of giving yet another time advice *to refuse, as I consistently did* when, solely in my capacity as head of the family, I was drawn into the matter. In your case where there is no question of this family position I have still less occasion to advise and must leave it entirely to yourself to make the decision. Your W[illiam]. B[erlin]."

Annex
Translation of Baron Gedelia's report

Copenhagen, 7.7.1870

YOUR HIGHNESS,

Pardon my boldness in approaching you thus in a certain matter although I am fully conscious that the right way would be for me to ask you personally and by word of mouth to grant me an interview.

I will be as brief as possible, hoping that at least my name and position will be known to you.

In confidential negotiations with one of the most influential members of the Spanish Government I have been empowered to approach Your Highness with the enquiry whether, if the Spanish crown were to be offered you from another quarter, you would be disposed to accept it.

Although I need not point out to Your Highness that there is no time to be lost and can confidently rely on the certainty of the necessary discretion on Your Highness's part, I beg your Highness in the event of your willingness to consider the matter to telegraph to me the following words:

"I wish to see you."

I shall then have the immediate honour of waiting personally upon Your Highness and submitting the official documents to you. In the event, however, of Your Highness being of the opposite opinion, I beg you to telegraph me as follows:

"The matter does not interest me."

With the highest esteem I have the honour to sign myself Your Highness's humble servant

BARON GEDELIA. Spanish and Portuguese Consul General

303. *Thile to the Director General of the Telegraph Service*

(Draft) [German]

Berlin, 28 July, 1870
A 2204

The Foreign Ministry has the honour herewith to return to the Director General, with thanks and after having consulted them, the originals of the two cipher telegrams sent from here to Madrid on 21 June of the current year and enclosed with your obliging letter of the 11th inst.[1,2]

Foreign Ministry of the N[orth] G[erman] C[onfederation][3]

[1] See Doc. No. 287.

[2] Marginal note: "*Attach hereto* the originals of the two cipher telegrams sent here in [cipher] *A 2204.*

(The enclosed attested copy of the first of these telegrams to be retained in the Foreign Ministry files.)" See Annex to Doc. No. 287.

[3] Marginal note: "Bü[low] 27th."

304. *Salazar to Baron von Canitz, Prussian Minister at Madrid*

(Original) [French]   16 Nov[ember], 1870

MONSIEUR LE BARON,

I have been unwell for the last month and have just returned from the Cortes with a heavy chill. I must have a word with you *this very evening* and I would beg you to be so good as to call at my house, Calle de Hortaleza 34, 2nd floor, the doctor having forbidden me to go out.

Yours ever
E DE SALAZAR Y MAZARREDO

*   *   *

311 votes.
191 Aosta   344—191—153
120 against among them 27 for Montpensier
33 absent

Almost all the ex-Ministers, including M. Topete, were among the minority of 120. Catholic emotion overexcited. Coolness of opinion—comparison with the prestige that Prince Leopold's candidature would have enjoyed.

305. *Baron von Canitz, Prussian Minister at Madrid, to Count von Bismarck*

(Telegram. Draft for cipher) [German]

Madrid, 17 November, 1870

Confidential. An hour after yesterday's vote in the Cortes in which M. Salazar voted for the Duke of Aosta, he made me the proposal to ask Your Excellency by telegraph to get Count Brassier to use his influence in Florence to induce the Duke of Aosta not to accept election in circumstances thus unfavourable to himself so that it might become possible to revert once again to the candidature of the Hereditary Prince of Hohenzollern.

I answered in a not unfriendly form that at this moment such a step did not seem to me appropriate. To my question whether he had been authorized by Marshal Prim to have the talk with me he replied in the negative.

306. *Baron von Canitz, Prussian Minister at Madrid,*
to Count von Bismarck

(Telegram. Decipher) [German]　　　Madrid, 21 February, 1871
　　　　　　　　　　　　　　　　　　A 945. pr. 28 February, 1871
　　　　　　　　　　　　　　　　　　No. 6874. pr. 3.3.71[1, 2]

No. 15

Two nights ago after a long illness Don Eusebio Salazar y Mazarredo, the active negotiator with the Hereditary Prince of Hohenzollern in the question of the candidature for the Spanish throne, died here.

　　　　　　　　　　　　　　　　　　　　　　(signed) CANITZ

307. *Count von Arnim, German Ambassador in Paris,*
to Prince von Bismarck

(Original)[3] [German]　　　　　　Paris, 14 January, 1873
　　　　　　　　　　　　　　　　　A 147. pr. 19 January, 1873[4]

No. 7

M. Olozaga narrated to me yesterday in talking of the death of the Emperor Napoleon that this event set him free to speak of certain incidents which had occurred here in the decisive days of July, 1870, and in which he had taken a part.

In the days of 5-7 July he had been above all in consternation over the disaster which threatened to befall his country if Prince Leopold's candidature were pressed. France, he said, was in a position to stir up a civil war in Spain which would have reduced the country to ruin. He had never felt any doubt that the Cortes and the nation would take up arms against France in defence of the elected King, but he, Olozaga, could not but acknowledge to himself that in the struggle everything would have been imperilled for the sake of the Hohenzollern dynasty. He had therefore busied himself for several days with the idea of making an appeal to Prince Leopold to use his discretion as to further action.

After making up his mind on this question he had gone on the evening of 7 July to the Emperor and asked him whether peace would be assured

---

[1] Marginal note by Bismarck: "Copy to be put in the files."

[2] Marginal note by Abeken: "Put in the files, 3.3.71."

[3] The document itself is not in the files relating to the Hohenzollern candidature, but they contain the following note: "A 147. pr. 19 January, 1873. No. 7, Paris, 14 January, 1873. Memorandum. The Imperial Ambassador, Count von Arnim, reports on a conversation with the Spanish Ambassador, Olozaga, about the decisive days of July, 1870. Original in the file: IA Bc 70. adh[ibenda] IX."

[4] Marginal note by Bismarck: "laid before H.M. 23.1.—Bu[cher]." Marginal note by Bucher: "Put in the files. Bu[che]r. 23.1."

R　　　　　　　　　　　257

if Prince Leopold withdrew his candidature. The Emperor had been extremely astonished at this question and had replied: "That is a question which does more honour to your patriotism than it is flattering to my intelligence. It is clear that if the Hohenzollern candidature were out of the way, peace would be assured, but how can you imagine that Count von Bismarck, who has engineered all this *de longue main* to provoke us, will let the opportunity slip?"

M. Olozaga put forward a different opinion and in the end obtained the Emperor's authorization to appeal to Prince Leopold and make him understand that his renunciation of the Spanish throne would undoubtedly avert a great disaster. "Perhaps—the Emperor had added—you judge the situation better than I. I have always had a great liking for the Prince of Hohenzollern. That is probably why they did not want to leave me to deal with him. He may well be willing to take heed of what you propose to say to him. By the way this is strictly between ourselves. Nothing must be said about it either to Ollivier or to Gramont."

Thereupon M. Olozaga wrote, as he says, either to the Prince of Hohenzollern or to Prince Leopold, I am not sure which, on approximately the following lines.

"I am not only an Ambassador but also a deputy in the Cortes. In this latter capacity I feel it my duty to go to Madrid and vote for Your Highness and call upon the country to take vigorous action on your behalf. But I know that by so doing Spain would embark on a course which would end in a great misfortune and I therefore cannot refrain from drawing Your Highness's attention etc."

By a trustworthy person—not a Spaniard—whom he could not name without permission[1] he sent his letter to the Weinburg.

M. Olozaga believes that the well-known telegram of Prince Anton[2] was the result of this letter.

On the return of his confidential messenger he went late on the evening of the 13th to St Cloud to communicate the messenger's report to the Emperor. The adjutant on duty refused to announce him because the Emperor was at a Cabinet meeting. In the end, on M. Olozaga's declaring that the matter was extremely important, he called the Emperor out.

Napoleon was most pleasantly surprised by M. Olozaga's communication. On returning to the Cabinet he met with much opposition but in the end the Cabinet dispersed in the firm conviction that peace was assured.

A quarter of an hour later the Emperor went to see the Empress and found the Duc de Gramont already with her.

"At a quarter to twelve, midnight, on 13 July peace was concluded [*geschlossen*]—at a quarter past twelve, midnight, war was inevitable."

"The Emperor never wanted the war."

[1] Marginal note: "By Strat."
[2] Marginal note: "of 12 July." See Doc. No. 297.

I may have misunderstood the Spanish Ambassador in certain details, as he speaks so indistinctly that he is difficult to follow. But on the whole I do not think I heard amiss anything essential.

His version does not entirely tally with the already known stories of others.

As regards the sending of a confidential messenger to the Weinburg Your Highness will no doubt already know the name of the person and whether it was this mission which caused Prince Anton's withdrawal.

ARNIM

APPENDIX A

Versen's Diary: 18 May–22 July 1870

18 May, 1870

Sent in name to the Crown Prince at the Palais. He came from a Cabinet meeting and was—after the Carlsbad cure—very excitable; he asked a few questions about Spain and said all he had heard was that the matter was at an end; he had just been seeing the "King of Spain" out riding. He told me to come tomorrow morning to Potsdam by the 10 o'clock train.

19 May

10 a.m. to Potsdam. One of the Prince's carriages awaiting me at the station. Major von Werner of the Belgarde Dragoons took me along. For more than an hour the Prince talked with me about Spanish conditions. He had read the report I had handed him yesterday and asked whether he could keep it longer; I begged him to keep it altogether as I had nearly finished copying another and would now complete it. He began by saying that he had heard from various quarters that I had been sent on ahead to Spain and that General von Goeben was to follow with the young Prince of Hohenzollern. I mentioned that I had avoided all questions and always gone to Dresden when I had to wait in Berlin; but many people had of course got to know of things. We talked over the whole affair, for which he showed much interest and understanding. He said that the position of his House had undergone a great transformation and it had to fulfil a great civilizing mission both in Rumania and elsewhere. (In the same way as the English with their mission in Corfu.) He took up the cudgels for the Prince of Rumania, who was still known only as "Little Charlie" in the family, just as Frederick of Augustenburg was called "Frederick, the Slowcoach" and thus rendered ridiculous with a flippancy that lacked all justification. I told him about my talk with the King. He said he thought that from the very beginning not only Russian but also Austrian money was working against him (the Prince of Rumania). I said that was just what the King had wanted to say to the Tsar. He said a thing like that could happen without the Tsar's knowledge. The Tsar is willing to show favour to the Germans and yet how are they being maltreated in the Baltic provinces! In Rumania the people are already very contented, only the Boyars are venial and contemptible. I once again clearly explained to him the position of the clergy, of the parties, of Prim as mayor of the palace, that of the Grandees, the artizans, everything. He was surprised at my regarding Spain, especially certain

261

provinces, as no less monarchist than Germany. We discussed one by one the Bourbons, Montpensier, Comte d'Eu, Duke of Parma, Isabella, Alfonso, the Iberian idea, the army. On all these the answers I gave and my replies to his objections were such that he said: "You are too sanguine about things; the new King will have no bed of roses, only a bed of thorns." But he was concerned for the greatness of his House. I explained how things were, namely that it was not the Hereditary Prince but the second son who was under consideration, whereat he added that since as a family they were not given to loose living their numbers would still go on increasing. I therefore said: "The Hereditary Prince can of course come home again when his eldest son comes of age, the second will become the heir and there would still be the third." He once again described his relations with Leopold and that of the ladies. He had hoped that the King would command Prince Frederick as Louis XIV had commanded his grandson or great-grandson. I said Frederick was not suitable, giving my opinion of him and telling of my recent conversation.

The Crown Prince with his wife had to go to the Dowager Queen's and asked me what I was going to do. "Nothing." He said he was sorry he could not offer me a meal, I was to go and lunch at the Lord Chamberlain's table. At lunch I had a conversation with Major von Normann and Fräulein von Below and sat between Countess Brühl and Major Mischke.

After lunch an hour again with the Prince. I talked with greater ease. I was able to meet all his objections and clear up many points. He enquired what the King had said, what he thought. It so happened, however, that Prince Frederick had been with him and had carried the day. It was all over and done with, he said. The Crown Prince had teased him but had realized that he would make a better cavalry captain than a king, a contrast to Carol of Rumania! I insisted that Spain would be easier to govern than Rumania—there was a Constitution and there would certainly be people on whom reliance could be placed. The whole thing gone over once again. I said the Margrave of Brandenburg had had more to contend with than the future King of Spain, and this crown would never be offered again, Civil List of 750,000 Marks; Spanish language etc. etc. The Prince said: "My ancestors began earlier than Carol of Rumania." Various interesting discussions by the way. Also the letter to Bismarck, opened by the King, had to be read aloud to him by me and my opinion given of Prim and his position. I said I thought I could easily renew contacts, asked for his backing, gave an account of how matters stood and of what the King, Bismarck, Thile and the Prince of Hohenzollern thought. *Prince*: "Have you not been in Düsseldorf?" *Myself*: "What would I, a Major from Posen, be doing there? Give me a letter. Send me there!" *Prince*: "Under whose command are you?" *Myself*: "Under Moltke, he can send me; give me a letter." *Prince*: "I will write to Moltke at once." He wrote and gave me the letter. I was to telegraph when I passed through Potsdam.

I went to Moltke at Berlin and briefly told him what I had effected. He was quite vehement about Prince Frederick and said he had told him the same thing straight out. It would be damaging for us one day if an Archduke or a Bavarian or an Orleans came to the helm there (this I had said to the Crown Prince too) or a republic was set up (which, by the way, Bismarck did not think the worst that could happen). He granted me leave. I telegraphed to the Neues Palais that I would be passing through Potsdam on the morrow 9 a.m. en route for Düsseldorf. In the evening I wrote. Bucher came and said that Bismarck, too, had thrown up the game because he got too irritated with His Majesty as soon as he came into conflict with the latter's personal feelings.

20 May

8.30 a.m. off to Düsseldorf; in Potsdam the two letters were handed to me. At Düsseldorf I learnt that the old Prince was at Nauheim. The Hereditary Prince intends to go to Brussels tomorrow; I telegraphed that tomorrow with the earliest train I would come to see him at Benrath.

21 May

8.30 a.m. off to Benrath. A carriage awaits me, I drive to the Hereditary Prince's. He has only half an hour to spare as he cannot postpone his journey. We drive together to Düsseldorf in his carriage but I have time enough to touch on the most important points, on which I was able to enlighten him. I noticed a willingness in him; he said he could not be a mere shadow of a king, he was not so constitutionally minded as the King of Portugal about whom actually today's dispatches are saying that Saldanha has made a Pronunciamento and stormed the Palace, whereupon the King has made him a Minister; he (the Hereditary Prince) could never make a man like that a Minister. He took the defence of Montpensier. I denied the latter's pretensions to a legitimate claim and told him that the House of Bourbon together with the House of Orleans had already been discussed and rejected by a large majority. We went on to discuss Prim, the clergy, the budget (he would refuse to begin his reign with state bankruptcy). All I had to say produced such a favourable effect on him that he begged me to make the acquaintance of the old Privy Councillor of the family. I spent some hours with him at the huntsman's lodge and entirely brought him round; of course the conditions in Rumania are always the bogey that makes them scared of those in Spain. In the end he asked my consent to his introducing me to the old Princess, his mother. I was half an hour with the rather deaf old lady explaining to her in particular that the new King could not possibly come into conflict with the clergy, that her protégé Montpensier possessed no claims and had no prospects. She asked whether the clergy were as uneducated as in Mexico, the people as wicked as in the Near East, the soldiery unreliable etc. etc.

She had gruesome imaginings and will not have let herself be persuaded by me, since she would be deprived of their lovely family life if the Hereditary Prince were to go to Spain: selfishness the whole thing! about noon I took the train via Cologne to Nauheim. I had arranged with the Hereditary Prince that he would come at once in answer to a telegram. That evening I sent in my name to Prince Karl Anton asking whether he had any messages to give me for Bucharest as I was on my way thither. He heard my name and at once received me. As ill luck would have it he had a letter of the 14th from the King saying that I had looked at everything through too rose-coloured spectacles. I replied that here everything was looked at as if it were a spectre and that I had conscientiously observed and reported all weaknesses and abuses. I liked the Prince very much, I have never met so much distinction, naturalness and frankness in a Prince. He settled that tomorrow at 12 I shall make my report to him and after that lunch with him, in the evening I could then leave by the express. I did not betray that I had quite other intentions. We touched superficially on the well-known points. He was interested in Lopez and I had to tell him a lot about Paraguay. At the end he began again about how much he had wished that his younger son would have more drive; what a misfortune it had been that Bismarck was ill, the Crown Prince absent and Thile the only adviser. I agreed that this was a misfortune and that otherwise it would all have turned out differently. He said that if he had been a bit younger he would have undertaken it himself, taking his younger son with him. The King had told him that Frederick Charles would willingly have gone, but for the religion. He enquired whether Bismarck were kept informed and added: To be sure, if Bismarck says it is an interest of the state it would then be his duty. (This I shall use tomorrow.) We talked a lot, he said it was strange that all this had been kept secret from him, he having got the impression in Berlin that such a thing was out of the question. Bismarck, he said, was irreplaceable; he must now reap what he had sown. We talked of the Rumanians and much else.

22 May

At Hotel Belle Vue bad dinner and bad night's sleep. At 12 in morning coat to Prince's. I always find I make a better effect in uniform than in mufti, probably because of the Pour le Mérite and the ribbons for courses of training! Here all sail will have to be hoisted or else I shall be travelling this very night via Berlin back to Posen! The Prince was most understanding, kind in every way and in agreement. He says: "You are putting the knife to my throat"; he asks for information on all sorts of questions, and I tell him how to make his Family Law in the matter of the entail since he asked me: "Shall I have to maintain the King of Spain? That would come too expensive." Further, it was particularly acceptable to him that the Prince would have to be supported by a two-third majority and could then stay on here for three or four months to learn the language and settle family questions. He asked how the thread could be picked up again, how he was to behave with the King so as not to seem fickle, what was the attitude of France, what were the ideas of the Crown Prince, Bismarck and Moltke. We discussed the most delicate questions: Schleinitz, Delbrück, Thile, the Queen, Frederick Charles, Rumania, Prince Frederick, in short everything. Much struck me as thoroughly funny. I lunched with him at 2, then we were at the concert and after it sat down on a bench in the promenade where again 100 questions were discussed. I reminded him of the Margraves of Brandenburg, the renown of the Family, duty towards the State; Spain could help Rumania better than Prussia, and Prussia could help Spain. He is afraid the press will be hostile, even the *Kreuzzeitung*; I dispute this, moreover France, where the Emperor had triumphed by a plebiscite, would keep quiet, if not, it would be all the better for us. I laid the main stress on its being his duty to make the sacrifice and part with his son. There was the railway and he could often go and visit him, moreover in 15 years from now the Hereditary Prince could come back home again when his son was of age; this moment would never offer itself again and by the time he had 12 grandsons he would be sorry about it. I told him I had talked with the Princess, his wife, and reached agreement with the Hereditary Prince that he would appear in answer to a telegram. I proposed Düsseldorf as a rendezvous. He thought it would be better here. In spite of my urging he could not make up his mind to telegraph the Hereditary Prince. He wanted first to write once more to the Crown Prince. I am to come and see him again tomorrow at 12. He went on to tell of Moltke's brilliant plan to raze 15 fortresses rendered useless by the railway; we talked about Blumenthal, he said he thought our generals ought to have a better political training, was impressed by the secrecy in the present question which from his own experience he would have thought impossible.—In the evening I wrote Moltke asking him to get Bismarck to write a letter to Prince Karl Anton saying that acceptance would be to the interest of the state.

23 May

Letter to Schneider [Louis Schneider, reader to the King, whose acquaintance Versen had made]. At 12 to the Prince's. He gave me the letter to the Crown Prince, which he read aloud to me as far as it related to the present matter. He does not want to seem fickle but says he will stand aloof and leave the decision to his son. Since the rejection his son had had two scruples: 1. as regards obligations towards the House of Hohenzollern, 2. as regards obligations towards his country and profession. He, the father, still viewed the matter as he had always done but left it to the Crown Prince and Bismarck to bring about his son's decision and be its advocates with the King. After that we only discoursed about the castle, the Princely stables, the servants, crown jewels, whether the Guards... etc. etc. I enquired how long the son would be staying in Brussels. A few days, then he goes to Benrath. We lunched together and talked again of America with his adjutant von Collas. At table I received a telegram from Moltke: "Please come at once." He was surprised and grew suspicious. I said I could see a reason, because Bismarck had returned I must report to him. *He*: "How does Moltke know that you are at Nauheim?" *Myself*: "I told him because I did not find Your Excellency at Düsseldorf and he must know where I am." He was reassured and asked me whether I would see Moltke or the Crown Prince first, making the time-table so that I should first see the Crown Prince; I said I would be staying at the "Windsor" and I would be at the Crown Prince's at 11; if I had time before that I would first go to Moltke.

24 May

Missed the connexion in Kassel, 3 hours late in Berlin. At once to Moltke at the Reichstag. He told Bismarck I was there and took me to a Minister's room. Soon came Bismarck buttoned up in his Cuirassier's coat. We sat down and I had to tell how I had found things in Berlin, what they all think: King, Crown Prince, Prince Karl Anton, Queen, Princess Karl Anton; he said he was now dropping the youngest Prince but intended to send me to Rumania. I explained to him that the Hereditary Prince was more ready than ever and that the Rumanian would not leave where he is. (Yes, but if Russian money works so that they oust him by intrigue.) I said that at Düsseldorf I had gained a better insight into conditions and how the Bulgarians were intriguing. I adverted to the Hereditary Prince again. I had to make him see what needed to be done and said that in the Prince's letter to the Crown Prince which I was delivering today he had written asking that the Crown Prince should take the matter in hand together with Bismarck. And also advocate it with the King; he, Prince Karl Anton, was standing aloof and did not mean to intervene so as not to give the impression of being fickle. Bismarck then commissioned me to ask the Crown Prince, provided the latter were agreed, to fix a time one of these days when he could have a talk with him; he asked me what day it was; I knew neither day nor date. He bethought himself that the day after tomorrow is Ascension day and asked that it might be the day chosen (circumspection with the Crown Prince, with the King he, as he says, does not need it). I was to say to the Crown Prince that his opinion remained unchanged, especially since he had heard from me that the army had improved; the political constellation on the other hand was less favourable than it had been depicted to the Crown Prince 2 months ago (!?)

He spoke of Thile, of his nervous agitation, weakness and lack of decision etc. etc. Finally he talked of Paraguay and said he thought I might consider myself lucky to have got out of there! I am to report verbally to him and would be received immediately. He began the whole conversation with apologies for feeling very tired and having to drink a bottle of porter; he sent home for another because the one they had sent had gone sour!—At the Windsor I receive a telegram to go to Potsdam if possible by the 5 o'clock train, and do so. The Crown Prince received me. I told him briefly about the trip, saying the Hereditary Prince was willing but had not yet been asked and had not yet seen my report; I handed him the letter and said I knew the part dealing with the question at issue; adding the commentary about how Prince Karl Anton was quite willing but did not want to recant what he had said to the King and therefore left the matter in the hands of the Crown Prince and Bismarck; the letter was, I said, diplomatically worded. The Crown Prince then told me what he had said to Princess Antoinette, but did not know why the initiative did not come from the Princely family seeing that the matter concerned it most closely. I said word might still be sent to the Hereditary Prince that he must come forward himself. I gave Bismarck's message about the Thursday meeting and that the political conditions were no longer so favourable as 2 months ago. If the Reichstag ends tomorrow the Crown Prince will come tomorrow, otherwise he will let Bismarck know when. Finally he expressed amusement that I was being used here so long while Steinmetz had to look on. I told him about my orders to be "at the disposal of Bismarck". I also had to explain to him how the thread could be taken up again at Madrid. It was most interesting what he said about often not being told of the most important things as soon as he is away from Berlin. He was furious with the King of Portugal over Saldanha. In cases like that, he said, the King ought to lay about him with his sword even were he to perish in the act rather than suffer such a Minister to be forced on him.

25 May

Now I have got things going again; for Bismarck had given the matter up, not wanting to come into conflict with the King's personal feelings, which always wear him out more than anything else. The Hohenzollern Princes were doing nothing, had declined with the utmost tact, and the Crown Prince had advised against, though wishing that the King as head of the family had commanded acceptance. Now things are as follows: the old Prince has asked the Crown Prince to raise the matter with Bismarck keeping his name out of it with the King, as he does not want to appear inconsistent; the Crown Prince, fearing that a Hapsburg or a Bavarian will get the throne, is more active especially as he notices willingness on the part of the Hereditary Prince, and Bismarck, who was wanting to be called in (on account of the King; to spare his feelings), has been so, as the Crown Prince wants to discuss with him. Both have been told by me about the Hereditary Prince's standpoint, also that it will be necessary to send me once more to him to request him to declare himself; *he* must do the asking.—At 10.30 to Moltke's. I am to remain for the present in Berlin.

27 May
>   Appointment with Bucher; off to Dresden.

28 May
>   Train to Dresden.

3 June
>   Letter from Bucher to say that the willingness is there, that, nevertheless, the many buts are threatening to wear out the patience of the friends, and that B. will be glad to see me at his place on Whit Monday, the 6th.

6 June
>   4 a.m. off to Berlin, Bucher not at home, a letter tells me that he has gone to Spain and that I should probably find employment in Germany.—Bismarck is besieged by Delbrück, Abeken, Bülow etc. But I have my name sent in. He sends a message of excuse that he is too busy and asks me to dinner at 5 p.m. I thought a lot of guests would be there but I was the only one with the family and had to take Her Excellency in to dinner. I sat between him and her; I had already met the daughter at the Shrove Tuesday party. The eldest son, a cornet in the Dragoons, the second, a student; the cousin, Privy Councillor Count Bismarck-Bohlen, Privy Counsellor von Obernitz (family friend) and a lady companion formed the party. Bismarck came in from a ride in the Grünewald and, as it was Whit Monday, had seen a lot of carriages in the Tiergarten, was talkative all day, in a decidedly good humour after his trip to Ems, where he had talked with the Tsar of Russia. While he was out riding a Berliner from the coachman's seat of a carriage had fired a volley from a revolver at him; he said he was at first in doubt whether to bring the man down from the coachman's seat with his Toledo sabre until he noticed that they were only blank shots (Berliners' letting off of firearms on holiday outings in the country).—Count and Countess Bismarck told about their misadventure in Bonn with the doctor who had sent for the whole family and given them unnecessary anxiety about a slight wound of their son's and had then sent in a bill for 100 Thalers. I had to tell about Lopez and America. Bismarck said that up to the age of forty he had a liking for travel; after that he lost his urge to see the world. He had no desire to visit North America, at most buffalo hunting and adventures with Red Indians.—I told him I had seen S.S. "Bismarck". She said many children now were being christened thus, and many little boys with this name were running about the streets. After dinner we went out into the park, he and

I alone. He told me of the further development of the Spanish business. The King and Prince Karl Anton had met on the Ems journey, the Prince being at first embarrassed when the King reproached him with changing his mind. The King had also been angry with him, Bismarck, for corresponding with the Crown Prince behind his back; he had, however, replied that this was natural at the stage at which he had found the affair, and that he had worked in harmony with the Crown Prince on this occasion when he had the same views as the latter. In the end the Prince confessed that his son would accept if in the autumn circumstances in Spain were as they are at present and if the Civil List were sufficiently handsome. Bismarck said he thought this latter seemed to play the deciding part and might yet make the whole thing fall through. He had now sent a cipher telegram to Spain asking them to send someone; the answer had been that someone must go there; he, Bismarck, thought this better on other grounds as well, and on 5 June had sent Bucher to Madrid. There he was to have a talk with Salazar, see whether those concerned would still entertain the idea on the stipulated terms and then return with Salazar. Bucher would stay a few days at San Sebastian as his health was affected and he, Bismarck, did not want this capable worker to come to harm over it all, for he thought a lot of him. The Spanish affair was not worth that. So we reckoned that both would arrive here about 16 June. He was now anxious to make sure by then that the Hereditary Prince himself confirmed his acceptance, but could not send an army officer without a command from the King. I saw what he was wanting and offered to go there on my own initiative, guaranteeing that I would bring him a written acceptance since I had seen how eager the Hereditary Prince had been etc. etc. I suggested that the Hereditary Prince by a letter to the King should apply for permission to accept, and to this he agreed. He gave me the further commission to report to the Crown Prince on this latest development. He said he would be grateful if I did so. I would have to go to Reichenhall where the Hereditary Prince is at present taking the cure and could defray all expenses. We spoke of many other matters and of the characters of the persons involved. He compared Prince Karl Anton with Frederick William IV, who had all sorts of desires but shrank from putting them into execution, [and spoke of] the influence of the Catholic environment of our Queen. On my remarking that the threat of a Hapsburg or a Bavarian was always effective, he said it was so with the men but not with the ladies. That is just what the Catholics want, for them the Pope and the Church stand higher than their own families and the state. He told me how he had urged on Carol of Rumania. I asked him what the future King of Spain could expect from Prussia, since the Hereditary Prince had told me he was not going to Spain as an adventurer like the Rumanian; he had a Royal Princess as his wife and must keep up his position. Bismarck replied: "He can expect nothing at all from Prussia; he has to be a

German in Spain, he is stationed in a Prussian warship. If Prince Frederick Charles were there we could count him as offsetting three French army corps." I replied that I would keep silence on that point and he agreed. Among other things he said to me at one moment: "As we have somehow [*künstlich*] kept out of war for the last three years . . ."; I said that Prince Karl Anton had told me he feared that the Minister Canitz's diplomatic support in Madrid would not be enough and that the King would keep Canitz there; could I not assure the Hereditary Prince straight away that his position would be rendered thoroughly strong? Bismarck said: "That would of course be done just as in Rumania where we use our ablest diplomatists such as Keyserlingk, Radowitz. Canitz is employed there because no more innocuous post could be found for an incompetent man," etc. etc.

After several hours of extremely interesting company and conversation I was home again considering whether to write to Moltke at Kreisau that he should send me or start off on my own account, as the affair was after all out of proportion with any such unauthorized step. I decided to ask for leave, reported to my superiors at Posen that my business would be settled in a few days and asked for 4 weeks' sick leave to go to Reichenhall and Potsdam. I asked for an audience of the Crown Prince on the 8th.

8 June

By the 10 o'clock train to the Crown Prince at the Neues Palais; I travelled with Major von Hahnke and Justizrat Lindstaedt.—I made my report to the Crown Prince and asked him to give me a few lines for the Hereditary Prince. He said the King was displeased at things being done behind his back; I said Count Bismarck had already told me so and had answered the King that it was after all quite natural for him to join forces with the Crown Prince since they thought alike and had not been present at the decision. The Crown Prince nodded. He asked why Bismarck had not attended the *Lehr battalion*[1] party on Whit Monday; I said he was besieged by Delbrück, Abeken and numerous Privy Councillors. We spoke of my journey to Reichenhall, he would have nothing to do with it. The King believed me to be long since in Posen busy with documents; I am not to let myself be seen here by the King, not, for instance, make an appearance at the cavalry review. He regarded the Hereditary Prince as having expressed his willingness to him in a letter of the 5th which said he would ask the King's consent if the crown were again offered him. I thought it desirable that he should make the request now and fix the autumn time limit so that everything should be prepared against Salazar's coming. The [Crown] Prince thought that the time limit depended on the father. However, he left it to Bismarck to achieve whatever he thought best in the circumstances. He had written a letter to Bismarck enclosing

---

[1] Of officers undergoing special courses at Potsdam.

in it the one from Hohenzollern which Bismarck was to return confidentially to him somehow or other. I asked whether he would give me a few lines for Reichenhall. He said possibly the day after tomorrow at the station, otherwise I was to give a verbal message that he thanked the Hereditary Prince for his letter and now regarded the matter as settled, moreover here at the Neues Palais something might crop up at any moment. Right at the beginning the Crown Prince had said what a funny way of doing business (nothing funny except that I am the intermediary between him and Bismarck). At the end as I was going away he said: "Hasn't it turned out as I said it would?" (he no doubt said it to the Hereditary Prince's wife, not to me). I went back to Berlin; Bismarck had gone off that morning to Varzin. I write to Bismarck that the Crown Prince has expressed his willingness to receive Salazar, but under a fictitious name.

12 June
No letter from Bismarck. I write again, registered, asking whether I am to go to Reichenhall, remain here or come to Varzin and saying I would wait here for an answer. At noon to Thile's, he gives me a telegram from Bismarck and copies of all the stuff from Madrid. He himself does not know what has gone on and learns certain things from me. I am to go to Reichenhall; we arrange about a cipher for telegrams; he still does not believe anything will come of it but thinks that if Bismarck had not fallen ill then things would have turned out differently. I said: "No doubt, especially with the Crown Prince away at Carlsbad at the same time." He asked who was now in favour of it. I said the whole lot of them, he seemed incredulous. After that I wrote Moltke. At 9 p.m. back to Thile, who had letters from Bismarck. He read them all out to me, also a fresh telegram from Madrid, which, however, I will not tell the Prince about, and also the reply to Madrid. He handed me Bismarck's letter to me. At 10.30 I started my journey.

13 June as far as Regensburg-Walhalla; in the evening went on via Passau to Wels-Salzburg.

14 June. Forenoon at Reichenhall. "Graf Dehringen" not yet here Family arrived towards noon. Brauschitsch says the Count has stopped in Munich and would arrive here tomorrow at the latest, his wife expects him today. Brauschitsch says he is not to be depended on, has nothing to do and likes to go off on side excursions.

15 June
In the forenoon Spa Director von Auer, Voss, Brauchitsch. At 3 p.m. to the Count's. He most astonished; I inform him of the state of things, also of the telegrams, and ask for a letter to the King. He is reluctant, does

not want to do anything without his father, tells me of his family connexions with the Archdukes of Tuscany and Salzburg etc., saying that he
could not continue the cure he has just begun if the election were now. I
suggest asking for the 25th instead of the 20th and that no one should
arrive before 10 July. He cites the telegram of the 11th in which Prim says
he has offered it to 4 and has hopes in 3 months. I tell him who the 4 are
and that the Cortes themselves are pressing, also the well-informed Bucher,
so that that must no doubt be how things stand, though not to be assessed
from here. Deputies go home for the hot season and later the broad basis
will not be there. The 3 months were to be a proof of a consolidated
situation. I said the 2½ years were so, the 3 months would have the opposite tendency. We finally agree to take the 6.45 a.m. train tomorrow to
Sigmaringen where the father is to arrive on the 17th. I telegraph: "He
has dawdled around for 2 days, will not settle anything without Werner,
we are just going off to Werner's." Brauchitsch has got wind of something, says he is not inquisitive and asks a lot of leading questions. The
Hereditary Prince tells me he is only doing it because they all tell him it is
a state interest; I replied: on the children's account. *He*: "They are excel-
lently provided for."
Myself: "But if you have 12 grandchildren."
In the evening a telegram from Thile—"Schmidt"—that "Braun and
Bock" are en route for Reichenhall. I telegraph during the night to ask
that Braun and Bock should await me in Munich, Hotel Four Seasons.
Long letter to Thile (Schmidt).

16 June
Letter for Braun in case he comes here.
2 o'clock lunch at the Hereditary Prince's. Morning coat. Yesterday
in my presence he received a telegram from the Crown Prince announcing
the birth of a daughter. At lunch I sat next the Princess; she is not only
beautiful but witty and agreeable. In the afternoon I left with the Hereditary Prince, all alone in the compartment. I read my report out aloud to
him, we discussed matters thoroughly, especially the things to be careful
about and how to conduct himself. He has familiarized himself with the
idea of the position but says he loves Germany too much and would come
back again some day, he also deplored the separation in a few years' time
from his 2nd son, who is to be educated here. I told him about Prim's
attitude, since he was under the impression that he would have a particularly difficult time in the first two years (which I denied) and because
in many ways he was in favour of absolutism. I told him he should pile
plenty of hard work on Prim to wear him out and make him old. We
talked of the Schlösser woman etc. As Montpensier is a near relation of
the wife's, he seems to have made a special effort here and won everybody's
good opinion. It is funny that it is always against him I have to work here,

in spite of his being of all the Pretenders on the other side the one I should most like to get the Spanish crown. Here I bring up against him that Montpensier backs Topete and thus has favoured the revolution if, indeed, he did not start it, that he has just as little legal claim there as Prince Frederick Charles would have to the throne here, that he has had two and a half years' free play wherein to win success and has failed in the end after all, that the Bourbon and Orleans question had been so thoroughly thrashed out and the whole family always ruled out by a clear majority, so that it could no longer come in question; now after $2\frac{1}{2}$ years the choice lay between a Hohenzollern and a Bavarian, or failing that, a Hapsburg. The Hereditary Prince mentioned a Bavarian Prince as having been sounded and refusing. I firmly denied this; Prim on the 11th had stated that the King of Portugal and the two Italian Princes had declined, negotiations with a 4th were proceeding, hence if anyone else had been sounded it had been by un-authorized persons without influence; I said I knew only too well that this was a last resort etc. etc. We changed carriage three times to Sig-maringen; besides an overcoat, umbrella and an overnight bag he had burdened himself with a trunk which he always carried himself, not taking a porter. He said he enjoyed when he could travel without attendance, he hated having a suite, which all officers love so, including Brauchitsch. At Ulm we each lay down on a bench in the waiting-room and slept for two hours.

17 June

Here we met the father and Collas and then took the line to Mengen, opened only yesterday; thence via Achse to Sigmaringen. The castle is over 1000 years old; i.e. the origin was a Roman tower on the cluster of rocks on which by degrees the castle grew up as a fort. The Princes were connoisseurs of works of art, the present one especially having greatly enlarged the collection so that it contains several million marks' worth of armour, porcelain, glass, engravings, picture gallery, rococo objects of all sorts. Now there is the railway it will have more visitors; till now the treasures have been practically buried. The Prince, who in Düsseldorf lives as a general, and on the Lake of Constance as a Swiss citizen, is here entirely the Prince. He owns practically the whole Hohenzollern territory in addition to estates in almost every German province, in Hungary, Bohemia etc. An exchequer, constituted as a Government authority, carries on the administration for him, with a Director at its head, so that he has not to give any further attention to it, like the King with his Treasury of the Royal Household. The Chamberlain, von Mainfisch, and the Councillor for Domains, Losser, conducted me to my apartments. At 1 o'clock banquet, tails and black tie. Excellent food, the Prince every inch a minor Great Power, at one moment all noblesse and dignity, at the same time full of wit and conversational ease and approachability—I do not know another so really distinguished a Prince. After lunch, over the coffee, he spoke a few words with me, I showed him the telegrams, he invited me to his room. I had to look at his collection of antlers, the largest in Europe. The Hereditary Prince took me to see a charming bastion overlooking the Danube in order to ask me what his father had said to me, and to tell me that till now he had only been able to say a few words to his father. Prince Karl Anton, lame as he is, climbed two flights of stairs to his apartments, round which he showed me himself (fine Titian, and a painting of his son, Prince Anton, who fell in the war). The son joined us and I had a difficult discussion; Prince Karl Anton said that the *Kölnische Zeitung* of two days ago had published a telegram that the Cortes had been prorogued until September. That, it is true, meant the collapse of my main proposal, namely to get the election carried through by the present weight of votes. He enquired about my instructions and I showed him in confidence the relevant telegram. He told me that the King had recently summoned him to Giessen and had been displeased, had however then said that, while he himself was against it, Bismarck said it was in the interests of the state and so he would not raise objections, but the Queen, who wrote him every week, had not written since then. I said she should be left out of account, she always bowed to a *fait accompli* but would never take an active part in anything; whereat he nodded. He, like his son, desired secrecy to be maintained, therefore the election several months hence. I said once the Cortes had dispersed it could not be held sooner, but preparatory steps must be taken now, since they would take several months more, and as Bucher was coming here with Salazar it would be best to await their arrival and then discuss everything needful with Salazar, so that Madrid could designate the person who could settle all matters with the advisory body to be appointed here (perhaps the Treasury of the Royal Household), it being necessary to settle every detail beforehand, every bed, every horse, whether Germans are to be taken along, crown insignia etc. etc. But the Hereditary Prince must now address the relevant application to the King, so that the King may then give the relevant commands to the Treasury of the Royal Household etc. The Hereditary Prince said: "But I am only accepting because everyone tells me it is in the interest of the State; I have not that ambition and I do not want to." I once more represented to him that one cannot expect the aged King to issue a command, or, what amounts to the same thing, express a wish. In him (the King) there were three different currents. But the father [Prince Karl Anton] would no doubt draft the letter in the light of the latest news reaching him and the Hereditary Prince need only copy it out. They agreed to this; the father said he could refer to the Giessen conversation in wording the letter but he had not slept last night and lacked elasticity of mind. He could not write it before tomorrow. He raised the further point whether by some state treaty the provision could be made that Leopold's second son should always remain a Hohenzollern prince; I said all that could be discussed after the son's letter to the King; he spoke again of the difficulties raised by the changing of the Family Laws. Besides deploring that Frederick Charles was not able, since Princess Charles herself had said that he was willing, Leopold further said that the best thing would have been for Ferdinand, the father of the King of Portugal, to be made King of Spain, which would not have excluded the possibility of his wife and himself succeeding (by sanction). Gratuitous assumptions without any grounds to back them up! Finally I offered to telegraph at once to Berlin the time at which Bucher and Salazar were expected at Reichenhall; we should then await them here. I would at the same time let Thile know, since owing to the dissolution or prorogation of the Cortes the matter was no longer so urgent! I did both things. In the evening at 8 o'clock to supper in tails. Before that a stroll round Sigmaringen—Gothic but the stables in Renaissance style. At supper besides Collas, the comic von Mainfisch and the slick Jewish Losser, the librarian, Hofrat Lenec. Prince Karl Anton every inch a Prince! "How are things doing with our neighbours in Württemberg?" Liberal in the Infallibility question, special train from Stuttgart to Hohenzollern and propaganda against those who were anti-North German. *Wiener Neue Freie Presse* involuntarily playing into our hands, difficulties in Austria, especially in Bohemia. The Prince unobtrusively expressed his leading views pretty clearly and accurately. Death penalty—penal code—ape theory—artistic taste in Sigmaringen—discourse on houses in Pompei—rates of interest in the world—value of landed property, very interesting talk. Acquisition of the latest art treasures, unpacking to be tomorrow morning. Good food, beer, wine, red wine. Everyone smoking his cigar. I have none. Gas lighting, observations thereon. Several present here have been in Bucharest and keenly cross-question me; I consequently act the strong silent man, say yes or no or stock phrases, with mysterious hints: "That is something I cannot talk about"; because of my arriving with the son they are all, including Collas (who seems to be very nice, decent and capable), to my great amusement extremely curious.

18 June

Expecting telegrams from Berlin and Reichenhall, I have copied the old ones for the Prince and will copy the new report to His Majesty. Collections marvellous. Telegram to say that Salazar and Bucher are at Reichenhall and will be here tomorrow at 10.

19 June

In the morning Hereditary Prince in my room, says his father wants to see me; he has finished the letter to the King but could not help saying again in the final sentence that he is making this sacrifice in the interest of the State. I once more made representations to him that after all the son of the house and the interests of the coming generations were also involved, that the task was not too arduous, nay even a rewarding one in view of the undoubtedly firm basis. He further said that his father wanted to discuss with me whether it would not be better to let Bucher and Salazar stay at the hotel in the town, because here at the castle everybody would be too curious. I went to Prince Karl Anton and offered to waylay Bucher and Salazar; he said that today he was having the leading officials to a banquet and I was to convey his excuses. Towards evening he would receive the gentlemen. I went to the Hotel zur Post; Bucher arrived with the mail coach: "Do you see that Spaniard there who knows not a word of German or French! What I have gone through with the pair of them would fill a novel. Salazar is as restless as fireworks. Go and see him; he has been here a long time, travelled here in the private carriage of a gentleman of independent means, a Herr Teufel, from the Hotel Bristol in Paris. He is irritated, Prim likewise: 'that press telegram a French intrigue, the last moment come, in fact past; I throw up the job; but Salazar insisted on leaving no stone unturned; that is why we came on here after all'." He went on to tell me that at Reichenhall they were not able to find the Hereditary Prince's house until towards evening; the Princess had then sent a wire; the Prince had not answered. Bucher had sent in his card, the servants had been very late in letting Brauchitsch know of it, so that he was late in giving Bucher my letter, whereupon they came on here. I told him I had finally managed so that the Hereditary Prince's letter to the King was lying ready. I then greeted Salazar, who after 4-5 night journeys was looking like a skeleton. He then told me that Madrid had received the telegram of refusal on Prince Frederick's behalf at the beginning of May but nothing at all with regard to the Hereditary Prince. He had read a press telegram in *Epoca* saying that Bismarck was ill. Finally came Bismarck's first telegram. In the meantime the French and Austrian Ministers had been intriguing in favour of Archduke Salvador, who had travelled all over the Balearics, knows the language, had written a very good book and was a candidate. Prim, he continued, was offended and impatient; the time limit had been reached, the Cortes were waiting on another few days in spite of the heat but must now be prorogued. Once the session was ended it would be all up and negotiations with the Archduke would be resumed at once, especially as Prim was going to Vichy and would be meeting Napoleon. Now or never! He was very excited; as Bucher said, he has involved himself so deeply in the affair that his position as a statesman is at stake because he has consistently filled Prim with false expectations and Prim would now drop him if nothing came of them. Salazar had ciphers for telegrams with him. I went to the castle, met father and son on the stairs and said: "I suppose it will be too late, but the matter is so urgent that it is a question of hours, if not of minutes.

Salvador is already bidding successfully; touring the Balearics, written a book, speaks Spanish!" "Is it too late?"

No, the Cortes have not yet closed down. The French Government through the Havas agency has published the bogus dispatch about the dissolution. Prim is waiting until the closure of the Cortes. But he must today receive a telegram from Salazar, otherwise they will be dissolved and then negotiations will at once begin with the Archduke. I knew from Bucher that Salazar had in his pocket the authorization from Prim to open negotiations at once with Archduke Salvador unless the Hereditary Prince accepted immediately. I therefore said to Prince Karl Anton and the Hereditary Prince that matters were back again where they were nine months ago when the offer to the Hereditary Prince was first made, and since he could not make up his mind negotiations with the Italian Prince had begun. The Prince and his son now made up their minds to accept immediately and realized that all that now mattered was to get the tele-gram off in time to Madrid. I asked permission to fetch Bucher in at once to give a more detailed account of the situation at Madrid. This was granted. I fetched him from the hotel. He did not regard himself as authorized to negotiate with Prince Karl Anton as he had no instructions to do so. I showed him Bismarck's letter to me in which Bismarck wrote: "All that matters is to bring the parties together." Bucher saw reason and came along at once. I led him to Prince Karl Anton's room by back stairs because the servants and all the castle inhabitants were thoroughly curious. Bucher once again explained the whole thing. When Prince Karl Anton said he must ask the King's permission Bucher said this was not legally necessary. The Prince, however, said he thought the Family Law laid it down that if anyone took service elsewhere or established his domicile outside the realm or took a wife he must ask the permission of the King as head of the family. Bucher pointed out that it did not mention the case of anyone accepting the crown of another country, and it was ancient Germanic usage for junior members of ruling houses to go forth to win crowns abroad. The Prince confined himself to saying that the King must be asked and read out the letter to the King which he had drafted with his son after prolonged pressure from me; it was brilliantly phrased. The Hereditary Prince said that with a heavy heart but with the consciousness of acting in the interest of the State he asked the King's permission to accept. The letter was worded in such a way that the Hereditary Prince intimated that he was making a sacrifice for the renown of the family and the weal of the Fatherland; but it was at the same time phrased so that the King only needed to reply: "no objection". The Hereditary Prince re-peated what he had said to me already several times, namely, that "he had to say this because he was not acting either from self-interest or on any special impulse, and he did not want to appear as a 'climber'." Bucher induced Prince Karl Anton to accompany this letter of the

Hereditary Prince's with one of his own to the King in which he said: "Only on grounds of Family Law did his son thus apply for permission and he trusted the King would have no objections to make." The question now arose who was to go to the King. Bucher looked at me as if I should be the one. I said the best thing would be for Herr Bucher to go, for the King is furious that I am not at Posen. Then there came various scruples on Prince Karl Anton's part. What would France say about it? Would it not give rise to complications? I said: "Bismarck says that is just what he is looking for." Karl Anton: "Yes, Count Bismarck may want it, but is it really in the interests of the State?"

Myself: "Yes, Bismarck's interests and those of the State are the same thing." *Bucher:* "I can only say what Bismarck has often said to me: if in these last years Napoleon had wanted war he could have found plenty of grounds for it."

Various other unimportant matters were discussed. Bucher was allowed to go, but there was to be a conference at 4 o'clock immediately after the banquet, not so late as the evening. I accompanied Bucher to the hotel and asked him to impress on Salazar that he must not offend Prince Karl Anton's *noblesse* and not say that he had instructions to negotiate already in his pocket. Bucher and I were of course more pleased than ever. I sped back to the castle. There was the banquet for the leading officials. They were already assembled, a groom of the chamber fetched me from my room where I just had bare time to get into tails. My late arrival was noticed, likewise my black tie. Everybody else was wearing white tie and decorations. I sat next President von Blumenthal and a Herr von Maisenbach. Of course I was questioned, but what I was pleasantly asked was whether I was on reconnaissance; I said: "Yes, along the Danube valley, the traditional route of armies." "When are you leaving?" "To-night." After the banquet the Prince withdrew and gave the signal for the party to disperse. He had asked me to have a word with his Director of the Board of Domains, but asked him to his own room. I waited for him, and the chamberlain, von Mainfisch, took the opportunity to cross-question me, but got nothing out of me. At 4 o'clock I went to the Hotel zur Post: Bucher was already pacing about agitatedly and asked me to get up steam beneath the Spaniard, who had not finished dressing. He said the two Spaniards (the second one was Salazar's secretary) had driven him half crazy on the journey with their excitability. When I had got up steam in Salazar I conducted him and Bucher to the castle to the astonishment of the promenading Sigmaringers (it was Sunday). Salazar admired the castle, exclaiming every minute: "This is where the deputation must come" etc. Prince Karl Anton received us in full royal style, seated in an armchair and to my joy (on the Spaniard's account) leaving us all standing. The conversation was all in French and turned on the dispatch and phraseology of the necessary telegrams and letters. Those present were Prince Karl

Anton, Hereditary Prince, Salazar, Bucher, the Prince's Director of the Board of Domains and myself. Prince Karl Anton once more explained that he was not head of his house, the King was the supreme head of the family without whose consent his son could not accept. Salazar on his part asked to be permitted to send the following telegram to Madrid: "The Hereditary Prince accepts: a few difficulties remain." He had concerted a cipher with Madrid by which he would telegraph: "The Carlists are conspiring. Have Deputy No. 3 watched." As the Carlists had their headquarters in Switzerland the French might be expected to let this telegram through since it seemed one from a Spanish agent who was watching the Carlists in Switzerland. It must not be dispatched from Sigmaringen, so the Director of the Board of Domains received the command to send a trusted official to Mengen in the direction of Switzerland whence he would dispatch the telegram this very day without fail. (In the evening Prince Karl Anton told me the official had not yet returned and had probably gone on further because telegraph offices closed early on Sundays.) Salazar thereupon insisted on a letter from the Hereditary Prince to Prim, saying that he would accept if he were elected. This formality was laid down in the law relating to the election of a king lest the case should recur of somebody being elected and withdrawing in the meantime like the King of Portugal. The Hereditary Prince expressed his willingness if the King granted permission. Bucher had made a draft of a letter in this sense and read it out to the Hereditary Prince. The Prince declared he would willingly make use of it since he had no experience in such things. The letter to Prim was read aloud, receiving some suitable additions. Now it was time for Bucher to leave, as it was 5 o'clock. The newspaper said that the King was on the way to Ems; so that was where Bucher must go. Prince Karl Anton said: "But at Ems the King has nobody, who is with him?"

I said: "Abeken."

"But he is not likely to know anything."

Prince Karl Anton lamented that Bismarck was not there and asked who was acting for him in Berlin.

I said: "Thile."

He said: "But he is against it. Then the affair falls into hands which do not know what has to be done."

I said: "I think Herr Bucher will be quite competent, since he has once already been received by the King in this connexion."

We continued to discuss how Bucher could best manage to obtain an audience of the King with all speed; he thought he could manage it through Abeken. I further told Prince Karl Anton that Bismarck would continue to act, using Thile merely as an instrument, so would he therefore give me a letter for Bismarck? and would the Hereditary Prince give me one for the Crown Prince? which they agreed to do. Bucher slipped away. I asked Prince Karl Anton whether I should leave him alone with Salazar but he said I was not at all in the way, so I stayed on. Salazar declared he would remain in Sigmaringen until the King had signified his approval and would then depart with the Hereditary Prince's letter to Prim. He intends to be in Madrid on the 26th. He told us that the Cortes were being kept in existence by the device of introducing several important new bills. He estimated that the election would take place about 8 July as the Cortes would have to receive a week's notice of the election. He talked of Archduke Salvador, his journey etc., the French Minister, Mercier, who, he said, did not stop short even at bribery to further his intrigues. The Prince at all events had one other confidential matter, for he begged me to ask Bucher to return the *Kölnische Zeitung* which he had lent him this morning and which for the first time stated: "It is reported that a Hohenzollern Prince is the candidate whom Prim has in mind and does not want to name in the Cortes." I went to the hotel and helped Bucher with his departure by fast mail coach; the Spanish secretary, who spoke only Spanish and with whom he could not make himself understood, owed him a few hundred francs. Seeing Bucher driving off he ran shouting and hatless after the coach to the amusement of the people of Sigmaringen. I shouted to him in Spanish not to do that, as I would settle the matter, but he went on shouting till the coach stopped. Some people came up to me saying: "He does not understand you, he speaks a funny language that nobody understands."

I said: "They are Rumanians", which was immediately passed round by the people of Sigmaringen. I went back to the house and telegraphed: "Parcel going off to Leipzig", i.e. the Hereditary Prince has accepted, the relevant letter is at once going off to the King. I went to Prince Karl Anton and took charge of the letters from him to Bismarck and from the Hereditary Prince to the Crown Prince; I then went to Salazar at his hotel; he had grown quite thin and nervy with the excitement and was at last dining in peace. We talked in Spanish about the successful issue; he was grateful to me for the telegrams to *Epoca*, talked of Bismarck's being ill, and how they had consequently marked time and had not yet approached Archduke Salvador. I offered to take duplicates of the Madrid telegrams and other such things along with me to Berlin, whence they would be dispatched in cipher. He agreed. The gendarmerie captain came into the room and said I was wanted, a telegram had come for me. I said goodbye to Salazar. At the castle I found there was no new telegram for me and that mine could not be dispatched because the telegraph clerk had closed the office an hour earlier than the legal time. I ordered fast post horses for 2 a.m., wrote my report for Bismarck, enclosed in it Prince Karl Anton's letter and one from Salazar and went to supper. Prince Karl Anton said he would never in all his days forget 19 June. I said: "It was a historically important hour this morning when we three were together and again when the six of us met this afternoon." I said to him that when the deputation arrived he ought to have a painter over from Düsseldorf. (He had begged Salazar that the deputation might be a small one; but Salazar had replied that the law laid down that it should be 15 strong in order to be fair to all parties.) At supper besides the chamberlains there was a Herr Teufel, the owner of the Hotel Bristol in Paris, who as a native of Sigmaringen had built a summer villa there and had arrived that very day from Paris. He had brought Salazar (travelling as a Brazilian from the province of Rio Grande) along in his carriage from Mengen to Sigmaringen, but fortunately did not mention it. He was a talkative, elderly, pleasant man who had thoroughly studied and understood the good things of life. I tucked in well. After supper Prince Karl Anton bade us goodbye with very friendly words, the Hereditary Prince likewise thanking me for my trouble and asking where I was going; I said: "Straight through to Posen." He said: "Well, I hope we shall meet again in summer!" I took leave of the other gentlemen, finished my letter to Bismarck, packed and went late to bed. Wakened an hour later, I drove to Mengen by express coach, then to the railway for Ulm; here I sent off the telegram: "Parcel going off to Leipzig immediately!" Took my ticket to Stuttgart; by mistake got into a wrong train at Bruchsal, having stayed on in the compartment, but at Durlach I happened on a train which enabled me to rejoin the right one at Heidelberg. At Frankfurt I registered and posted the letter to Bismarck with enclosures. Not until *21 June* in the forenoon did I get to Berlin (some 30 hours in the train). I went to Thile's; he had received my letter and said he would at once telegraph Bismarck asking whether I was to go to Varzin; he did so although I told him I had sent a full report to Bismarck, at the same time enclosing letters from the elder Hohenzollern and Salazar. I delivered to Thile 3 telegrams from Salazar to be sent in cipher to Madrid, one to Prim saying that the Hereditary Prince had accepted, one to the President of the Cortes to say that Salazar would be back in Madrid on 26 June, and one to his wife. Thile had them sent off immediately. I told him that the French had been again on Bucher's tracks and had all sorts of spies after him; he refused to believe this, saying that, if so, they could have rendered our telegrams to Madrid unintelligible. He wanted me to stay in Berlin until Bismarck replied.

On *22 June* the Crown Prince received me at the Potsdam town castle. I told him the whole story; he was much interested; I gave him the Hereditary Prince's letter. He asked me, smiling: "Where are you off to now?" I said: "Straight on to Posen." He nodded. I returned to Berlin.

On *23 June* to Thile's. He told me that after a great struggle the King had given his consent. I then departed for Posen. Steinmetz was greatly amused.

In the papers I read of the adjournment of the Cortes without the election of the Prince. I wrote Bucher at Varzin. He answered that the French had garbled my Salazar telegram, changing the date of Salazar's return from 26 June to 9 July; thereupon the Cortes dispersed, having been kept hanging on only by expedients. From Moltke on *27 June* I received a letter of commendation for what I had done in this matter. On *28 June* unveiling of the monument to Nachod at Posen with festivities. On that same morning I received from General Staff Adjutant de Claer at Berlin (Moltke was at Kreisau), on instructions from the Cabinet, a summons to report immediately by whose request or command I had entered into negotiations with the Prince of Hohenzollern and had gone to Düsseldorf. I could have named the Crown Prince; but as the King might have taken it amiss of him I reported: "On my own initiative!" By chance Claer came that very day to Posen for the unveiling of the monument and learnt that Moltke had written appreciatively to me. I handed him my report, which he sent on to the Cabinet with his own comments. Nothing more was heard of the matter. As is known, the war developed out of it.

14 July. All that the King said is literally true; but the semi-official newspapers are ingenuous when they declare that Bismarck, who was at Varzin all the time, knew nothing of the negotiations. In the night of 15-16 July came the order for mobilization. For five days and three nights I was continuously busy at Command Headquarters with the mobilization of the V Army Corps.

On *22 July* I was appointed General Staff officer of the IV Cavalry Division, the only one in the II Army.

signed MAX VON VERSEN

APPENDIX B

The Sigmaringen Archives

UNTIL recently the archives of the Hohenzollern-Sigmaringen family have remained closed to historical research apart from a few revelations due to Zingeler, keeper of the Sigmaringen papers, in the years preceding the First World War. The Introduction to this book shows how Berlin put pressure on Prince Leopold to prevent any leakage from Sigmaringen on the Hohenzollern candidature.

Since the end of the Second World War Prince Frederick of Hohenzollern,[1] grandson of Prince Leopold, the candidate for the throne of Spain, has agreed, on the advice of Dr Johannes Maier, now in charge of the family archives in Sigmaringen, that the secret files should be opened to historians. One cannot be too grateful for this decision.[2]

*   *   *

The Spanish diplomatic archives revealed that the Prince of Rumania had written to the Spanish Regent in all probability before the official offer of the Spanish Crown was made to his brother Leopold on 17 February 1870. Was this initiative by the Prince of Rumania taken in connexion with the Hohenzollern candidature, or did it merely concern the affairs of Rumania for which he had come to Paris in the autumn of 1869?

The answer to this question can be found in the Sigmaringen archives in Charles of Rumania's letter of 1 April 1870, from which it appears that he had written to the Spanish Regent to notify his marriage.[3]

[1] Since the extinction of the Hechingen line the Prince of Hohenzollern-Sigmaringen takes the simplified title of Prince of Hohenzollern (3 September 1869).

[2] The main series of files used here is:

> Rubrik 53. Nr. 73. Sigmaringen 1870–1895. Zwei von Sr. K. H. dem Fürsten gesiegelte Pakete mit der Aufschrift "Personal Akten Familien Archiv 1870". Es sind Akten auf die Spanische Thronkandidatur bezüglich. Ein drittes hier beiligendes Faszikel enthält hauptsächlich Briefe und Gesuche vom Jahre 1870 in Zusammenhang stehend mit der Spanischen Thronfrage.

When not otherwise indicated, the documents reproduced in the following pages come from this series.

[3] Charles of Rumania's biography contains the text of this letter but with several omissions, among which is this essential passage: [German] "Serrano's letter in answer to my notification was specially sympathetic and cordial"; it included, however, concerning the letter of the Spanish Regent, these words which I did not read on the original: [French] "in reply to the notification of Your Highness' marriage" (see Fester, Briefe, Aktenstücke . . ., docs. 109 and 132).

[German] Bucharest, 1 April, 70[1]

DEAREST BELOVED PAPA,

The departure of a courier gives me the desired opportunity to reply immediately to your letter of the 20th ult. with its weighty news. Radowitz sent it to me this morning. I have for some time suspected that Spain was again taking under consideration the candidature of a Catholic Hohenzollern. On the 12th ult. Strat wrote me from Paris the following: [French] "I think it my duty to point out to Your Highness as something particularly flattering both for Y.H. and for our country that the Regent of Spain's letter was presented to me in person by the Spanish Ambassador who, against all the rules and customs of diplomatic etiquette, came and called on me yesterday asking me to deliver the letter to its august destination. In this country ambassadors do not call even on accredited ministers plenipotentiary holding an official position, and Spanish ambassadors are pre-eminent as to their strictness in matters of formality and ceremonial, hence yesterday's call took me entirely by surprise and I can only attribute it to some special instructions which the Ambassador must have received from Madrid. It is true M. Olozaga, the present Ambassador, a friend of the Emperor's and a leading Spanish statesman, is also extremely affable and courteous and has accorded me an exceptionally gracious reception whenever I have had occasion to see him at his Embassy, but that does not seem a sufficient explanation of his yesterday's call and I am inclined to think that this excessive politeness is not entirely unconnected with certain rumours which have again been circulating for the last few weeks ascribing to the men who are at present masters of the destinies of Spain the intention of raising once more the question of offering the Crown of Spain to L. . . . . [2]"

[German]

Serrano's letter in answer to my notification was particularly sympathetic and cordial. I still hope that Leopold has not said his last word in the Spanish affair; the fact that he has three sons makes the solution of the question much easier and he would not be obliged to forsake his native land for ever. He would still have the chance after ten or twelve years to renounce the throne in favour of his son.

Judging by conversations I had with Fritz and what I know of him, he is hardly likely to be willing to undertake the task. What he would lack would not be intellectual ability but experience and knowledge of human nature. A few days ago I met someone who had seen Fritz in Rome and Naples and had known him previously; that person

---

[1] Received in Düsseldorf on 11 April 1870.
[2] Leopold.

was quite amazed how much Fritz had developed mentally and physically. This news gave me uncommon pleasure. If he *has good advisers* he will certainly be equal to this great mission. In the event of acceptance of the Spanish Crown certain conditions would have to be laid down. First and foremost the dissolution of the army, which at present would be more a danger than a support, and the subsequent creation of new corps; the army need not be on a large scale, but on the other hand efforts must be made to develop the navy very considerably. Further:—a modification of the Constitution voted last year with retention of the absolute right of veto contained in it; a severe law of repression and finally, means at hand to curb the harmful influence of the various parties; party intrigues in Spain always remaining a great danger and making all government very difficult. If my two brothers were definitely to reject the offer I should not be sorry if the Crown were offered to me though of course I neither would nor could accept it. But I could use it to scare the parties in this country and rid myself of much that is irksome; I would then formulate the conditions on which I would make my remaining here dependent.

The insolence of the Reds is beyond all bounds, they insult Elizabeth and myself in articles and cartoons so that against my will I am unfortunately obliged to go to law with them. . . .

Your most obedient Son,

CARL[1]

So it seems that Charles of Rumania was not involved in the early negotiations for the candidature. Did he, however, mention the candidature when he met Napoleon III on several occasions during his stay in Paris in 1869? Sybel affirms that Karl Anton informed Napoleon of the Spanish offer of September 1869: [*German*] "Prince Anton, who for the moment saw no occasion to report to Berlin, informed his old friend and near relative the Emperor Napoleon of the episode. (Prince Leopold's two grandmothers were cousins of the Emperor's.) The Emperor wrapped himself in profound silence, and from the absence of all dissuasion or warning the Prince drew the conclusion that Napoleon would not be unfavourable to his cousin's candidature. . . ."[2]

As far as could be ascertained from the Sigmaringen archives, Karl

[1] Sigmaringen archives: *Rubrik 53.* Nr. 1433, Rumänien Bd. VI (1870). This file is part of a series of eight covering the period 1866-1875. All eight were sent during the Second World War to the King of Rumania, who took them to Lisbon when he left Rumania. Some years later the files were sent from Lisbon by diplomatic courier to Bonn and thence to Sigmaringen, where they arrived on 26 May 1954. Volumes 4 and 5 (which cover the year 1869) are now missing and are believed to have been taken by the Russians and to be now in Moscow.

[2] Sybel, article in *Die Zukunft,* 20 April 1895, p. 103.

Anton did not write to the Emperor in 1869 about the candidature. The Sigmaringen archives contradict Sybel's statement that the Spanish offer of September 1869 to Leopold was the second offer.[1] Several memoranda written by Leopold himself, which were intended neither to be published nor even to be forwarded to Berlin, confirm the chronology suggested by the German Foreign Ministry secret files. In a letter of 4 June 1870 to the Crown Prince, Leopold wrote that the candidature question was coming up for the third time; this meant that the offer of February 1870 was the second and the offer of September 1869 the first.

Had Bismarck told Benedetti on 8 May 1869 that Leopold had already been offered the Spanish Crown, Sybel would have been justified in saying that the offer of September 1869 was the second one. In fact, Bismarck merely said that Leopold had been sounded.[2] The German Foreign Ministry files reveal that Karl Anton had forwarded to William I this extract of a letter he had received from Brussels.

[French]   Brussels, 19 April, 1869
... The Belgian Government has had word from Spain that if Leopold were to present himself as a candidate for the throne, he would have prospects. ...

signed PHILIPPE[3]

Karl Anton was asking the Prussian King to give his son permission to refuse the offer of the Spanish throne, *should an offer be made*. The King's answer on 23 April 1869 was:

[German]
... that Leopold would not accept the Spanish Crown and I fully understand your not persuading him to do so; I shall certainly not advise it.[4]

★   ★   ★

The unfolding of the story of the secret negotiations follows the same pattern in the Sigmaringen as in the German Foreign Ministry archives. Indeed, many of the documents of the Sigmaringen archives came from Berlin or were communicated by Berlin. From the Foreign Ministry files

[1] Sybel, article in *Die Zukunft*, 20 April 1895, p. 103.

[2] For Benedetti's account see: Benedetti, *Ma Mission en Prusse*, pp. 307-8. Dispatch of 11 May 1869. For Bismarck's account see: Thimme, *Bismarcks Gesammelte Werke*, Bd. VIb, doc. 1389. Wertheimer was sceptical. See Eduard von Wertheimer, "Kronprinz Friedrich Wilhelm und die Spanische Hohenzollern-Thronkandidatur (1868-1870)", in *Preussische Jahrbücher*, Bd. CCV, Heft 3, 1926, pp. 273-307. Wertheimer's main source was Das Preussische Hausarchiv in Berlin, Charlottenburg.

[3] Philippe was probably the Comte de Flandre (1837-1905) who had married Marie, Princess of Hohenzollern (1845-1912). In German Foreign Ministry file *IA Bo 28, Bd. 4*, A 1558.

[4] Ibid.

it is apparent that Bucher had transmitted to Karl Anton a number of important documents; even before consulting the Sigmaringen archives one could guess with some accuracy what was to be found there.

The Sigmaringen archives, however, help one to understand better the parts played by Karl Anton and Leopold in the negotiations and how they were influenced by the statesmen in Berlin. Platzhoff and Rheindorf, in their report of 1924 on the German Foreign Ministry files, took an unfavourable view of Leopold's attitude:

> The role played by Hereditary Prince Leopold in the whole affair appeared in an unflattering light in the material already published. The diplomatic files reveal that in the whole question he had virtually no will of his own, allowing himself to be led by his father whatever his personal scruples.

The Sigmaringen files make this view appear oversimplified, for Leopold was not influenced only by his father. Furthermore, the attitude of the Hohenzollern-Sigmaringen family, seen from Berlin and particularly by the King, seemed hesitating and changeable. In the Sigmaringen archives Karl Anton's attitude looks much more consistent. His reaction to Salazar's démarche of September 1869 was to take no step which would show a desire to accept. He wrote on 23 November 1869 to von Werthern, the Prussian minister in Munich who had introduced Salazar:

[German]
MOST HONOURED BARON,
    With deep interest and with no less deep appreciation I welcome your kind communication on conditions in Spain. The account given of them is not of a nature to awaken any great desire for the possession of the Crown. I fully share the opinion of those who live in the belief that an absolutely clean sweep must be made of the Spanish chaos before a new build-up can emerge from the ruins.
    Unless the personage were to possess the courage to defy all hazards he would into the bargain have to accept the condemnation of Europe, for it is a fact that if there is no agreement of opinion anywhere, at least there exists unanimity in the general judgement as to non-acceptance of the Spanish Crown.
    Let us therefore await events and take not the slightest step that might show inclination in this direction.

C[ARL] A[NTON]

After the official Spanish offer Karl Anton's attitude was not far different, for he wrote to Leopold not to show any enthusiasm or any ambition—advice which Leopold was only too ready to take literally:

[*German*]   submitted Berlin, 26 February, 1870

. . . I regard it as my duty to place the decision in the hands of the King,—if for reasons of high policy and statecraft he so wills, then it is incumbent on us to join with him in making world history—if he does not so will, it would be folly to venture into a situation in which the support and goodwill of Prussia would be lacking.

Above all keep perfectly cool and collected, no foolhardiness and no agitation. First of all what is needful is a purely *objective* weighing up before proceeding to a subjective decision, and this latter must be taken without impetuosity and with a steady pulse.

Let me know the King's impressions at once,—for he, like Bismarck, will be receiving the letter today.—The King will obey his first impulse and immediately reject the whole thing out of hand, but that is not the end of it all,—not emotion but grounds and reasons must be the deciding factors.

Least of all must the affair be viewed in the light of your own ambitions. If for higher reasons of state the King rejects—well and good—you categorically refuse, but if he enters more fully into the matter then let him command me to come to Berlin. The Crown Prince too must be consulted since the future belongs to him. There ought to be a so-called Family Decision on it all. With Bismarck in any case you must endeavour to have a word. In a matter like this all qualms and niceties must be cast overboard. . . .

Karl Anton's attitude may seem strange. He wanted his son to become King of Spain but he did not say so. He put forward instead the principle that acceptance must be recognized as being in the Prussian interest. Was it to dissimulate an unavowed ambition under the veil of civic duty? Or was it mere prudence, to be certain of Prussian support in case something should go wrong later in Spain?

There is room here for several hypotheses. It may be no more than a coincidence that the idea of a Prussian interest in having Leopold as King of Spain was the conclusion of an article in the *Uckermärkische Zeitung* of 13 October 1868, the earliest press-cutting on the Hohenzollern candidature to be found in the Sigmaringen archives:

[*German*]

Consequently the candidature of the Hereditary Prince of Hohenzollern for the Spanish throne is the only possible one and a necessity in the interests of Spain, of Prussian North Germany and of Europe.[1]

Leopold did not try to dissimulate his reluctance to accept the Spanish Crown. He was a family man, a good son, a devoted husband, and he

---

[1] On possible foreign reactions to the Hohenzollern candidature, the article said: "Frankreich und Oesterreich sind zu schwach um ernstliche Schwierigkeiten zu machen."

lacked the imagination and enthusiasm of his father as well as the ambition of his younger brother, Charles of Rumania. He much preferred to become *Fürst* in Sigmaringen and stay in his castle overlooking the Danube than to exile himself as a King in Madrid. Leopold saw coolly the difficulties which he would encounter in becoming and remaining a King. The German Foreign Ministry archives contain, too, the memorandum Leopold sent to the Prussian King (2 March 1870) enumerating all the reasons against accepting the Spanish offer.[1]

Leopold, rightly or wrongly, felt from the beginning that the Spanish throne was an adventure into which Bismarck wanted to throw him. As early as February the Crown Prince had warned him against Bismarck's capacity for promoting for immediate purposes a plan which he might drop entirely later; this is mentioned in a letter of 27 February 1870 from Leopold to his father in Düsseldorf, recounting his consultations in Berlin:

[*German*]

. . . The King with whom I did not venture to take the initiative in this matter said to me yesterday evening just as he was going away that he had received a letter from you, clasping his hands and asking me if I had known of the matter for any length of time. I replied that except for an interview with the gentleman[2] in the autumn I had heard not a mortal word and for my part felt a deep repugnance towards the move. That was all that was discussed. But today I gave the copy of the letters and Prim's missive to the Crown Prince to read. He expressed no clearly formulated opinion but thought the business very risky if only because of the many families putting forward pretenders—Don Carlos, Asturias, Parma, Montpensier with the Orleanist following, and then he warned me against Bismarck who at the bidding of a whim for the momentary attainment of a definite purpose would commit himself to a project which later on could in no way count on his support.

It was also Leopold's own impression that Bismarck was not entertaining the plan with the requisite seriousness and objectivity:

[*German*]

. . . I should prefer to avoid having another conversation with Bismarck before knowing what the King's views are. The grounds alleged by him the other day certainly did not produce the impression of the completely disinterested objectivity and solidity which could convince me.[3] . . .

[1] See Doc. No. 6, Annex.
[2] Salazar.
[3] Letter of Leopold to Karl Anton, 3 March 1870.

The chances were then that Leopold would refuse Prim's flattering offer. His mother, Princess Josephine,[1] did not want him to go to Madrid as she feared to be separated from her grandchildren, and she wrote to him again and again in Berlin to dissuade him. Here is, for example, a characteristic letter from her of 16 March 1870, written at a time when she did not yet know the outcome of the Crown Council held in Berlin the day before.

[French]   Düsseldorf, 16 March

MY VERY DEAR AND GOOD LEOPOLD,

You will perhaps think I overwhelm you with letters, but I need to talk to you of what weighs on my mind and occupies almost all my thoughts in spite of many distressing things which combine at this moment to fill me with sadness. I do not ask you to reply, knowing that at Berlin it is not always easy in the midst of all that fills up the days to find a moment to write letters when one wants to, especially those dealing with a matter as serious as the one which engages our attention. In the solitude of my daily life I have the time to do so and it soothes me a little to write you. I sometimes fear that the two of you, you and Antoinette, would like to accept, [German] for if you really felt so strong an aversion against acceptance as you write I do not understand why you should not decide your fate yourself but have to follow the great statesman's policy as if you were his tool and had no will of your own. Forgive what I write you in my anguish of heart. But you did say you were against the affair and that it was repugnant to you if only on account of the many pretenders to the throne. Dear Papa is not in favour of acceptance either, the King, the Queen, the Crown Prince are all against it, the only one in favour is Herr von Bismarck. From his point of view I understand it, but cannot resign myself to the thought that for the sake of a historical fact such a sacrifice should be asked as that of seeing you set forth into so uncertain a future, and against your own wishes, too! It is very hard to be far from you both just now. If you do actually accept this gilded misery, which God forbid, I shall never cease to lament having been separated from you at this fateful moment.

But I still hope that the great sacrifice will not be imposed upon us and that you will neither of you regret it. Today I do not feel able to write about anything else so will end with warmest greetings to dear Antoinette. Werner will tell you how well and lively the two dear

[1] 1813-1900. Born Princess of Baden and a daughter of Stéphanie de Beauharnais, adopted daughter of Napoleon I. Her letters were usually written in French with German breaking in here and there.

children are. With the most fervent wishes for the welfare of you both, my dearly beloved Leopold,

Your devoted Mother,

JOSEPHINE

These admonitions from his mother did not leave Leopold unmoved, and he referred once to the grief his acceptance would cause his parents.

What made Leopold almost waver in his resolution not to accept was the Crown Council of 15 March 1870. Bismarck denied in his memoirs that this Crown Council ever took place, but its existence has been known in fact for a long time[1] and the German Foreign Ministry documents provide supplementary proof to it. The Sigmaringen archives contain, however, a document of particular interest: the detailed minute written by Karl Anton the day after the Crown Council[2]:

[German]

On 15th March H.M. the King commanded that a dinner be given in my apartments at the Royal Castle.

To this dinner at 4.30 p.m. were bidden at His Majesty's command: (10 covers)

H.R.H. the Crown Prince.
Hereditary Prince Leopold.
Minister-President Count Bismarck.
Minister in Attendance, Baron von Schleinitz.
War Minister von Roon.
Infantry General von Moltke.
Minister Delbrück.
Under State Secretary von Thile.

The subject under discussion was the question of the Spanish Throne, as it now presented itself to us. At the end of the dinner H.M. commanded a private discussion with the proviso that no decisions were to be taken for the time being. The party having adjourned to H.R.H. Grand Duchess Alexandrina of Mecklenburg-Schwerin's apartments in the angle of the castle, which for the moment have been assigned to me, the King opened the discussion in the following terms:

H.M. the King said he had convoked the gentlemen here assembled in order to submit the question at issue to a confidential examination.

---

[1] See bibliographical note above.

[2] The designation "Crown Council" for this meeting of 15 March 1870 is not quite traditional. Lord (*The Origins of the War of 1870*, p. 20) criticizes both the French writers who asserted it was a "session of the council of ministers" and German historians who used to speak of a "family council". The latter expression conforms with the Sigmaringen point of view that the King of Prussia was to give his assent as head of the whole Hohen-zollern family.

H.M. was deeply conscious of the importance of the matter and all its implications but could not conceal the pitfalls which stood in the way of acceptance of this offer of the Crown. Conditions in Spain were still too unsettled and the attitude of foreign Powers still too unknown to expose a member of his Royal and Princely line to the "inconnu".

He fully appreciated the reasons of a political nature speaking in favour of it but they were not such as to outweigh the other obstacles. He now threw open the discussion and desired to hear the views of those whom he had summoned *ad hoc* to this meeting as men enjoying his full confidence. He thereupon called on Count von Bismarck to lay before them an account of the historical development of the whole question, beginning by reading out aloud to the meeting the documents that had been exchanged.

Count von Bismarck: After a brief introduction Count Bismarck read out the following documents:

1. Prim's letter to the Hereditary Prince,[1]
2. to H.M. but not laid before His Majesty except only in copy,[2]
3. Prim's letter to Count Bismarck,[3]
4. my letter to H.M,[4]
5. my letter to Count Bismarck,[5]
6. a memorandum of the Hereditary Prince,[6]
7. Bismarck's report to H.M. the King.[7]

After brief concluding remarks H.R.H. the Crown Prince expressed his views.

H.R.H. the Crown Prince said he must confess that although he fully appreciated the political exposition given by Count Bismarck there were other and very substantial grounds in favour of non-acceptance, namely the existence of opposing, intrinsically justifiable claims on the part of legitimate pretenders to the throne, the uncertainty as to the ratio of votes in the Cortes, ignorance of the attitude and behaviour of the Great Powers in the question.

The very fact that preference for the election of a Catholic Hohenzollern had been emphasized was in itself sufficient satisfaction for legitimate Prussian pride without the necessity of acceptance seeming an inexorable command.

To see a flourishing branch eliminated from the community of the family group and handed over to a future that is still obscure was a serious step wherein not alone reason should say its word but also,

[1] See Doc. No. 3.   [2] See Doc. No. 1.
[3] See Doc. No. 2.   [4] See Doc. No. 4.
[5] See Doc. No. 5.   [6] See Doc. No. 6, Annex.
[7] See Doc. No. 9.

room should be allowed for the rights of the heart. While reason spoke in favour of the idea, feeling strove with all its might in the opposite sense.

Minister von Schleinitz said he did not overlook the weight of the reasons in favour of acceptance of the Crown. Faithful to his principle that, as a former Minister at the Foreign Ministry he felt it did not *now* lie within his province to intervene in the difficult deliberations of the present head of the Foreign Ministry, he avoided further examination of the political considerations. Called upon, as Minister in Attendance, to uphold the dynastic interests of the Crown he, too, saw in the accomplishment of the project a satisfaction of patriotic Prussian and German sentiments but in no less a degree the possibilities of danger ahead. To sum up his views, he assigned the final decision in the last resort to the free will of the Hereditary Prince who, following his own inner voice without external influence, should arrive at a decision pro or contra.

General von Roon began by stressing the political interests advanced in Count Bismarck's exposé. If a Hohenzollern on the Spanish throne would be bound in the first place to feel and act as a Spaniard he would nevertheless be able in taking decisions to throw Prussian and Hohenzollern sympathies into the scales. The army was thirsting for a manly king, and if until now it had been drawn actively into the maelstrom of revolution this was only because for lack of a compass it was placed in the hands of its generals and withdrawn from the directives of its Monarch.

For political and dynastic reasons Roon was in favour of unconditional acceptance. Moreover, acceptance by the Hereditary Prince would provide a guarantee that conservative interests would receive due consideration and that the danger to Europe of a republic would be averted.

General von Moltke associated himself with the above opinion. He, too, pointed out the characteristic qualities of the army and the advantages of a German dynasty in that country. The name of Germany had a good sound in the ears of this proud people, and the greatest age of Spanish power and glory was the period during which the ascendancy of the House of Hapsburg was at its height. He was in favour of acceptance.

Geheimrat von Thile was of the same opinion, drawing attention to the fine qualities of the nation and its readiness to welcome a progressive spirited amelioration of its conditions.

Minister Delbrück has first-hand knowledge of the country and its people and held out favourable prospects for its future; in his view the founding of a Hohenzollern dynasty would offer powerful guarantees for important developments in trade and intercourse and therewith for favourable repercussions on Germany as a whole. He voted for acceptance.

After this last expression of opinion the King closed the meeting, thanking those present for their advice but intends to reserve the decision to himself and the Hereditary Prince in order, as he expressed it, to sleep on this highly important question.

Written down from memory,

Berlin, 16 March, 1870,

CARL ANTON OF HOHENZOLLERN

Leopold was very much impressed by this high-level discussion and noted with dismay that every one of the King's advisers had spoken in favour of acceptance:

[German]   Berlin, 17 March, 1870

After the discussion of the Spanish question held on 15 March in the presence of His Majesty, and now that not only the Minister-President but also the most experienced and influential members of the Crown Council have all spoken in favour of acceptance of the Crown, some of them bringing forward weighty grounds in support thereof, it becomes more and more difficult to bring forward those reasons of the heart which have hitherto been preponderant. Since reason must acknowledge the force of the grounds for acceptance brought forward above—and even the Crown Prince, who up to the present has concurred in my views against acceptance, now thinks that the more deeply one ponders over the question the more decidedly reason comes down on the side of acceptance—I am prepared to make the sacrifice but must adhere to my decision expressed from the beginning that acceptance must be made easier for me by the express wish of H.M. I owe that to myself and my parents, to whom I am thereby causing deep sorrow.

The King himself, however, was still reluctant to take any responsibility in the Spanish affair and squarely refused to bring any pressure to bear on Leopold by saying that his acceptance was in Prussia's interest. As the King was refusing to give the desired *command*, Karl Anton turned to Bismarck and the Crown Prince[1] to obtain at least an *authoritative declaration* that the acceptance of the Spanish Crown would be in the interest of the Prussian State. This double démarche reveals how keen Karl Anton was on the success of the candidature and how much he needed to appease his conscience before trying to persuade Leopold to accept. Yet Leopold still refused for the time being, and at the end of April 1870 anybody at Sigmaringen would have considered the Spanish dossier finally closed.

[1] Letter to the Crown Prince of 2 April 1870.

The negotiations with the Spanish Government were not revived by Bismarck until the beginning of June and Leopold's acceptance was not raised again until that month. During May, however, the stage did not remain absolutely empty. A new actor appeared—a Prussian General Staff Officer, Major von Versen, whose diary for the period 18 May-22 July 1870 is reproduced in this book.[1] Originally the King had requested that an officer be sent to Madrid to counterbalance the optimistic reports sent by Bucher from Spain, but Versen became, as it happened, an enthusiastic supporter of the candidature, claiming in his diary to have played a decisive part in securing Leopold's acceptance. The Crown Prince, in sending Versen to Leopold, had warned the latter about the ebullient Prussian officer, who was "zu sanguinisch":

[*German*]   19 May, 1870

Versen wishes for a few lines of introduction to you. So be it. More I will not say since he himself has the gift of the gab in plenty and will be able to talk away to you at any length about Spain. I think he prides himself on his powers of persuasion as he finds conditions there enchanting. Give him a hearing, post festum, since it seems now to be all up, does it not? But let me warn you that he is a hotspur with a lot of restless blood in his veins.

Karl Anton also thought Versen "sanguinisch":

[*German*]

. . . Major von Versen was very interesting although his views are probably sanguine. . . .[2]

Versen understood the position of the Hohenzollern-Sigmaringen family. He noted in his diary on 21 May this reflection by Karl Anton: [*German*] "To be sure, if Bismarck says it is an interest of the state it would then be his duty." And Versen added in a parenthesis: [*German*] "This I shall use tomorrow." In fact, Versen was in possession of the magic formula which could sweep away all objections from the candidate and his family. On the following day (22 May) Versen's diary says: [*German*] "In the evening I wrote Moltke asking him to get Bismarck to write a letter to Prince [Karl Anton] saying that acceptance would be to the interest of the state."

On 23 May Karl Anton told Versen: [*German*] "He, the father, still viewed the matter as he had always done but left it to the Crown Prince and Bismarck to bring about his son's decision and be its advocates with the King."

Now well informed of Karl Anton's disposition, Versen went to Berlin on 24 May, immediately saw Bismarck in the Reichstag, and told

[1] See Appendix A.
[2] Letter Karl Anton to Leopold (submitted Benrath, 28 May 1870).

him that he and the Crown Prince should take the affair in hand. Bismarck readily agreed to meet the Crown Prince at an early date. Later in the day Versen went to Potsdam and handed to the Crown Prince a letter from Karl Anton:

[*German*]

If it is still in accordance with your ideas and those of Count Bismarck to return to the matter again, I, in the interest of the state and with dutiful regard for the undoubtedly great historic moment, will no longer in any way influence the decision which Leopold is called upon to make and on the contrary—heavy as is the sacrifice the family will have to bear—will *leave him an entirely free hand*.[1]

Versen added that Karl Anton wanted Bismarck and the Crown Prince to assume responsibility in the affair. This visit of Versen to Berlin made the resumption of negotiations possible. We know Bismarck's letter to Karl Anton of 28 May from the Foreign Ministry files.[2] The Crown Prince also wrote to Leopold telling him that now was the moment to accept:

[*German*] Neues Palais, 31 May, 1870
presented Benrath, 1 June, 1870

. . . H.M. thought the whole matter over and done with and was therefore at first indignant to find what was "dead and buried" brought to life again. But then H.M. said that having been unable to command any of you to go there and having therefore in your name declined he could not today unconditionally bar the way in view of the fact that the reopening of the question originated with you two, but he would, nevertheless, first have a word with Bismarck. Bismarck is, as he has always been, in favour of *acceptance* on your part, he thinks the situation no longer so favourable as two months ago, but does not anticipate complications in the event of election.

The upshot is that there is little likelihood of difficulties being raised by him, especially as you yourself now say you feel more inclined towards acceptance than two months ago. . . .

If in these conditions you are willing to tell your Father unreservedly what you wish to do, you can do so without fear—but there is no time to lose!

Understandably this turn of events filled Karl Anton with joy, for the interventions of Bismarck and the Crown Prince were, as he had wished, a substitute not only for the King's command to accept the candidature but also for the King's declaration that acceptance was in the interest of

---

[1] The published text of this letter (Fester, *Briefe*, doc. 180) did not contain this sentence. [2] See Doc. No. 135.

the Prussian State. Karl Anton's letter to his Chef de Cabinet von Werner is a cry of triumph and he could proudly say that the acceptance of the Spanish Crown was a sacrifice to *raison d'état*:

[German]   Nauheim, 1 June, 1870

. . . *Alea est jacta!* It is no longer possible to hold the affair back—it is a *duty to the state* to acquiesce in it. I would not have answered so categorically if delay were not dangerous and if in the event of a categoric refusal we would not in the future have to count Spain among our certain enemies. . . .

As my son's intentions to defer to overriding reasons of state policy and make the grievous sacrifice became very well known to me in the course of the negotiations I was able with a good conscience to answer as I did.

It is a tremendous sacrifice I am making; the visions of my own future dissolve in an uncertain future—but Providence seems to will it so. . . .

Karl Anton was no less emotional when writing to Leopold on 5 June:

[German]   Nauheim, 5 June, 1870

First of all I want to send you a written welcome to Sigmaringen on your arrival.

It is *perhaps* the last time for many a long day that you will greet your native town and homeland. I just cannot bear to think of it! It breaks my heart. But outpourings of emotion are of no avail in this place—present times demand realism and the days of ideal conceptions are in my mind already merging with the categoric imperative of today. . . .

So far, however, only Karl Anton had expressed his agreement.[1] Leopold himself had also to accept, and Versen was sent by Bismarck to obtain his formal acceptance.[2] It was now an easy task, though Leopold, still lacking enthusiasm for the task ahead, refused to say one word or to write one line without having consulted his father.

The Sigmaringen archives show, especially if read in conjunction with Versen's diary, that Karl Anton definitely wanted his son to become King of Spain and that Leopold was until the end reluctant to accept. He did so only under pressure when Karl Anton succeeded in showing that acceptance was in the interest of the State. Later in his life Leopold suffered from being regarded, so he thought, as responsible for the 1870 war, and it is clear from the Introduction that he wished the documents on his candidature to be shown to historians. He rightly considered that he had nothing to fear from a revelation of the true course of events.

[1] See Doc. No. 141.   [2] Versen's diary, 6 June 1870.

INDEX

The following names have been omitted: Bismarck; William I, King of Prussia; Prince Leopold von Hohenzollern, the candidate for the throne of Spain; Prince Karl Anton von Hohenzollern, his father; Eusebio Salazar y Mazarredo, the Spanish negotiator; and Lothar Bucher, Bismarck's right-hand man.